Dear Pitman Publishing Customer

IMPORTANT – Read This Now!

We are delighted to announce a special free service for all of our customers.

Simply complete this form and return it to the address overleaf to receive:

A   Free Customer Newsletter

B   Free Information Service

C   Exclusive Customer Offers – which have included free software, videos and relevant products

D   Opportunity to take part in product development sessions

E   The chance for you to write about your own business experience and become one of our respected authors

Fill this in now and return it to us (no stamp needed in the UK) to join our customer information service.

Name: Position:

Company/Organisation:

Address (including postcode):

                                                   Country:

Telephone: Fax:

Nature of business:

Title of book purchased:

Comments:

-------------------------- | **Fold Here Then Staple** | --------------------------

We would be very grateful if you could answer these questions to help us with market research.

1   Where/How did you hear of this book?

☐ in a bookshop

☐ in a magazine/newspaper
   (please state which):

☐ information through the post

☐ recommendation from a colleague

☐ other (please state which):

2   Which newspaper(s)/magazine(s) do you read regularly?:

3   When buying a business book which factors influence you most?
(Please rank in order)

☐ recommendation from a colleague

☐ price

☐ content

☐ recommendation in a bookshop

☐ author

☐ publisher

☐ title

☐ other(s):

4   Is this book a

☐ personal purchase?

☐ company purchase?

5   Would you be prepared to spend a few minutes talking to our customer services staff to help with product development? YES/NO

PITMAN PUBLISHING

The Business Publisher

Written for managers competing in today's tough business world, our books will help you get the edge on competitors by showing you how to:

- increase quality, efficiency and productivity throughout your organisation
- use both proven and innovative management techniques
- improve the management skills of you and your staff
- implement winning customer strategies

In short they provide concise, practical information that you can use every day to improve the success of your business.

FINANCIAL TIMES

PITMAN PUBLISHING

Making Change Happen

Making Change Happen

A Step-by-Step Guide

GRAHAM WILSON

FINANCIAL TIMES

PITMAN PUBLISHING

Pitman Publishing
128 Long Acre, London WC2E 9AN

A Division of Longman Group Limited

First published in Great Britain 1993

© Graham Wilson 1993

British Library Cataloguing in Publication Data
A CIP catalogue record for this book can be obtained from the British Library

ISBN 0 273 60259 4

10 9 8 7 6 5 4 3 2

Phototypeset in Linotron Times Roman by
Northern Phototypesetting Co Ltd, Bolton
Printed and bound in Great Britain by
Biddles Ltd, Guildford and King's Lynn

CONTENTS

LIST OF ILLUSTRATIONS

ACKNOWLEDGEMENTS

This book results from the experiences of colleagues and myself during our work as consultants to a very wide variety of organisations throughout the UK, Europe, the USA and the Gulf Region. We have not referred to each of our clients by name but we should like to record our appreciation to all of them – without the richness of experience and variety that they have provided this would be a strictly academic tome. I should also like to add my personal thanks to my colleagues, past and present, with whom I have enjoyed many hours of constructive debate and whose observations, ideas and thoughts are bound to have been incorporated.

Writing a book is never an easy task when you are trying to respond to the demands of a thriving consultancy practice. My partners and colleagues have been enormously supportive. In particular, Liz Morrison, who founded the Tactics Group, has been a source of inspiration throughout.

The index was prepared by June Morrison and I am very grateful to her for her thoroughness and most constructive feedback.

Finally, I should add a word of thanks to the relatives and friends who have lent me their homes as a place to escape to concentrate. Long may your holidays continue!

Graham Wilson

INTRODUCTION

The word 'Audit' brings to mind images of accountants labouring away for days on end dotting 'i's and crossing 't's in company accounts. Of course, this is not the only type of audit that one comes across. From the 1950s to the 1970s there was a whole discipline of management services which incorporated 'Work Study' and 'Time and Motion' analysis. Their origins go back much further and historians of management science and organisational behaviour often cite the work of the 'Scientific Management' gurus in the late 19th and early 20th centuries.

Audits have been carried out for a variety of reasons. In our experience most have been concerned with policing – attempting to catch out wrongdoers. In the work study arena, of course, the idea was to help everyone identify better ways of performing their tasks. Unfortunately, few managers ever subjected themselves to this discipline and experienced the anxiety that it provoked. Nowadays, although there are some remarkable exceptions, the number of organisations employing time and motion (T&M) specialists has shrunk dramatically. In the 1970s, when they were still quite common and the new style of management was only just emerging, Edgar Schein published his pivotal books on Process Consultation.[1] These two books firmly established the new approach to management though it would still be some years before the organisational implications became apparent. By this time management consultants around the world, especially those working within accountancy-based practices, had developed a tool known as a 'Diagnostic'. In most cases this consisted of a series of structured questions which required very little effort to answer but which, when the answers were collated, produced a picture of the organisation's strengths and weaknesses. Critics of the diagnostic approach, which is still widely practised, point out that the weaknesses are simply a shopping list for further consultancy work. Schein raised a more significant concern.

In performing a diagnostic the consultants had to ask questions of the employees throughout the organisation. They were often not highly skilled in interview techniques, and even if they were, they would be making many substantial interventions into the organisation's way of thinking. Let's consider a simple example. The consultant asks the Personnel Manager for a copy of the organisation chart. A simple enough question. The Personnel Manager probably has one and gives it to the consultant. In doing so, however, the consultant is saying: 'You should have an organisation chart, or you are no good as an organisation, and what's more you're not much good as a Personnel Manager'. Of course there will be exceptions, but in most circumstances the Personnel Manager would provide a chart even if they had to prepare it specially.

When he wrote his first volume, Schein recognised the problem of Internal Audits and incorporated an appendix specifically dealing with their problems.

Superficially this book is about Internal Auditing. However, we hope that you will quickly see that we are talking of a very different approach. The methods described are intended to overcome the objections that Schein voiced by involving the right people in the process, equipping them with the skills to do their job sensitively and skilfully and to see the results of their work put into practice. There are actually four themes running throughout the book. These are illustrated in Figure 0.1.

The skills and concepts that we discuss in the first three chapters apply to

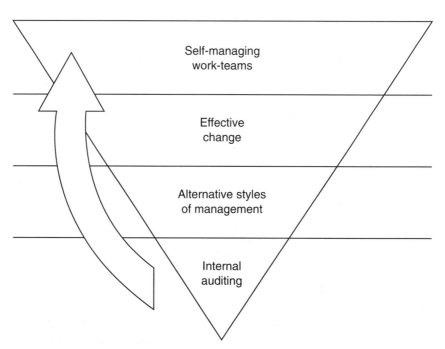

Figure 0.1   Making change happen

anyone in an organisation today. They are not restricted to auditors. In fact, one of the jobs of the auditors is to provide a role model for a new approach within the organisation. So, at a second level, this book is about styles of management and about styles of behaviour within an organisation.

When writing about organisations it is easy to lapse into the area that you feel most comfortable with. Coming from a commercial world we have slipped in words like company and business. Inevitably, too, we have spoken of production and manufacturing. We have also tried to give a wide range of examples drawn from our experience of non-commercial and service organisations. The approach applies just as well in this environment as it does anywhere.

Why write about Auditing? What is the purpose of Auditing? And why call the book 'Making Change Happen'? The answers are simple. No matter what the organisation is, if it is to change at all it has to be exposed. It has to see itself, 'warts and all'. It has to acknowledge that change has to happen if it is to survive. Organisational Development specialists acknowledge two kinds of pressure acting in this way: stimuli and triggers. Exactly which trigger will provoke change to happen cannot be predicted. If it could we would have made our fortunes and retired by now! The purpose then of Auditing is to focus a wealth of information in the knowledge that one or two of these many stimuli will prove to be the trigger that is needed. At a third level, therefore, this book is intended to introduce the principles of effective change in organisations and to provide the resources for 'Making Change Happen'.

In late 1991, a senior manager in a well-known company called me into his office. I had been engaged as a consultant and had been working there for some time. He lambasted me for suggesting in a conversation with one of his colleagues that their Total Quality process was all about culture change. He said that their culture did not need to change, that they were already very successful, that 'there's no point in change for change's sake'. If you were to visit them now you would not recognise them. Everything has changed and there is universal agreement that it was for the better.

Part of the senior manager's problem was that he had no picture of any alternative. He had been brought up believing that there was only one way to organise a business and as his own ideas matched this model it must be all right. This is not meant to be critical of him. None of us can be expected to prophesy alternatives if we have not experienced them elsewhere. Although there are a good many who would disagree with him about the need for change 'for change's sake' this is not the point of this book. However it does have one other objective.

Slowly, over the last twenty years a new way of managing and of organising businesses and non-commercial operations has emerged. It is still far from widespread. Most of us believe, though, that it will be the model for organisations in the 21st century. It involves making use of all the talents of the employees – it is about giving them opportunities that might otherwise be denied, about giving managers and non-managers a more satisfying job, while at the same time being much more productive and more efficient. The concept is known as Self-Managing Work Teams. It is radically different from almost any other organisation structure, and yet it is the natural development of the Total Quality movement with which most of us are familiar. The fourth level of this book then is to introduce the idea of Self-Managing Work-Teams, to provoke questions about the effectiveness of our existing organisation and to pose the question 'could it be better this way?'.

At the end of each chapter are summary diagrams, the first for the chapter contents and the second for the activities in the Audit. These summary diagrams are based on the concept of 'Mind-Mapping' developed by Tony Buzan.[2] Mindmaps are an increasingly popular way of summarising information, especially with groups that have been given problem-solving training. The three main reasons for their success are that they convey information in a form that appeals to our visual sense, that they do so in a non-linear form that appeals to a much larger proportion of the workforce (namely those that are manually dextrous – right brain dominant) and incorporating only key-words and concepts rather than the non-essential constructions that are retained in formal linear text.

References

1. Schein EH (1988) *Process Consultation. Vol. I: Its Role in Organization Development* (2nd Edn). Addison-Wesley, Wokingham, and Schein EH (1987) *Process Consultation. Vol. II: Lessons for Managers and Consultants* (2nd Edn). Addison-Wesley, Wokingham.
2. Buzan T (1978) *Use Your Head*, BBC Publications, London.

THE NEED TO RESPOND

INTRODUCTION

For the last twenty years the 'gurus' have been telling us that 'change is the only constant'.[1] In almost every industry the pace of change is accelerating. Figure1.1 shows the almost exponential pattern for the printing industry. The sources of this change are widespread and multifaceted – they vary from business to business, from industry to industry. Even in the same High Street, although there will be many similar experiences, for almost every shop there will be a myriad of unique pressures to change. Every organisation has been affected to some extent and most have tried to respond in some way. Whether your sector is commercial, industrial, public, private, charitable or social, your organisation will have to 'change with the times'.

Over the last decade there has been an assumption that years of complacency have led to a *status quo* – a steady state – which needed to shift. The theory goes that years of plenty have led people to be blinkered now. As one authority put it: 'In the 1950s you couldn't have screwed up a Fortune 500 company if you tried!'.

Change of any kind is threatening. Not only is there the uncertainty of the new, but there is also the loss of a trusted friend – 'the way we have always done things around here'. It was this last reaction to change that led many of us to use the analogy of a grieving process. To help managers deal with the reactions of their employees as they implemented new technology, new cultures, new conditions, we drew on studies of bereavement.

For most of us the threat of rocking the boat was much too severe. As Caleb Fowler who is President of the Property & Casualty Group of CIGNA has said: 'Our original inclination was to start in the back room and fine tune the system'. The group began its change process in 1986 and spent nearly two years fine tuning before they *really* embarked on substantial improvement.

CIGNA were far from unique. Many of us chose to address internal issues rather than tackling major customer interfaces. Universal widgets are being made better now than they have ever been made before. This has produced real benefits for the organisations that have tried – and they were in the minority! Sadly many more businesses did nothing. They either did not

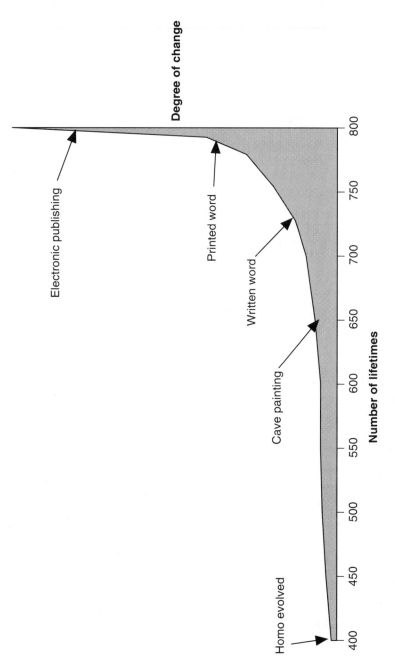

Figure 1.1   Pace of change in the printing industry

appreciate the need, or they could not generate sufficient energy to overcome the *status quo*.

THE CASE OF THE NEVER-CHANGING COMPANY!

For many good reasons, as a preliminary to change most senior management
teams will spend time developing a picture of the business in the future.
They are encouraged to encapsulate this in a phrase: a mission statement, a
corporate philosophy, a vision. These phrases are often communicated to
the workforce to motivate them to work towards a common goal. So
widespread are they that your own organisation probably has one. You will,
like us, have seen others used in company advertising. Collect them – they
tell you all you need to know about the survival potential of their creators.
For example, how would you rate the following business?

'✶✶✶✶✶✶✶ ✶✶✶: For all your conventional . . . requirements'

The extent of the shift in the steady state that was needed was only really
appreciated by a few people. As Fowler of CIGNA adds: 'You can have a
great system, but it's not worth anything if it isn't meeting the customer's
needs'. The enlightened few had a vision of dramatic change, of radically
rewritten rules, of organisations that bore no resemblance to their former
shadows.

Among the exponents of this step change were the authors Tom Peters
and Bob Waterman.[2] In their first book, and in Peters' sequel,[3] they
described a new type of organisation, a new steady state, a condition of
'Excellence'. Whether it was a reflection of the times, or a misinterpretation
by their readers, most people drew from these books a model of the ideal
organisation. They spelt out four aspects critical to survival:

- customer obsession;
- transformed leadership;
- empowered employees; and
- innovation.

The power of Peters' and others' messages was their simplicity and the
abundance of examples that they provided.

THE DINOSAUR ANALOGY

Equipped with this new 'body' the organisations had evolved to suit a new environment. As long as the environment persisted they survived. Rather like the dinosaurs, whose earliest forms struggled to fit into a changing world, when the environment was right they came of age. Contrary to popular belief the dinosaurs were undeniably successful. They dominated the earth's environments for longer than any other animal. While one species was successful there were others biding their time, waiting for an opportunity. Only when the environment changed did they get their chance. But eventually there were no new forms that could step in when the environment changed again and so the dinosaurs became extinct. Their successors were the mammals. They had been present for a long time, but they too were biding their time until the correct opportunity arose.

Sadly, for many of those 'Excellent' organisations of the 1980s the sources of change never abated. The new *steady state* that they had introduced served them well for a while, but they were no longer equipped for the new environment and (like the dinosaurs) they perished. The only survivors had evolved long before and, rather like the mammals, had been waiting for their opportunity.

The messages have been consistent throughout but have needed reinforcing – there is no ideal organisation; there is no safe steady state. If we are to survive in this changing world, we have to change constantly though not necessarily randomly. We need to predict the future, to prepare for it, and despite our own success we have to change again – even if it seems the most irrational time to do so just when everything is coming right.

This book is not about change. It is not about a new steady state. It won't tell you how to manage people through the grieving process. This book is about the changing environment in which you need to compete. It is about understanding that environment and preparing your organisation to respond to changes before they happen or when they take effect.

THE NEED TO RESPOND

Before we look at the aspects of your business that will enable it to respond to this changing world we are going to see what has been affecting it in recent years. This may seem pointless. It may appear facile. Yet a common cry from Chief Executive Officers and senior managers is that they wish they had taken stock *before* they initiated change. Not because the route or extent of their own actions would have changed necessarily, but because they have lost the chance to measure their own progress.

Begin with an inventory of change over the last ten years by following Activity 1.1 on page 11.

TASK VERSUS PEOPLE: THE TWO ELEMENTS OF A CHANGE PROCESS

Responding to change is a two-part process. Often an external change involves some physical event. These physical events and how we handle them are known as the 'Task' issues. The 'task' may be a new market opening or a new competitor or a new product launched by a competitor. Whatever the task is, there is a need to consider tangible actions in response. We shall be looking at this area, and how you can prepare your organisation for it, throughout the book, but especially in chapters 4 and 5.

While it is obviously very important to address these physical issues there is another set of issues which also needs to be managed if our organisation is to be responsive. These issues are to do with human reactions to change and, not surprisingly, are known by Organisational Development specialists as 'People' issues. Again we shall be concerned with these throughout the book, but especially in chapters 6 and 7.

So far we have mainly talked about the physical changes, the Task issues. While we are still looking retrospectively it would be useful to spend a few minutes considering the emotional side-effects or the People issues.

SELF-ESTEEM AND CHANGE

Your self-esteem determines how you will feel about an event affecting you. Self-esteem is difficult to define, but it can be summed up as the way you feel about yourself. Self-esteem is influenced by all sorts of things: how you feel physically (whether you are well or run-down); how things are at home or at work; and how other people are responding to you. Sometimes things are going well – everyone cooperates and you are achieving your own personal goals. You feel positive about yourself and this affects how you feel about little obstacles thrown in your way. If you've had a good day at work and then drive home, traffic jams are less irritating than if you've had a bad day at work. On a good day you may shrug off cynical comments from colleagues, while on a bad day you'll swing back at them.

The ebb and flow of self-esteem is always present and most of us have our own average level. Some individuals may have relatively low self-esteem most of the time. They have developed this for a reason and (if they want to be helped) they can usually be encouraged to raise themselves. Others are almost always on a high. They too have developed this attitude for specific reasons and it is conceivable, though pretty unlikely, that they might need help in reducing it! For a few people, their brain chemistry can get out of balance and their self-esteem can undergo dramatic changes. They may spend some time being very high and other times very low. Such mood changes are characteristic of depression and can again be treated, although these people often have to have the chemical imbalance corrected first.

For all practical purposes there is a parallel between self-esteem and morale. In organisational terms morale can be high, low or inbetween. When an organisation experiences change it is morale which is affected.

Whatever our resting level of self-esteem, when we are confronted with a change we experience a shift in its balance. These shifts have been well documented and found to break down into seven stages. Before we look briefly at the stages it is worth remembering that throughout this book we are not assuming that all change is for the worse. An equal amount is for the better. The reactions it provokes, however, are the same.

THE SEVEN STAGES IN REACTING TO CHANGE

Figure 1.2 shows how self-esteem varies while we come to terms with change. From your researches so far, pick a significant incident from the last ten years – one that you have experienced or, at least, one for which there is a lot of detail available. As we look through the seven stages try to identify the symptoms and how they appeared at the time. Activity 1.5 on page 13 provides a form for collecting this information together.

1. Numbness

The first phase is usually characterised by shock. We feel lost, overwhelmed. We don't know what to do or say. We freeze. The extent of the numbness varies from person to person and situation to situation. If the morale in a factory is high and redundancies are announced then the numbness is likely to be greater than if morale is low when they are announced. The outward symptoms of this stage can include the lack of response expected to an announcement or people hanging around afterwards for no apparent reason.

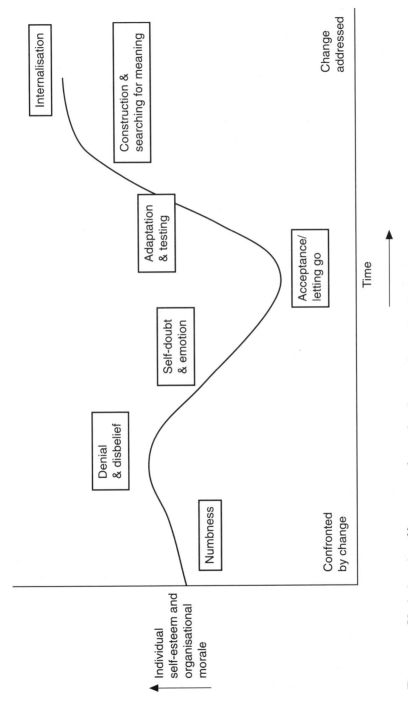

Figure 1.2 Variations in self-esteem and morale when confronted with change

2. Denial/disbelief

We next begin to minimise the change either by trivialising it, denying it completely, or trying to joke about it. The disbelief stage is often linked with high energy. Sometimes people will go overboard with their reactions. The celebrations of a father of a new-born baby can sometimes show these signs. Equally, people who have been promoted may refuse to acknowledge the changes in responsibility that the new position will bring. Occasionally, an individual who has been made redundant will continue to get up, leave home and make the journey to work. They are probably stuck at this step.

3. Self-doubt/emotion

As people become aware of the changes that they must make to adjust to the new situation they often become uncertain. If this feeling develops it can lead to a feeling of powerlessness, of things being out of control. This is just as likely to happen when the change has been positively anticipated for some time. Have you ever had a promotion and wondered whether you are up to it? This step is often associated with high emotions too, though here people are angry. Frustrations at an inability to control the situation can be vented by individuals and also by groups. Of course, groups can be incited to behave in this way.

4. Acceptance/letting go

The lowest ebb of self-esteem is when we begin to accept the change for what it is. This process can involve a lot of ups and downs with set-backs being triggered by simple events. The reality of the situation is accepted slowly as the connections with the past are finally severed.

   The difficulty of overcoming this stage is why many consultants recommend that redundancies are made quickly and once only. If people continue working together when they know that one is going to leave then those left behind can have great difficulty adjusting in the end. Similarly, if the redundancies are only made once then people will adjust more quickly than if they have that nagging doubt that they may be next.

5. Adaptation/testing

As people adapt to their new environment they become more energetic, trying out different ways of working. For example, divorcees will now start dating again. This step is also fairly emotional. Young people at college – often exploring relationships away from home for the first time – can become distressed, lose attention, and threaten to drop out. At work this is the stage where even quite experienced managers can devote hours to devising theoretical models of how to tackle their new job.

6. Searching for meaning

On the way up, as individuals begin to feel that they have got to grips with the change, they can 'see the bigger picture' but may begin to wonder where it is going to lead. Often when we are approached at work to take on a new job we have to negotiate our package at the outset. As we begin to understand the full implications we can either be happy with the package or not. If we are not then this is the time when we will probably begin looking for other jobs. Have you ever had an employee who has taken on a new role, been in it a short while and then handed in their notice? Often such employees will move into a position that is radically different from their original path.

7. Internalisation

At last, we accept the changes that have happened, we adapt to suit, and our behaviour changes too. In a plant where substantial changes have occurred the managers will report that the place is running on a high. They say that morale has never been so good and that production and efficiency are better than they had expected.

People very rarely move from stage to stage effortlessly. Most authorities believe that people have to experience every stage. However, we sometimes try to suppress steps or, at least, do not provide the opportunity for them to be expressed. If you are about to introduce change – no matter how small – to a group of people, try keeping a log of the behaviour they demonstrate. You will find a chart in Activity 1.6 in which to make these notes concisely.

Why bother looking into the People issues? The Task that has to be achieved is pretty clear. Few people would deny it – or so you would think . . .

STUFF QUALITY – Number 1

A recent survey[4] by Ernst and Young and the University of Michigan asked senior executives from the automotive industry in the USA to describe the car company of the future. Despite the universal recognition that the US car industry is losing to Japan entirely on the basis of product quality, despite the fact that the home and export markets are in decline due to foreign competition, and despite the efforts of the 'Quality' gurus over the last twenty years to re-educate American manufacturers, one in twenty of the respondents didn't even rate quality as 'quite important' to the car maker of the future!

STUFF QUALITY – Number 2

Remember Gerald Ratner? He was the owner of the UK's largest chain of jewellery shops. Then in 1991, speaking at the Institute of Directors' annual conference,[5] he described his own products as 'absolute crap'. He poured scorn on the public's bad taste and enumerated the way in which he had ripped off his customers through a not-so-generous discount scheme. Since his revelations his business has collapsed – a cost which has been calculated in £100,000s per word!

STUFF QUALITY – Number 3

There was a business in the North West of the UK. It had a turnover of £35m and employed 600 people. It made building products. In September 1989 it made two new appointments. The first was Quality Control Manager whose job was to introduce new ways of working on the shopfloor. But the company didn't really believe that this was achievable. At the same time the company appointed a Customer Service Manager who was responsible for a 30-strong national service organisation handling warranty claims. The new role was to develop the department into a cost-effective profit centre.

We can only conjecture how well these two individuals got on with one another, constantly striving to put the other one out of work!

QUALITY AS A BUSINESS PREREQUISITE

We are not going to try to justify quality as a basic business prerequisite in this book. If you need to be convinced we recommend that you look at almost any business book published in the last two decades and certainly the sister book to this publication.[6] Nobody consciously buys something that they want to break down. Fortunately the examples above are increasingly rare.

Companies like Motorola, IBM and Digital are setting the standard. They have embarked on vigorous campaigns to improve continuously their performance. So dramatic are their efforts that they have set a goal of experiencing only three defective operations in every million.[7] Known as 'Six Sigma' this is a far cry from the Acceptable Quality Levels of the 1970s which were typically 95 per cent or five defects in a hundred. This goal is just the latest expression of a long process of development for these organisations. For most businesses, achieving a defect rate of three in one million would be exceptional. The Motorola goal is not for assembled units but for each component that goes into them and every administrative procedure that leads to their production.

THE NEED TO RESPOND: ACTIVITIES

Activity 1.1: How much has changed?

Ask the Personnel Department to tell you who is your oldest employee and who is the longest serving. Take them out to lunch – use the canteen or a pub.

Get them to describe the business as they remember it when they joined the company. Really encourage them to reminisce. Take notes. Get specifics. When was new technology introduced? Were pay and employment conditions always the same? Which changes do they remember? What were they doing when Kennedy was assassinated, when the Queen Elizabeth II was launched, or when man walked on the Moon?

Activity 1.2: The pace of change

Take the annual reports from your organisation and identify the major events in its history. Plot them on a timescale to see if any patterns of change emerge in the industry, in technology, in markets, etc. Show mergers, acquisitions and so on.

Histories presented graphically can be far more revealing than prose. ARCO, the Atlantic Richfield Oil Company, displays its history as an evolving chart in the reception halls of the head offices around the world.

Activity 1.3: The *status quo*

Load up your camera with a roll of film. Walk the job taking snapshots. The technical merit of the photographs is totally irrelevant so don't get the company photographer to do the job. Just make sure that every aspect of the work your organisation does is captured. As a minimum, the snaps need to include:

- The salespeople
- Goods inwards
- Any raw materials holding yards
- Pre-production processing
- The production line itself
- Scrap heaps and rework piles

- Goods outwards storage
- The loading bay
- Distribution
- A delivery being made
- The accounts department
- The head offices

For some reason CEOs and senior managers are sometimes uncomfortable doing this. If you are it's worth asking yourself why. A common reason is embarrassment at being seen doing something that is considered inappropriate for someone in authority. To help overcome this, one favourite trick is to take a young son or daughter around on a weekend. This doesn't get quite the same results because there are usually fewer people around, but it is better than nothing.

Activity 1.4: The inventory of change

Now that you have begun gathering information, think back to ten years ago. Use the inventory of change (below) to summarise these events.

AN INVENTORY OF CHANGE

- How have your main facilities changed?
- How has the product range changed?
- How have the numbers, types, mixture of employees changed?
- How have working conditions changed?
- How has the production process changed?
- How has the company funding changed?
- How have production statistics changed?
- How have the customers changed? Are they the same or different?
- What sorts of product do these customer buy and in what volumes? How have these changed in the last ten years?
- How has the remuneration package changed across the range of employees?
- Have there been any significant disputes? What were they about, how long did they last, and how were they resolved?

How do you *feel* about these changes? Have they been positive or have there been setbacks? Were they avoidable, inevitable or deliberately engineered? Are there any that you would rather forget? Some things will have remained the same. Should they have, or would you rather some had changed? Make a note of some of these. Finally, jot down any of the things that you already expect to happen in the next decade. Do you see these as positive or negative? Do you think that they are inevitable or do you have some degree of control over them?

Activity 1.5: Changes in morale

For each of the seven stages of reacting to change, identify some symptoms that you have observed in your organisation at one time or another. Complete the symptoms of change grid on page 14.

Activity 1.6: Plotting the seven change-steps

If you are about to introduce change to a small group of people, or are witnessing such a process, try to record people's reactions on a chart like the one shown in Figure 1.3 on page 15.

SYMPTOMS OF CHANGE

1. Numbness

Situation:

Circumstances:

How long did it last?

2. Denial/Disbelief

Situation:

Circumstances:

How long did it last?

3. Self-doubt/Emotion

Situation:

Circumstances:

How long did it last?

4. Acceptance/Letting Go

Situation;

Circumstances:

How long did it last?

5. Adaptation/Testing

Situation:

Circumstances:

How long did it last?

6. Searching for meaning

Situation:

Circumstances:

How long did it last?

7. Internalisation

Situation:

Circumstances:

How long did it last?

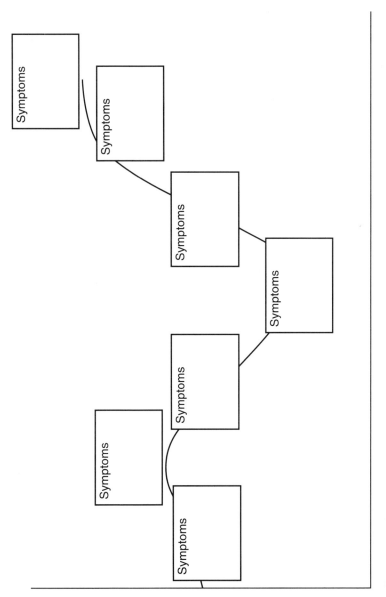

Figure 1.3 Reactions to change

References

1. Toffler A (1970) *Future Shock*, Bantam, New York.
2. Peters T and R Waterman (1982) *In Search of Excellence*, Harper & Row, New York.
3. Peters T and N Austin (1985) *A Passion for Excellence*, Random House, New York.
4. Rock M (1991) The car company of the future, *Director Drive*, Winter 1991, pp. 32–34.
5. Ratner G (1991) This business is surviving, *Director*, Special Convention Issue, pp. 66–72.
6. Munro-Faure L and M Munro-Faure (1992) *Implementing Total Quality Management*, Financial Times/Pitman, London.
7. Wilson GB (1993) *The Route to Perfection*, IFS Publications, Bedford.

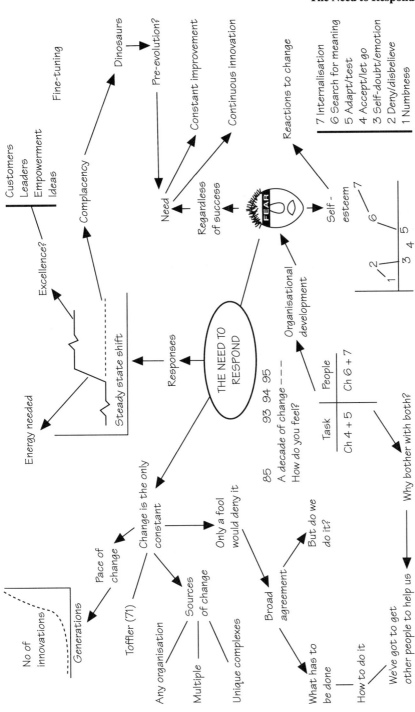

Summary Mindmap 1: The Need to Respond

2 SELF-ASSESSMENT FOR CHANGE

INTRODUCTION

How do you prepare your organisation to become more responsive?

For any organisation to be able to respond it has to be aware of what is going on around it. It needs to listen to its customers, watch its competitors, and monitor the markets. It has to have the means to interpret the information that it gets. Then it must decide whether to respond and if so, how. It has to have the facility to work with ideas.

If the organisation has not provoked the change itself then it must respond very quickly. To do so calls for a lean set of systems, procedures and working practices that together help turn ideas into reality. There is no point having the best mousetrap if your own people will not let you make it or sell it until their own paperwork is completed. Similarly, the best ideas in the world won't get translated into actions if your people are demotivated, under-performing, and not properly focused.

Responsibility for all these rests with the management team. That doesn't mean that they have to do all the jobs, but it does mean that they have to create the right environment, prepare people, set the standards and lead. In brief, the following have to be right:

- customer focus;
- ideas;
- administration;
- employees; and
- leadership.

SELF-ASSESSMENT

The idea behind self-assessment is simple. Before making decisions on tangible changes to the organisation the senior management team commissions studies of critical aspects of the business. Rather than calling on an outside body, they do so by briefing, preparing and supporting a small group of people from inside the organisation. This group of employees does not have an open-ended brief, but does have considerable responsibility. Several features will influence its success:

- the make up of the team;
- how they are prepared;
- the way in which they tackle the assignment;
- the support that they are given;
- the way in which they present their findings and recommendations; and
- the response of the senior management team to these.

So what is special about self-assessment and why is it so important when becoming a responsive organisation?

SENIOR MANAGEMENT OWNERSHIP AND THE 'NOT-INVENTED-HERE' SYNDROME

Very few organisations confronted with change are starting from scratch. Most will have been operating for sometime; they have an established workforce, defined products or services and the means of getting them to their customers. For these organisations there may be no obvious reason for change or there may be substantial ones. Whatever the case, we know that they will not change if the whole of the senior management team doesn't 'buy into' the reasons. Ownership is a very important word when it comes to major change. In today's environment there are all sorts of exceptions to such 'rules', but there seem to be none to *this* one. If the senior managers do not fully buy in, then either the change process will stall or the senior managers concerned will go.

The issue of ownership is a tough one to write about. Unfortunately the term is grossly over-used and abused. Consequently, it has become a jargon word that is likely to turn many people off. There is a well-researched, psychological phenomenon that is known popularly as NIH or 'not-invented-here', which explains both why ownership is so important and why the self-assessment approach is so effective.

From birth, individuals are progressively developing their images of the world. To make sense of the vast amounts of information available to it, the brain has to impose some structure. It does this by heavily prioritising information that comes from a source that it can trust. This is probably one reason why our parents, and in western society especially our mothers, are so important in shaping our personalities during our first two years of life. It is also why the loss of a parent in our early childhood is so devastating. The second source, and increasingly important through childhood and early adulthood, is the individuals themselves. If I have decided something, if I have a view, then I am going to take much convincing before I believe a different one.

If you visit the office of many senior managers you will see on their bookshelves extensive reports, beautifully bound and presented, documenting all sorts of issues of importance to their business. Very often these have cost a remarkable sum to produce. They have often involved outside agents and certainly haven't involved the senior managers themselves, except in a minor way.

If you were seeking evidence to support a decision that you had already made (at least in your own mind) then you probably will regard the information in the report highly. If the brief was to explore alternatives, but not to make a recommendation, then you probably will be interested. However, it is only if you were closely involved in its preparation that you will act on its recommendations. Of course reports prepared by outsiders do have a very useful role when trying to provide stimuli for change. It is at times like this that outside consultants can bring a credibility that insiders often lack, especially in technical disciplines or when seeking a wider range of alternatives.

The success of the self-assessment approach to change is really due to NIH. At the outset the decision to review is much easier than deciding what to do. If the senior managers have agreed that a subject is worth reviewing then they have reached agreement without opinions about the correct solution getting in the way.

In preparing the brief and commissioning a group of people to do the work, the skilful leader will be building ownership into the less committed members of his team. Once the work is underway, if they do not intrude, the senior managers can supply as much information and support as they wish. They run the operation and so they feel less threatened than they would if outsiders were involved. If no individual senior manager has influenced the group strongly then the whole senior management team has equal ownership for the resulting report. We shall look at how to prevent such influence in the next chapter. If the senior management team fears that the investigating team is straying beyond its brief and has no cause to do so, they can control the situation. Senior management attitude and timing, therefore, are critical to the decision to use self-assessment. They also influence the process by which the self-assessment is carried out.

SENIOR MANAGEMENT ATTITUDE AND NON-STARTERS

For every case of change in organisations that we have examined there have been at least two that were non-starters. According to senior management attitudes there are four types of non-starter organisation. These are where:

- no one really appreciates the need;
- senior management paid lip-service to the change;
- senior management did not share the need with the Champion;
- the Champion was ostracised and left the organisation.

To these add the case of the slow-starter where:

- the senior managers concerned were removed or left.

Whereabouts are you? In the previous chapter we looked at the changes that were confronting your organisation and those that had affected it in the past. You are interested in achieving some change. Where do your colleagues stand? The first two activities in this chapter provide a quick picture of the senior managers in your team. The first asks you to rate the members of the team on their likely exposure to new ideas. It looks at how willing they are likely to be to share views and ideas with you. There are no right or wrong answers. A team that is open to new ideas, and routinely shares views and interests, is much more likely to support individuals from within when they propose change. It is in your own interests to be as objective as you can.

The second activity looks at the maturity of the team as a whole. It is widely held that effective change will only happen if the senior management team behaves as a team. The scales show different aspects of a team's ability to work effectively. Once a team is open to discussion about its own performance (which it may not be yet), then this can provide a good medium for group assessment.

THE STIMULUS TO CHANGE

Often organisations are reacting to outside influences. Of course this need not be the only case. There are plenty of times when a business will create its own niche in a marketplace and, while expanding to fill it, has to cope with change because of its own growth. Changes of key players due to promotion, death or retirement are all examples of internally generated change. This doesn't mean that these organisations do not have to respond, nor that they can do so without regard to the outside world.

Nonetheless the commonest expressed cause of change has something to do with events outside the organisation. Organisational Development specialists distinguish between the myriad of stimuli to change and the single event that triggers change. The SGB Case Study (see page 30) provides a simple example of change beginning.

Whatever their situation almost all organisations embark on a stage of self-assessment. This may provide the trigger or it may be a later stage of activity that triggers change. The introduction of change into organisations is a subject that has been widely studied since the 1930s. The lack of widespread business education means that few managers are aware of the principles involved. This situation is changing and it will be interesting to see the effect when the present generation of MBA students reaches senior management positions. However, the steps that organisations need to plan and progress through, as they carry out change, are consistent under most circumstances. They occur because of the underlying principles of Organisational Development and are not invented for specific applications. Whether you are introducing new technology, new pay conditions or a new culture (such as Total Quality Management) you have to allow for these steps. The process of the steps varies from one organisation to another, but the content and the pattern remain the same. These common elements are shown in Figure 2.1.

Does Figure 2.1 highlight any stages that you have slipped beyond? Could the gaps be filled now? What would be involved? Self-assessment forms an important part of this sequence. To illustrate the steps we look at an example of highly successful change – how a medium-sized electrical company, Zytec, won the US Baldrige Award (see Case Study 4 on page 31).

The activities that are described in the rest of this book are intended to allow you to instigate and carry out a self-assessment phase for your organisation. They can be used whether you are doing so to provide a trigger for your own senior management team or as part of an ongoing process of change.

WHAT DO ORGANISATIONS ASSESS?

The subjects chosen for assessment depend on the priorities in the minds of the senior management team. Nonetheless there are some striking but

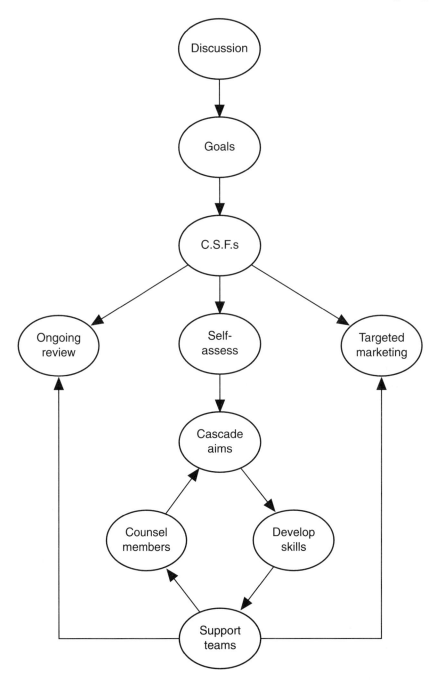

Figure 2.1   The successful implementation of change

obvious similarities between organisations. A survey of 26 organisations shows the commonest subjects (see Table 2.1).

Table 2.1 The subject of self-assessments

Customer focus	14
Organisation structure	10
Business processes	7
Employees' attitudes	5
Leadership	2
Innovation	2
Cost of quality	1
Physical environment	1

Source: Survey conducted by Tactics, 1992.

There is clearly some overlap between the material covered under different headings. In particular, a review of business processes will often highlight changes which need to be made to the organisation structure. There are also many activities which result in a review of these subjects without being recognised as such by the participants. Currently, the commonest of these is probably the preparation of a company to reach certification for the ISO9000 series of standards. Properly done, the development of a Quality System should lead to a thorough revision of a company's business processes.

WHY BOTHER WITH SELF-ASSESSMENT?

So far we have emphasised the value of self-assessment as a way of building senior management ownership for change and providing the trigger for change. When self-assessment approaches are used later in the change process they serve several purposes.

Prioritising change

Most obvious is the need to provide priorities for change. In the case of Zytec, (see page 31), the initial self-assessment based on employee attitudes showed the importance of changing the reward system so that it reflected the changing role of employees. The Cost of Quality analysis carried out by some companies is pointless unless it is used for this purpose.

Communication device

In some organisations the trigger to change is being experienced by everyone. The recent recession has highlighted this. Frequently the whole organisation is aware that the market has changed, money is scarce, and sales dropping. In manufacturing organisations few employees come into contact with paying customers. In the service sector too, most people inside the organisation feel powerless to do anything about these conditions. There is little that they can do to respond. The self-assessment approach, which we are going to describe, helps to address this problem by involving people within the organisation in the decision-making process.

Internal marketing

While the process of carrying out the self-assessment brings clear messages of intent to the employees, the content of the assessment also can be used to 'market' the key issues. Because involvement in a survey, for instance, is often individual, it allows the employee to dwell on the topic. It can let them contribute genuinely to the growth of the business. It may be just as powerful, if not more so, than the typical briefing carried out by organisations when the senior managers begin to cascade their vision of the future. Once the work of the self-assessment team is completed their findings too provide very powerful material for the internal marketing process.

Experiment for new ways of working

For many organisations the vision, which has been developed by the senior management team to allow them to respond effectively, involves higher levels of employee involvement than before. For these teams the self-assessment is often the first opportunity that they have to try out the new approach. They are as interested in the way in which it works as they are in the subject area that is chosen. If they do not build up unrealistic expectations, given the lack of preparation that their 'guinea-pigs' will have had, then this can be a very effective way of testing alternative approaches. For several organisations, despite initial scepticism, the results of the first attempt at self-assessment have been so productive that they go on to repeat the process with other subjects. The success or otherwise of this approach provides material for the senior management team to review and to plan around before setting up permanent teams.

Role model for the new style of working

A common mistake that is made when introducing a new approach is simply to change to the new way and then expect others to respond positively. The Managing Director of a major steel company, for example, decided that he wanted his senior managers to be more 'independent', 'to challenge more' and 'not to take things so passively'. He did not ask himself why they seemed to lack these qualities, but instead set out to role model the new style himself. At the next management meeting the first person to raise a question was subjected to a torrent of questions from the MD. This was repeated throughout the meeting every time anyone questioned anything. At the second meeting a month later the process was repeated. At the third meeting no one asked anything.

The example may seem improbable but it was very real to the individuals involved. When we want to change the way people work we have to do so progressively. As they take up the challenge we reward them with positive encouragement and by creating more situations for them to grow into.

As we have said already, the characteristics of a responsive organisation include highly autonomous teams of employees working with a common goal of satisfying their customers. If your organisation currently favours individuals who work alone most of the time then changing the culture is going to require effort. The first step is to give people some appreciation of the benefits and the sincerity of the senior management team. They need to see this for themselves and so a high-profile, team-based activity is called for. The self-assessment process provides this.

WHY NOT TO BOTHER WITH SELF-ASSESSMENT

It would be unusual for a management team to do anything without a few dissenters. Unfortunately some people will never take the survival issue seriously. The self-assessment process is one step in the complex sequence of events that will progressively transform the business. Dropping it means building on an unsound foundation, without an opportunity for the senior management team to test alternatives and without preparing the rest of the workforce for the change in approach. What are the commonest reasons for self-assessment to be dropped from the agenda once it has been tabled?

Better things to do

This excuse is usually given by management teams who have forgotten or mistaken the importance of the subjects under review. If their initial discussions on the subject have trivialised the brief then they will soon find other things to do that are genuinely more important. This calls for a review of the topics chosen and a look at the possible range of solutions that they may recommend. Once the senior management team has appreciated the scale of change that could occur they should see that the self-assessment is more important than anything else that they could do.

We already know the answer

'Let's get this straight – you accept that there need to be changes made to help this organisation become more responsive. You also accept that these changes need to be in the area of say, customer focus. But you already know what needs to be done so there is no need to get a team to study it. Okay. Why haven't you done it?'

'Oh! We're sorry. Of course we've started. But it's early days yet and you couldn't expect any results. Besides you don't want to do it again. After all, that would just disrupt people and they'd lose confidence in the senior managers.'

'Well, I'll tell you what. When *do* you think we'll see some results? In about six months? Let's add six for safety – we all know how budgets get in the way and delay things. So, if nothing has happened in twelve months' time can I have your *irrevocable* agreement to go ahead then? No? So what is the *real* problem then?'

We've studied this already

'Great – this means that the self-assessment team have something really positive to work with. Can we get copies of the report so that they can review them in their first couple of meetings?'

We can't afford the time or the cost

If the senior management team has understood the subjects to be reviewed then they should be able to see the benefits that can be achieved realistically. The costs of running the self-assessment group for three or four months will depend on several factors. These include the size of the organisation, how widely distributed they are geographically, and the scope of the brief given to the team. You can easily quantify these. Does it make sound commercial sense to go ahead?

If it doesn't then something is very seriously wrong. Either the group are not being given credit for their potential or the costs are disproportionately high. Would adding the presence of a senior manager onto the team make its potential any greater? Does the brief need reviewing to make it more significant to the business?

Why study this particular topic?

If this is a serious question then two things need to be done. Firstly, the senior management team needs to review the subject very carefully and redefine the brief until the choice is logical. Secondly, the anticipated benefits need to be reviewed. The team will present cost-benefit justifications for any recommendations that they make. Some senior management teams deliberately split the brief into two parts, asking the team to report having assessed the potential benefits of change before they consider the nature of the changes.

Nobody else does this, why should we?

We hope that there is sufficient material within this book to persuade the senior manager that this is a commonplace process that can occur under different guises. There is a growing mass of evidence that self-assessment is the most important step in achieving real change within an organisation.[1] The only real solution to this problem is for the management team to visit a few other organisations and see what they have done. Asking this question usually suggests a management team that has not spent sufficient time in initial discussions. This may mean that any teams that do start self-assessment will run into difficulties later through a lack of support. It is probably worth helping the senior managers to reassess their plans and commitment before going ahead.

Case Study 1

UK Food Manufacturer

One major UK food manufacturer with a very traditional range of products at the quality end of the market was waking up to the threat from foreign importers. During the late 1960s and 1970s they had correctly predicted the growing interest in foreign foods, especially those with a higher spice content. They launched a very successful range of products emulating the dishes from India and Asia, making use of the ingredients that they had been importing and selling raw for many years. In the late 1980s a new threat was emerging both from the increasing number of importers from these markets and from their European competition.

Though they had always majored on the quality of their products this couldn't justify their premium pricing and the Managing Director began to look for ways of reducing operating costs. Whether he had always been a conceptual thinker or not, this process began to create a divide between himself and his management team. They felt that he was losing control – he felt that they weren't sufficiently progressive.

Eventually he decided to begin a Total Quality process. He engaged consultants, who advised that the first stage should be a workshop for his senior managers. Within two hours of a two-day programme the senior managers were in revolt. They did not object to the idea, or the way it was to be carried out, but they did react to their lack of involvement in initiating it.

Within twelve months the Managing Director had left to head (very successfully) a quango concerned with management concepts and the senior managers had restarted the change process themselves (again, very successfully).

Case Study 2

US Systems House

The Information Technology industry has undergone more growth in recent years than any other. At one end of the spectrum are the giants: IBM, DEC, and Motorola. At the other are small businesses staffed by highly qualified enthusiasts. Somewhere between the two are larger businesses that have grown on the success of their initial products. The skills of their creators have often been in the development field and they have bought in business skills as they needed them. Some have adjusted well, others have become dominated by the new style of manager.

One such company, based in the US Silicon Valley, began to expand into Europe. Retaining all development activities in the USA, the European operations were almost exclusively sales based. The prevailing culture in Europe was therefore driven by the quarterly sales targets imposed by the US base. The senior managers were recruited for their ability to meet these targets. These targets became increasingly aggressive as the recession took effect among the larger businesses that made up the bulk of their customer base.

Meanwhile, in the USA the climate was changing; confronted by a mature market and a growing demand from the IT industry for quality products and services. The US parent declared its intention of winning the US National Quality Award, the Baldrige Award, within a period of less than four years. President Reagan's Baldrige Award has fast become the most prestigious for US industry. The criteria of the award are intended to identify those few businesses with exceptional achievements in quality improvement, with a positive, cooperative culture based around empowered employees and a supportive management style.

While the decision to win may seem of itself arrogant, the main problem that it created was one of little ownership for the target in Europe. To the European subsidiaries of this US company the Baldrige was irrelevant. Their senior managers continued to work only to the quarterly sales targets and within a year all efforts to change the culture of the company had virtually disappeared.

Case Study 3

SGB Contracts Division

SGB is one of the largest suppliers of access facilities to the construction industry in the UK and around the world. The Contracts Division is primarily concerned with the erection of scaffolding. It began its change process in 1988. At the time the senior management team was a very stable group with many years of experience of working together. The industry was undergoing massive adjustment. Terms of contract were changing with changes in the basis of calculation of effort. Terms were changing to allow contra-charges for failure to meet the exact terms of the contract.

Scaffolding is a complex activity involving considerable practical engineering skills. The complexity of the task, coupled with its physically rugged nature, had led to a policing style of supervision. A fully qualified scaffolder will have served several years apprenticeship and have attended expensive training courses through the CITB – the Construction Industry Training Board. Through the boom years for the industry the number of skilled scaffolders had progressively risen. In the late 1980s, Prime Minister Thatcher's policies were favouring the entrepreneurial smaller businesses. With relatively low entrance costs and strong local markets many scaffolders left the larger companies and began working for themselves.

As the recession in Britain took hold the construction industry was the first to be hit. Simultaneously, changes within SGB's parent company, The Mowlem Group, all influenced the thinking of the senior management team within the Contracts Division. With so many stimuli to change there should have been little to hold them back.

Nevertheless, the Divisional Director at the time, Richard Morley, pinpoints one event that finally triggered the change for the team. They were attending a Personal Time Management course when a small group of them began to think of the implications of what they were learning at a corporate scale. They didn't realise it then but they were rediscovering the ideas of Cost of Quality.

Returning from the seminar, Richard Morley quickly initiated a full-scale change process. Over four years this lead to an empowerment culture with employees responsible for their own self-management and the supervisors adopting a coaching role rather than the traditional controller-cop style.

Case Study 4

Zytec Corporation

A joint venture, Magnetic Peripherals Inc., formed by four electronics firms and based in Eden Prairie, Minnesota, was the subject of a leveraged buyout in 1984. The factory facility is slightly less than a hundred miles away from the HQ and is the base for ⅞ths of the 750 workforce. The company, which took the name Zytec, has two principal markets. Its core business is the manufacture of power supplies (PSUs) for original equipment manufacturers (OEMs) of computers, medical and test equipment. In addition, 10 per cent of revenue comes from the repair of cathode-ray tubes and power supplies, including those of the company's manufacturing wing's competitors!

After the buy-out the senior managers spent some time reviewing alternative strategies to develop their business. Their experience of the industry told them that service, quality and price were going to become dramatically better. For a while they looked at different approaches to achieve the dramatic standards they felt the industry would need. Eventually the group felt that they could identify well with the '14 points' of Quality guru, W. Edwards Deming, and decided to apply these within Zytec. The senior management team set itself tough targets for productivity and quality improvement with a vision of becoming the driving force in their two market sectors.

In 1984 the business depended almost entirely on orders from one of its former owners. By 1991 they represented only 1.5 per cent of orders, as their market position had risen to fifth in the USA in the AC-DC power supplier sector. Nevertheless, they have not adopted a scatter-gun approach. One of their original goals was to achieve long-term partnerships with their customers. Since 1990 they have supplied twenty customers – 18 of which have single source contracts – representing a turnover of $50m. In repairs and maintenance, Zytec are now the largest in the USA turning over nearly $6m.

The initial goal that was set was to fulfil the requirements of the US National Quality Award, the Baldrige Award. The company had achieved this by 1991 when they were awarded the prize. They have now embarked on the second phase of their improvement process.

Discussions

From their exposure to the eight-year quality improvement process and having achieved the Baldrige award, the senior managers were obviously in broad agreement of direction. They have now decided to pursue the same 'Six Sigma' standard that is being sought by the likes of Motorola, DEC, and IBM.

Goals

The Six Sigma standard cannot be achieved with traditional approaches to management. The Zytec team recognised this and began to formulate their vision of the future by building in many radical transformations. The lynch-pin is a programme known as 'Managing Through Planning' (MTP) – replacing the traditional management responsibility of goal-setting and planning with an employee-based one.

For the organisation to achieve Six Sigma it has to give its employees sufficient authority over their work that they genuinely manage themselves. The goal of the MTP programme is for the 33 distinct departments in the organisation to liaise effectively and work in a coordinated fashion without removing this autonomy.

Critical Success Factors

The senior managers do not lose sight of the criteria for the success of their business. But they do make them clear for all to see and update people on them. Among the factors identified by the team at Zytec are:

- sales per employee: they currently average $100k, against an industry benchmark of $80k;
- manufacturing yield: since 1988 they have achieved a 50 per cent improvement;
- manufacturing cycle time: in the same period they reduced this by 26 per cent;
- design cycle time: reduced by 50 per cent;
- product costs: reduced by between 30 and 40 per cent;
- product quality: (based on customer-supplied data) has risen to around four sigma. Specific measures are used for different products and services, therefore:
  (a) mean-time-between-failures of PSUs is over 1m hours;
  (b) on-time delivery now occurs on 96 per cent of orders.

Self-assessment

It became clear to the senior management team that highly motivated employees were crucial to the success of their plans. The team carried out a survey of employee attitudes. The success of this process and the benefits from its results have led to its adoption as a regular annual process.

Cascading aims

The introduction of new ways of working has built on earlier activities and so an initial cascade process was not really necessary. However at Zytec the CEO, Ronald D. Schmidt, holds face-to-face meetings with teams throughout the business as part of the MTP programme.

Developing skills

Many organisations mistake the cascade process, in which basic corporate goals are communicated to all employees, for training. The latter calls for a transfer of genuine skills. Zytec did not fall into this trap. Instead they have a basic requirement for employees to attend 72 hours (10 days) of quality-related training each year.

This links to a revised employee reward scheme. Although some authorities would argue about their effectiveness, Zytec has adopted a reward system that increases an individual's pay rate according to the number of job skills that they can use. The reward system, known as MFE or Multi-Function-Employee, encourages multiskilling for each person.

Supporting teams

As they develop their skills so teams of people are encouraged to run their own departments. These self-managing teams are a characteristic of highly responsive organisations, but they are not the only example of teams at Zytec. Teams are also responsible for coordinating other key business processes. For example, it is a cross-functional team that manages new product design and development. This work passes on to other teams for implementation. These teams are all empowered to resolve customer and supplier issues and anything affecting quality performance.

Counselling members

The role of the manager at Zytec has changed. Unlike their peers in many other businesses, the Zytec managers rarely get involved in day-to-day fire-fighting. Their job throughout is to provide the support and coaching that individuals or teams need to develop their own skills.

Ongoing review

Besides the annual survey of employee attitudes, teams routinely review performance of the various parts of the improvement process. The MTP programme, for example, calls together 150 employees for a two-day planning event. At this session the proposed five-year plans of six cross-functional teams are reviewed and revised in line with, and leading to, corporate goals. Once drawn together to form a coherent package these plans are then reviewed with selected customers and suppliers in an almost unprecedented partnership arrangement. In several areas the organisation has contacted other businesses to provide a benchmark for their own process. Again the results of this are regularly reviewed by the senior managers.

Marketing: internal and external

Most organisations can benefit internally from the systematic use of their marketing activities. Zytec clearly gained a tremendous boost in its profile when it was given the Baldrige Award. This coverage, and subsequent interest in the company, provides a great incentive internally too. Using such impromptu material the management team constantly reinforces the key messages to its employees.

The activities that are described in the rest of this book are intended to allow you to instigate and carry out a self-assessment phase for your organisation. They can be used whether you are doing so to provide a trigger to your own senior management team or as part of an ongoing process of change.

SELF-ASSESSMENT FOR CHANGE: ACTIVITIES

Activity 2.1: The current senior management team

On the chart on page 36 list the members of your senior management team on the right hand side. For each person, ask each of the questions, scoring 1 for a 'yes' and 0 for a 'no'. Add the total and calculate as a percentage of the senior management team.

- If close to 100% the team will be likely to respond constructively to your initiative.
- If less than 50% you need to do some serious groundwork before introducing anything radical.
- If between the two you need to gain the support of the lower scoring individuals carefully.

Activity 2.2: The current senior management team

The chart on page 37 is intended to give the senior management team an opportunity to assess its own performance in terms of group process. It also introduces them to some of the issues that are involved.

EXPOSURE TO CHANGE

Keeps in touch with new strategies

Regularly attends seminars/professional meetings

Has discussed the changing marketplace with you

Discusses non-operational issues with peers

Discusses strategies with peers

Discusses changes in own area with peers beforehand

Socializes with peers

Is known for creative solutions to problems

								Sum	TEAM MEMBER'S NAMES
								TOTAL	
								PERCENTAGE (%)	

GROUP PROCESS REVIEW

Participation

1	2	3	4	5	6	7	8	9	10

Uneven, some dominate, quiet members ignored

Undirected comments, full participation throughout

Influence

1	2	3	4	5	6	7	8	9	10

Evidence of rivalry, dominance of one person's ideas

Shifting influence, no rivalry, quieter members drawn out

Styles of Influence

1	2	3	4	5	6	7	8	9	10

Tendency to be autocratic with few other styles of influence

Balance of autocrat with democrat, peacemakers etc

Decision Making

1	2	3	4	5	6	7	8	9	10

Consequences poorly reviewed, steam-rollering, majorities used

Impacts well considered, group accepts all decisions, no drift

The Job In Hand

1	2	3	4	5	6	7	8	9	10

Drift off course, analysis paralysis or over task driven

Stick to goal, base decisions on essential facts, people & task OK

Maintenance of the Group

1	2	3	4	5	6	7	8	9	10

Little done to support others, some ideas are lost forever

Support given to all; all ideas are discussed

Group Atmosphere

1	2	3	4	5	6	7	8	9	10

Excessively congenial or openly sharp

Business-like with all involved and interested

Membership

1	2	3	4	5	6	7	8	9	10

Subgroups, cliques "against" outsiders

Subgroups do not interfere; full team membership

Feelings

1	2	3	4	5	6	7	8	9	10

No expression of feelings; Excessive emotions showed

Balanced emotions shown if appropriate

Group Rules

1	2	3	4	5	6	7	8	9	10

Excessive politeness or formality, taboos exist

Flexibility, no constraints or constraining rules

Using Activity 2.2 as a group review tool

1. Transcribe the scales on to a flip-chart.
2. At the end of a meeting ask people to spend five minutes in a review of the team and its performance.
3. Introduce the diagram and explain where it comes from. Explain why the questions it asks are important.
4. Get people to read the scales and on a separate piece of paper rate the team on each.
5. Collect the bits of paper – without consciously tracking who says what.
6. Mark with large dots the scores from each person on the chart.
7. If any patterns emerge – either common views (especially to the left of the chart) or widely differing views – discuss these and why people think they have arisen.
8. Finish by thanking people and offering to pass around some suggested reading on the topic.[2]

Activity 2.3: Your progress so far

Figure 2.2 represents the generic model of change that we have described above. Using the research, which you did for the activities in chapter 1, identify the various steps that you have gone through in recent months or years. Remember that you can expect to have to go through this sequence for almost any change. If you have introduced any strategic process recently you should spot them. Alternatively, you may feel that your organisation has already begun its current change process and you might want to record events so far.

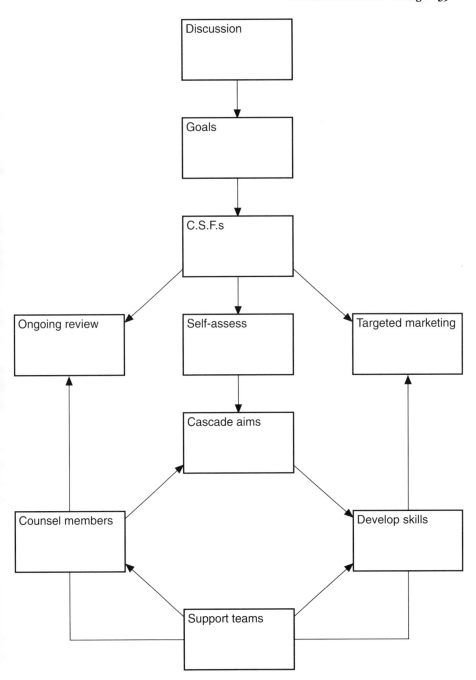

Figure 2.2   Successful change model

Activity 2.4: An inventory of surveys and diagnostics

From the research that you completed for chapter 1 you probably will have high-lighted several surveys, reviews and diagnostics conducted in the past for your own organisation. If you have any difficulty tracing these reports try:

- the Chief Operating Officer's Secretary;
- the Information Centre or Library; or
- the Purchasing Manager.

In our experience these are the most reliable sources, although most senior managers who have been involved will retain copies of necessary documentation. Try to summarise their process, findings and the resulting actions on forms such as the one shown in Figure 2.3.

TITLE OF REPORT:

SUBJECT AREA   Service ☐   Ideas ☐   Leadership ☐   People ☐   Admin/Syst ☐

CONDUCTED BY   External Consultants ☐   Senior Management ☐

Middie Management ☐

Junior Mgmnt/Supervisors ☐

Non-Supervisory Employees ☐

ORGANISATION   Individuals ☐

Team ☐   Within Dept | Cross Function

	Imposed Topic
	Team Choice

Date Commissioned	
Date of Report/Presentation	
Duration	
Cost	

METHODS USED   "Committee" ☐

Interviews ☐

Questionnaires ☐

Focus Groups ☐

BACKGROUND

SUMMARY OF CONCLUSIONS

RESULTING ACTIONS
Description   By Whom   Date   Time from Rpt

Figure 2.3   Summary of surveys and diagnostics

References

1. Beer M *et al.* (1990) Why Change Programs Don't Produce Change. *Harvard Business Review*, Nov/Dec 1990, pp. 158–166.
2. Schein EH (1988) *Process Consultation. Vol. I: Its Role in Organisation Development* (2nd Edn). Addison-Wesley, Wokingham.

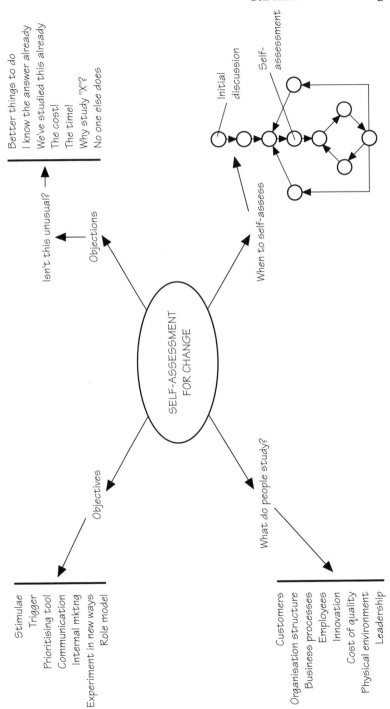

Summary Mindmap 2: Self-Assessment for Change

3 GETTING THE 'RIGHT' RESULTS

INTRODUCTION

In this chapter we shall look at the mechanics of self-assessment teams. What they need to do and how to ensure that the results they obtain are the best that can be achieved. To do so we are going to look at four aspects of any team-based activity and apply them to the self-assessment approach.

Whenever a group of people meet together there are a number of aspects of the group that decide how well the meeting will go. Some of these features will depend on the *task* that they are tackling. For example, a council meeting may proceed without incident until a particularly contentious topic crops up. Then the normal decorum may be shattered. As well as the task itself, the *people* who are present may influence the meeting. The contentious issue at the council meeting might have passed unnoticed if there had not been people of two different political persuasions present. In both cases we can distinguish between influences simply due to the *content* and those that are due to the way in which this is dealt with, the *process*. For instance, at the council meeting again, the two political groups could handle the contentious topic in different ways. Under some circumstances even the most radical issue could be passed by both groups without a murmur, when on another occasion it could lead to a revolution. We have all attended meetings where an agenda item has been expected to cause a rumpus. The way in which it is handled by the chairperson can make all the difference to the end result. These are all examples of *process* – the way things are done.

Having an agenda, using a flipchart, keeping minutes are examples of *task process*. Two people coming to a meeting together, whereabouts people sit around a table, how one person talks to another, are examples of *people process*. Choosing a select group of people to attend the meeting, screening attendees with a psychometric test, giving an open invitation, formally inviting guests or holding the meeting in a public place will all control the *people content*. Defining the items on an agenda, giving people a brief before a meeting, and training them in certain problem-solving techniques are all ways of influencing the *task content* (see Figure 3.1).

	TASK	PEOPLE
CONTENT	Formal agenda Goals	Who is doing what to whom
PROCESS	How the task is done	How members relate to each other
STRUCTURE	Standard operating procedures	Recurrent personal relationships & roles

Figure 3.1   Task vs people and process vs content

We shall use these distinctions to understand how a self-assessment team works and how the senior management team can ensure that they produce the best results.

WHO TAKES PART AND WHAT IS THEIR ROLE (PEOPLE CONTENT)?

The coordinator

The first person to be appointed by the senior management team is usually the coordinator. The coordinator will help the team achieve its goals. The role involves coordinating efforts, balancing resources, exerting influence outside the team to gain support, teaching the team new problem-solving skills if appropriate, and ensuring that the final report not only addresses the original brief but contains a well argued and supported case for any changes.

Do coordinators need training? Only if they lack the skills that are needed. These fall into three areas:

- basic problem-solving skills;
- specific techniques (such as survey design or statistical methods); and
- group behaviour and process skills.

We look at the basic-problem solving skills later in this chapter. Most rising managers will have been introduced to these during their earlier management careers. You can decide for yourself whether the individual concerned has a sound understanding of these. The specific skills are almost impossible to enumerate until work on the topic has begun as they will depend on the topic and the way in which it is tackled (task process). Usually the group would identify any weak areas and co-opt people as 'experts' for the short time that they need them. Interpersonal skills can always be developed and enhanced, though they are not often focused upon in traditional management development. The facilitator's role (described below) is intended to supplement the coordinator in this area. Indeed facilitators have a responsibility to help coordinators develop their skills. If anyone needs training it is probably the facilitator.

Leading self-assessment teams is frequently an assignment for potential high-fliers. They need the respect of the senior management team and the support of their line manager(s). Usually individuals will be identified and one of the members of the senior management team will approach their line managers clearing the appointment. This is an important preparation. Coordinators will inevitably find that the self-assessment activities conflict with their day-to-day tasks. When this happens they need the full cooperation of their managers.

- Positive attitude to the changing business.
- Interest in supporting the change.
- Supportive (not highly directive) leadership style.
- Good people-coordinating skills.
- Experience of leading teams (not necessarily at work).
- Awareness of basic problem-solving skills.

Figure 3.2   The characteristics of a good coordinator

You will possibly notice the emphasis on supporting the team. There is no room for a strong-willed and highly opinionated coordinator. In fact it is difficult to see a role for this sort of person in the responsive organisation at all! In the section on team members below we look at the roles people take in groups. In these terms the coordinator's style should be that of a coordinator.

The Facilitator

The coordinator's job, then, is to manage the task process. Coordinators do so by exerting influence over the task content, i.e. the material that the team works on. They will also usually have had influence over the people content – who gets invited to join the team. This responsibility is certainly enough for one person to handle, and inevitably they will get embroiled in the problem and the solution.

But far more can go wrong, even when the team is sensibly chosen, understands its brief and has all the technical skills to tackle it. People meeting together frequently do things that affect the contribution of others.

The Working Party

I remember sitting in on a government working party once. A union representative had been co-opted after the group had been meeting for a while. The individual was not very well briefed and joined the team one morning. As he introduced the chap to the other members, the chairman explained; 'This is . . . He's come along to put the views of a unionist'. I could see the chap cringe, but he was obviously weighing up the situation, looked slightly nervous, and didn't say anything. After an hour or so coffee arrived. The group broke into little gaggles, leaving the 'rep' to himself. After a minute or two one of the younger engineers walked over and started talking to the guy. At lunchtime the two of them went off together. In the afternoon the meeting carried on. By the end of the day the 'rep' had said nothing. When the group had dispersed I was left in the room with the chairman, the young engineer and one other person.

The chairman expressed surprise that the 'rep' had said so little. The young engineer countered by saying that it was his first meeting in this role, having been elected only the previous week, and that he hadn't been told anything about the working party. As we left the chairman was confiding in the other man, who it turned out was an old school friend he was staying with. 'I don't know' he said, 'these youngsters are all the same – all b****y left-wingers!'

The chairman had done a very poor job of coordinating the meeting in that he had been oblivious to the lack of contributions by some members. He had also clearly pigeon-holed the young engineer into a political niche, simply because he felt sorry for someone who was obviously nervous and had bothered to find out something about them.

It goes almost without saying that the final recommendations of the working party reflected the ideas of the chairman with very little input from others except those that felt the same way. The report suffered and, not surprisingly, had to be redrafted by a new team only three years later. The other members left with a very poor impression of the workings of the organisation, and the union man left feeling a little sour and having learnt nothing. What went wrong in that meeting was that the chairperson had a very strong interest in the solution – he'd virtually written it himself. He didn't understand his role in developing the ideas and contributions of others and he kept going back to his own interest, the task in hand.

The failings illustrated in the 'Working Party' example are very common. Coordinators of groups are usually the last people to see how they are steering the decision in favour of their own preferred solution. Good coordinators are rare. To make up for this and to help the chairperson develop as well as the team members calls for a special role. This is usually known as a 'facilitator'. Some people use the title differently, however,[1] so beware. In this context they are not a teacher, coach, tutor or another coordinator. The job of the facilitator is to manage the *people process*.

The task is not easy, and calls for some very specific skills. Facilitators are usually people with good powers of observation and are usually exceptionally good listeners. Facilitators have a good understanding of the dynamics of people in teams, both in terms of the individuals' personalities and how they work together, and in the way they communicate together during a meeting. In Belbin's terms (see below), facilitators are likely to have a combination of styles. On the one hand they have to be very people-focused, especially in groups, and so they are likely to be a Team Worker. On the other they are usually very good at seeing the pattern behind events, building on what they have learnt and constantly adding to it. This is a trait of the Shaper. This sometimes seems a contradiction in terms. Good facilitators though, will not get drawn into shaping the problem that the group is tackling, they will probably be shaping the group's behaviour instead.

As we've said, a good facilitator will never get drawn into the task, but will always concentrate on helping the others to be heard fairly and without prejudice. Most organisations have a few individuals who are either natural facilitators, or need little training to make very significant contributions. Outside the self-assessment process, the facilitator is often asked to help other teams and on many occasions they become a mentor or counsellor to the CEO. So valuable is the facilitator's contribution that one major steel company has removed most of its management layers (about 300 people) and replaced them with a small team of facilitators (numbering no more than 24). They are confident that productivity will increase!

The team members

So the senior management team will have appointed a named coordinator, and may have appointed a facilitator, or indicated to the coordinator that they should do so. It is then the job of the coordinator, armed with the brief which we shall discuss later, to choose the other members of the team. The senior management team may make recommendations, but it is usually best to leave the final choice to the coordinator. The only time when the whole team should be selected by the senior managers is when the coordinator is unlikely to know a broad enough range of people to be representative. Even then it is probably better for the senior managers to define the likely functions or other criteria rather than naming the people.

How do we choose the team? Each individual should be interested and have a positive attitude. There may be in-house experts with relevant experience or skills that the coordinator wants. There is also the need to have representatives from all areas affected by the subject or likely changes. These should be representative not only of functions (e.g. Accounts) but also of levels of employee in the hierarchy. There should never be a token person, however, especially from the shopfloor. In this case there should always be at least two.

But representation and experience are not enough. The team has an important job to do in a relatively short time. They need the right balance of team roles too. Team roles is the name given to the contribution that people bring to a group. They probably bring the same contribution regardless of the setting. The study of team roles has been extensive, but the most popular approach has been developed by R. Meredith Belbin.[2] Belbin studied students at Henley – The Management College over many years. Using a number of psychometric tests and other personality instruments he created artificial teams and gave them tasks to do. He and his co-workers then observed and recorded the behaviour and performance of these teams. Eventually they developed a simple questionnaire to help people identify their main strengths in a group and a model of these contributions so that a highly effective and complementary team can be pulled together.

Belbin's work showed that people contribute in a combination of three different ways. They may bring with them a wide variety of *ideas*, thereby being the people most likely to contribute new approaches to a problem. Alternatively, they may have a strong *people* focus, being concerned with helping to win other people to the team's cause and making new decisions stick. The third dimension is a strong *task*-driven approach. These people are good at getting things done, on time and to a budget. They may not be too concerned with the longevity of the solution but at least they've done something. In practice people do not have just one strength. They have combinations and Belbin identified ten of these. Figure 3.3 shows the strengths of the different roles.

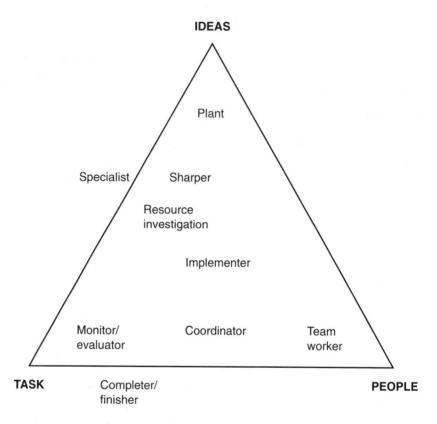

IDEAS

Plant

Specialist   Sharper

Resource
investigation

Implementer

Monitor/   Coordinator   Team
evaluator   worker

TASK   Completer/   PEOPLE
              finisher

Figure 3.3   The different strengths of team members
After the work of R. Meredith Belbin at Henley Management College

What is your natural role in a group and what roles do the other members of your management team take? The tables in Activity 3.1 on pages 73-4 show the characteristics of the various roles with an explanation of each and include a diagnostic chart for you to list your own team, to see what strengths they show and what impact this may have on the team.

Should we have a sponsor?

Senior management teams usually debate for a long time how they will relate to (and control) the self-assessment team. There are several options:

- have a member of the senior management team on the self-assessment team;
- hold regular reviews with the team or its coordinator direct to the senior management team;
- hold regular reviews with the coordinator through a senior manager;
- have a member of the senior management team act as sponsor of the self-assessment team; or
- use an external consultant as the liaison between the two teams.

The senior management team needs to discuss the implications of each of these and decide for themselves which one they want. Often their decision will reflect how far their own thinking has progressed in understanding the consequences of empowering employees.

When an organisation is widely dispersed with a large number of employees working for local managers a more senior 'sponsor', who maintains regular contact with the coordinator, can be very useful. Most often a sponsor's support is sought when there are conflicts over resources at a local level. If the business is smaller, say less than 500 employees, and based on one site, then occasional contact between the coordinator and the CEO is sufficient. In this case the CEO has to be very sensitive that they do not give subtle messages to the coordinator thus influencing the outcome of the study.

When a senior management team becomes locked in a discussion about 'sponsoring' the team, there are usually one or two individuals who are particularly emphatic about the need. If this is the case the facilitator, often an outside consultant, will assess the situation and decide whether these individuals are speaking for the group or just for themselves. Once the facilitator has begun to form an opinion, depending on time constraints, they will probably test out their view with the senior management team. If the team does not share the concern, then the facilitator will take time to work with the individuals, helping them to understand why they feel this way. If it is a team problem then there needs to be a discussion about it – otherwise any recommendations that are proposed are unlikely to be endorsed.

WHAT DO WE STUDY (TASK CONTENT)?

The second part of this book looks separately at each of the following five topics.

- Customer focus
- Leadership
- People
- Innovation
- Administration

The coordinator needs to be properly prepared to take on the task. This is a two-stage process. First, the senior management team needs to prepare a written brief and then needs to hand this over to the chosen coordinator. The written brief is very important as it provides the whole team with the framework in which they are going to be working and to some extent determines how ambitious they can be. The brief should not be very long – most are less than two sides of A4 paper.

The basic content of a briefing document is shown in Figure 3.4. It is very important that the senior management team have shared in developing the briefing documents.

Developing the Written Brief

Once the idea of self-assessment has been voiced we suggest that the briefs for each of the five areas are studied by the senior managers and they then come to a meeting prepared to discuss the topics and their relative merits with the organisation. It is useful to clarify the goal of the self-assessment; it is not intended to recommend simple fine-tuning, but equally it isn't to make recommendations that can not be substantiated. The senior managers have to appreciate that real change is only going to be achieved through radically re-examining what the organisation does today.

It is sometimes surprising how quickly the team can decide on their priorities for review. The argument often goes along the lines of: 'There's no point doing anything until we've understood . . .'. Provided that there is real consensus around the table then this is fine. On other occasions there will be one or two camps around the table with some people choosing one topic and the other a second. Usually some form of compromise is reached.

- One can be given the go-ahead with a specified review date to decide on the other.

AUDIT TEAM BRIEFING NOTES

TITLE	Reduction of Paperwork

KEY DEPARTMENTS INVOLVED	Depots Regional Offices Head Office
OBJECTIVES	To reduce the quantity of paperwork, while improving quality, effectiveness and systematic control.
SCOPE	All Divisional business activities, nationwide, including Regional and Head Office functions.

KEY TASKS	Select Audit Team
	Train team
	Develop project plan
	Liaise with Steering Committee to
	  verify scope, resources etc
	Identify data collection requirements
	Establish methods of data collection
	Gather data
	Evaluate data
	Develop alternative improvement actions
	Establish priority areas
	Present preferred solution(s) to
	  Steering Committee
	Implement when approved
	Monitor effectiveness of solution
	Identify new areas for action
	Produce subsequent Briefing Notes

RESOURCES	Leader: 18 days Members: 84 days (12 days by 7 members) Initial Duration: 13 weeks Further resources may be identified by the Audit Team
BENEFITS	Reduced cost of service delivery Improved morale in depots Improved systematic control in depots Improved financial control Reduced demands on managers

Figure 3.4 Example of a briefing document

- Both may be given the go-ahead.
- One team can be formed with a brief which includes aspects of both subjects.

If a review date is agreed it should not wait until the first matter has been reported on. The review date, say two months later, should be agreed there and then. This usually coincides nicely with senior management meetings, allows the first group to begin work, and any problems that they have encountered will be known and can be avoided with the second group.

Where both topics are chosen and two teams are given the go-ahead it is always sensible to make sure that the briefs very clearly define the limits of any overlap. The two team coordinators should be encouraged to have reviews together after most of their team meetings. They should also be encouraged to share plans so that any economy of scale can be achieved, and duplication of effort avoided. All sorts of imaginative arrangements arise under these circumstances, especially when the two teams independently decide to carry out questionnaire-based surveys.

If the teams are to look at a subject across more than one location it is important to consider how you would like them to operate. Are the locations so independent that it would be better to have one team at each, working separately? Or is the topic sufficiently central to the business that only one set of recommendations can be expected. Would you rather pilot the approach in one location – this won't necessarily be any less expensive and in the longer term could be twice as expensive, but there may be advantages. All of these questions need to be discussed before a decision is made and the brief(s) are prepared.

Usually, one member of the senior management team will agree to draft a brief and circulate it before the coordinator is contacted. Sometimes though the team will recognise that logistically this will take too long and they will prepare the brief, in committee, there and then.

Handing over to the coordinator

Once the written brief has been prepared the senior managers need to decide how to hand over to the coordinator. Obviously the extent of any handover depends on the organisation. Most medium to large organisations will arrange a meeting of the coordinator with a representative of the senior management team – preferably the CEO. If the senior management team has decided to name the facilitator too then a separate meeting will also be held with this person. In the handover the coordinator will be talked through a written brief and allowed to discuss any immediate questions that they may have.

A second meeting is often a good idea to clarify any points that the coordinator is unsure of, especially once a facilitator has been chosen. The coordinator should be given the option of meeting the CEO alone or with the facilitator.

HOW DO WE TACKLE THIS TOPIC (TASK PROCESS)?

Timing and the calendar for the team

A self-assessment may last for up to six months. This often raises eyebrows among senior managers and needs some explanation. The team itself will meet for between one and two hours each week, preferably at a regular time and location. They are asked to provide quantifiable recommendations – in other words to deal with facts and not opinions. This will involve properly designed data-collection, appropriate analysis, and valid interpretation. It may involve formal experiments and trials of ideas before they are recommended. Once the conclusions have been drawn together, the team must prepare itself for a formal presentation to the senior managers and practise what is effectively a critical sales opportunity. It is vital that the team's findings reinforce the trust which is being placed in them, and cutting short the preparation time causes trivial issues (such as a misspelt word in the report) to interfere with the task itself.

Given the nature of the subjects under consideration and their long-term impacts on a business it is difficult to see how any group could make its presentation in less than 20 to 25 weeks. A senior manager who still insists that this is too long cannot properly understand the importance of the work. In Figure 3.5 we show a typical calendar for a self-assessment team. This is only provided as a guide – teams will vary, as will events between meetings.

Of course teams can complete their work in much less time, if the senior managers are prepared to allow them the time to do so. The six-month average reflects the fact that these people are still fully occupied on their regular jobs. If they can be relieved of these duties then the self-assessment process can be much quicker. The slowest step is the data collection activity. Any survey usually takes at least three weeks to complete for logistic reasons and this effectively limits most self-assessment processes.

This is a guideline only. Circumstances can change and teams may find they work faster or slower. If you are the leader or coordinator of a team, do not be pressurised into reporting back until you are all ready.

Week	Content
1	Review of brief between sponsor and coordinator.
2	Review of brief by whole team; explanation of process including calendar and administration by coordinator.
3	Brain-storm of issues to be studied; discussion of methods.
4	Selection of key topics; selection of methods to study.
5	Design of data collection process.
6	Design of questionnaire (if used): classification variables.
7	Design of survey; design of questionnaire: comparative variables.
8	Review of survey; review of other data needs.
9	Review of data collection progress; trial survey(s).
10	Review of data collection progress; commissioning full survey.
11	Write up expansion phase of problem-solving structure.
12	Review of data collected; agree responsibilities for analysis.
13	Review of analysis; initial discussion on interpretation.
14	Establish consensus of interpretation; brain-storm solutions; agree additional data requirements to assess prospective solutions.
15	Review additional data; agree solution(s).
16	Agree methods of evaluation of solution; describe process.
17	Document solution selection process and recommendations.
18	Document evaluation process; agree responsibilities for presentation.
19	Review individual contributions to the presentation.
20	Review of report before copying and binding.
21	Rehearsal of presentation.
22	Full rehearsal of presentation.
23	Senior management presentation.
24	Review and celebration.

Figure 3.5   Example of a self-assessment team calender.

Agendas, minutes and other paperwork

Does a CEO really need to read about agendas, minutes and other paperwork? Organisations differ enormously in the amount of paperwork that they accumulate. There are countless reasons for doing so and someone can usually find a justification for each piece of paper and every form. We shall look at the consequences of this in the chapter 8 on self-assessment of administration. We explained at the start of this section that one of the objectives of a self-assessment team was to try out different ways of working, or to reinforce the new role models that have already been developed. If a self-assessment team, handling a subject of serious strategic importance to the organisation, operates effectively with a particular style of administration, then most other activities in the organisation should be able to do so too. For this reason the records kept by the team should be well thought out and reflect the future style for the whole organisation.

In Britain most civil servants can be recognised by their characteristic briefcases. Simple, black, single flap folios with a small brass-like catch immediately below the gold-embossed crown and plastic-covered name label. Most maintain daily sequential records in a plain buff-coloured, hard-backed A4 (or is it foolscap?) book. The briefcases and books have become a part of the organisation's culture. No doubt a historian somewhere will know how this arose and when.

When Marcus Sieff took up his post as Managing Director of Marks & Spencer he took a one-year 'sabbatical'. In this time he eliminated 80 per cent of the company's paperwork. The volume was estimated at 27 million pages per year. At the end of the year he lit a ritual bonfire heralding the new culture!

Bureaucracy appears to be proportional to the size of the organisation. For many larger ones the amount of paperwork is disproportionately large. For some smaller ones it can prove inadequately scant. The first meeting of the team should look at alternatives and agree how they will handle administration.

We include two examples of simple forms which are intended to capture all the relevant information without creating a hierarchy of administrative support for every meeting. These could be used to stimulate the discussion in the first meeting (see Figures 3.6a and 3.6b).

Using the skills and experience of the team

As we have said, one of the benefits of the self-assessment process is the development of the people in the team. The coordinator should make this

MEETING RECORD:		#:
(Group, Team or Project Name)		

Date:	Participants (draw plan of table):
Time (from):	
Time (to):	
Location:	

Summary of Agenda	
1	6
2	7
3	8
4	9
5	10

Agenda Item	Summary of Conclusions and Discussion	Action By	Action When

Next Meeting:

Figure 3.6a   Meeting record form (linear)

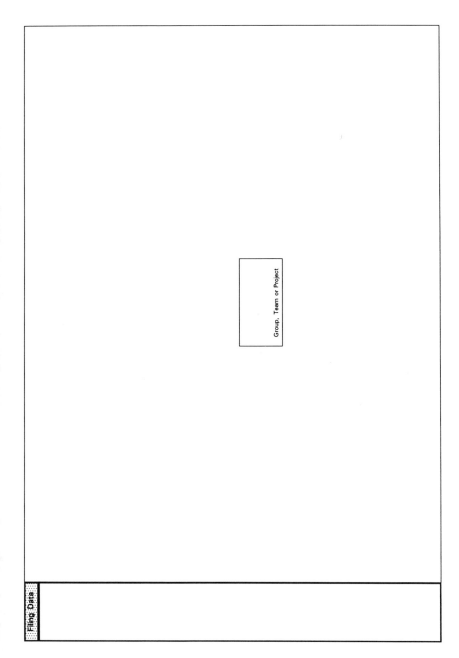

Figure 3.6b   Meeting record form (mindmap)

clear at the outset, letting the facilitator explain each role and how they will work together. It is often a good idea for the coordinator to help the team create an inventory of skills and experience during the first meeting. This can then be used to pair people for tasks so that someone with experience of interviewing, for example, can work with someone who has none.

The coordinator should also make it very clear that the group has been chosen because of the combination of members' experience and skills. It is everyone's responsibility to indicate where they think they have some special abilities that the team could use.

The problem-solving process

There are many different systematic problem-solving processes taught on management development courses. They are all essentially the same, despite the claims of their proponents. Any problem-solving approach begins with a definition of the problem, then uses divergent thinking techniques to develop possible solutions before using convergent techniques to identify the best solution, put it into place, and test its effectiveness. We frequently find that these models are taught on courses early in a person's career but are not adequately understood and applied later. To help recall your own training and see the similarities between approaches we have included a comparison table of the commonest approaches (see Table 3.1). Use the grid in Activity 3.2 on page 76 to analyse a recent project or problem which you have tackled.

The commonest difficulties with problem-solving techniques and the reason why most solutions do not eventually work is that people omit stages from the process. They may jump from identifying the problem precisely to deciding on a solution without exploring alternatives, or they may not include an evaluation process at the end. The approach which we prefer is the PRIDE model. This is a variation on the PRICE model developed by Ken Blanchard.[3] We recommend this not because it has any magical powers – being a mnemonic it is easier to remember without notes and therefore more likely to be used. Listed below are the basic stages of this approach.

PIN-POINT the problem: Before trying to tackle anything it is important to move away from symptoms of the problem – which are usually perceived as the problem by most people – to the underlying issue. For example, early in my own career I was asked to help reduce tanker driver absenteeism for a company. Even phrased more positively – improving tanker driver attendance – this was not the real issue. The real problem lay in a number of

Table 3.1   Comparison of problem-solving models

	Blanchard	Francis	Coverdale	GOAL
Pinpoint	Pinpoint	Tuning in	Purposes	To decide which problem will be addressed first (or next)
		Objective setting	End results	To arrive at a statement that describes the problem in terms of what it is specifically, where it occurs,
Record	Record	Success measures	Success criteria or results	when it happens, and its extent
Inform ourselves and others	Involve	Information collection	Information	To develop a complete picture of all the possible causes of the problem
Decide	Coach	Decision-making	Plan	To agree on the basic cause(s) of the problem
Effect and evaluate	Evaluate	Planning	Action. Do it!	To develop an effective and implementable solution and action plan
		Action		
		Review to improve	Pinpoint	To implement the solution and establish needed monitoring procedures and charts

policies which the drivers perceived as undermining their status within the company. Even with a very clear brief most self-assessment teams will have a range of ideas on the *real* issue.

RECORD the facts: With a clear problem definition we then gather information to help us understand it better. Unless we are considering an attitudinal problem we are not interested in opinions, just real facts. The facts that we require need to be decided by the team. For example, in reviewing Innovation, they may feel that information has to be gathered about previous suggestion schemes. Or they may feel that this is pointless and that they need to analyse a typical product to see how it has developed and how modifications have been introduced. There are many different approaches.

INFORM ourselves and others: Armed with a list of information needs the group sets about gathering the details. The object is to expand their understanding of the problem. In doing so they will be involved in contact with other people. This is often an opportunity to prepare the ground for trials of solutions and to improve people's understanding of the change process. For some reason, some groups develop elaborate plots to avoid telling others what they are doing and why. This doesn't work and needs to be avoided.

The selection, collection and analysis of data are all important steps in the development of an effective solution. They are also potentially the most expensive and easiest to foul up. The team need to prepare themselves carefully by looking at techniques of question phrasing, questionnaire design, and survey planning.[4] Modern problem-solving books are intended for use by teams of this kind and contain practical tools and techniques to improve the effectiveness and efficiency of surveys.[5]

DECIDE on a solution: The last phase of divergent thinking that the team get involved in is in devising solutions to the problem that will respond to the facts that they have gathered. This process is often not as difficult as it sounds. Solutions tend to suggest themselves from the data collection process.

EFFECT it: Although the self-analysis teams are not expected to put their recommendations into place they do need to devise appropriate ways of introducing them. Sometimes this can call for considerable effort and should not be underestimated. After all, many businesses recognise the need to reduce their bureaucracy. The real problem is how to do so.

EVALUATE the results: No solution is complete without the means to assess its impact. The second by-product of the data collection process is the identification of a small number of key indicators which will show whether or not the teams recommendations have been successful.

Reporting back

Once they have completed their study, developed their preferred solution(s), and devised plans for its implementation and monitoring, then the team are ready to report back. The coordinator will agree the meeting arrangements with the senior management team. By the time the study is over, the members of the team will have put in a considerable amount of personal effort beyond their normal work. They deserve to be present at the presentation. One or two people at the most should be appointed spokesperson(s), but the rest should be ready to respond to questions. Usually the team's report will consist of three elements:

- a physical presentation;
- copies of the materials used in the presentation; and
- a supporting document, containing the important data and evidence.

The presentation is crucial. A poorly made presentation will turn off the senior managers, may reinforce in the minds of any doubters there that this approach will never work, and can set the organisation back a long way. Most teams resort to straightforward presentation materials, but there are many exceptions. Among the alternatives are videos, scale models, site walkabouts and visits to other organisations (Disney seems very popular!).

You will have seen from the calendar in Figure 3.5 that some time needs to be set aside for the preparation of the presentation, and the preparation of the report should begin almost as soon as the team has agreed its primary tasks. It is important to provide the members of the senior management team with copies of the presentation materials. One question which is often asked is whether this should be done before or after the presentation. Usually teams prefer to give the materials at the outset so that they can be annotated by the audience.

Unfortunately there are a few people who will turn to the back of the pack, read the conclusions and then start asking questions about information that is going to be given later in the presentation. If you suspect that you've got one of these people in your senior management team, prepare beforehand and be ready to put them politely in their place!

Questions are probably best handled at the end, when they can be directed to other members of the self-assessment team. Finally, the report should be given to the senior managers. It is usually best to take a copy for everyone rather than allowing one copy to go on circulation.

Senior management response

The senior management team is not a passive recipient of the report. There are several things that they need to do before, during and after the presentation.

At the presentation it is important for every senior manager to be there, and for all to be ready with questions. It is also good practice for the managers to ask their questions at the end and to all the members of the team so that it doesn't become the spokesperson's show.

Beforehand, the senior managers should discuss whether to reward the members of the team for their efforts. Normally they would not; however, if the team are known to have invested their own money in the project in order to overcome some obstacle, have given up excessive amounts of their own time, or have made some other contribution 'above and beyond the call of duty', then some reward is perhaps appropriate.

Recognition, on the other hand, is much more common. How do we recognise the group's achievement and contribution? Everything from badges and plaques to inscribed scrolls have been used. At the Bank of England, for example, inscribed glass paperweights were prepared by one of the senior managers and only issued on special occasions, such as this. In a very different setting, Tremorfa Steel Works in Cardiff, commissioned one of their production operators, who was an accomplished artist in his spare time, to prepare a small number of local landscapes, which were then presented to the team members.

Unless you have a major event planned, the best time logistically for any act of recognition is immediately after the team presentation. This saves organising a repeat gathering so it may be worthwhile arranging for the company photographer to be ready when called. If the event has been arranged for, say, 11.00am, it gives the team a couple of hours for last minute preparations, allows an hour and a half for the presentation and questions, a half hour for the 'ceremony' and then can finish in time for a buffet lunch for the team with the senior managers. It also means that, after lunch, the senior managers can continue their own meeting to discuss the conclusions reached while they are fresh in everyone's mind.

Immediately after the presentation it is usual for the CEO to write to each of the team members thanking them for their efforts and promising to keep them informed of developments that arise from their work. The most important part of the senior management response, however, comes later. Armed with the report of the team, there may be questions which it raises and for which the senior managers want clarification. There may also be areas which the team have explored and dismissed, but for which the senior managers want to see more detailed information. Most of these issues will be channelled to the team coordinator who will decide whether to respond alone or to call the team together again for one or two more meetings.

Eventually the senior managers will have discussed and debated long enough. They should then respond to the self-assessment team, giving a detailed explanation of the actions they intend taking and asking for any further feedback that individuals would like to give them on their plans. Once this process is over the senior managers need to act quickly to put the changes into place.

How long this process takes depends on the senior management team. Some will set themselves a target of responding within a specific time. These vary from 'by the start of the next financial year' to 'by tomorrow morning'. Of course, if the team are serious about the need to be responsive, this is the opportunity!

HOW DO WE WORK TOGETHER (PEOPLE PROCESS)?

Attendance

Throughout the self-assessment team's activities it is important to remember that the group members were chosen for their skills and experience. The coordinator, and especially the facilitator, should be managing these throughout. The easiest to deal with is attendance. When people become disinterested, demotivated, or uninvolved they naturally look for reasons not to join in. With an activity which will be seen by some as outside their 'real' work it is particularly tempting simply to not attend. After all, you only have to explain why if someone asks and then it is usually easy to pass the buck. The coordinator and facilitator should be monitoring attendance. Although they can do this from meeting records we usually find that a simple table summarising attendance is useful. This is because discussions about anyone not arriving usually happen as the meeting starts. Rummaging through meeting reports is a waste of time and effort.

People who simply do not turn up should be followed-up and offered the chance to drop out. There should not be any pressure exerted, either directly or through an individual's line manager. If the skills or experience for which they were originally selected are needed then an alternative should be chosen and very carefully prepared to join the team.

Group dynamics in meetings

We have already looked at the different team roles; part of the *people content* of the meetings. The most important job for a coordinator is to make sure that everyone has the opportunity to contribute and that particular individuals are actively encouraged to do so.

The role of the facilitator is to improve everyone's ability in managing the contributions of others in meetings of all kinds. The facilitator calls on a

---

The Short General Manager

Not long ago, we were introduced to the General Manager of a Northern manufacturing company who was particularly short. He had inherited a large management team from his predecessor and hadn't done anything to reduce its membership because he was concerned that this would be demotivating.

Whereas his predecessor was quite tall and could effectively control the large team by sitting at the head of the boardroom table the new General Manager could not see most of his colleagues. His first effort was to import a larger (and higher) chair, but he still found controlling meetings difficult. He then had the table, quite crudely, elongated to spread the people further down it; unfortunately this just left people having to twist their heads more to see him and so worsened his feeling of loss of control.

When the company began its change process, flip-charts became a more popular accessory in meetings. For everyone to see a flip-chart it had to be placed alongside the middle of the table. On a team of this size there were bound to be a number of ideas people (Shapers or Plants, in Belbin's terminology). The General Manager was one. The other in the group used to sit halfway down one side. By switching sides of the table he retained his preferred position but also took control of the flip-chart. Within a couple of meetings he had begun to dominate.

When the facilitator got the group to discuss the flow of the meeting several people commented that they felt the General Manager was taking a back seat role and questioned whether he was doing so because he knew he was leaving. Talking to the General Manager later, the facilitator helped him see that his role was not under threat, but that he could influence the group more effectively if he moved to the position beside the flip-chart. The impact was immediate and, without realising why, the group confirmed this in a similar review after the next meeting.

number of specific skills and knowledge to allow them to do this effectively. We shall look at just a few aspects which illustrate how much more complex this is than many people realise.

Earlier in this chapter you looked at the roles adopted by your own senior management team during meetings. In Activity 3.1 on page 72 you will try to identify the characteristics of the team members and considered whether there are any gaps or imbalances in the existing team. Let's take this one step further. In most regular meetings we begin to do things consistently. For example, people tend to sit in their favourite places. This can have a dramatic effect on the contributions which people make (as 'The Short General Manager' story shows).

Activity 3.2 uses the decisions that you made in Activity 3.1 to look for any people process patterns in your senior management meetings.

What makes you say that?

(a) Observation

It's a busy street, with lots going on. Heavy traffic is moving slowly with pedestrians on either side of the road walking along, carrying their shopping bags. The shops are all lit up with Christmas signs and bargains galore. It's at a time like this that pickpockets are rife and on a street corner the police are using a loud hailer to warn people to keep their handbags in front of them all the time. From a side street a youth runs into the crowd. He's wearing a greasy looking jacket, with his hair flying around him. He looks violent and is. He shoves the passers-by out of his way, as he runs across the street dodging the fronts of the cars and a bus. Someone yells at him, but he carries on running.

Stop most of the people in the vicinity at the time and they will describe him in a negative way. They will have already drawn many conclusions from his appearance, his clothes and his behaviour. This is a clip from a training film made in the early 1970s. It was used to highlight the problems of sexual and ethnic discrimination in the workplace. The clip finishes with the youth taking a flying tackle at a woman pushing her clear of an object falling from a building.

In most regular meetings we arrive with our own pre-conceived ideas about what will happen and especially about the people who are going to be there. We all know the person whom we dread making a comment, because we know too that they will drone on for hours! In more subtle ways we do the same for everyone there.

Behavioural specialists have a way of describing the thinking process which we go through in a meeting. This is repeated hundreds of times during a meeting and it has a dramatic effect on how the meeting goes, how we feel at the end of the meeting, and what other people think about us. If you want to achieve results with a team you need to become very skilled at managing this process in yourself and with others.

When something happens, an event, we *observe* it using one of our senses. It may seem obvious that if one of our senses is not very good we risk missing some events or some of the details about an event. Some people have developed one or more of their senses better than others. The Sherlock Holmes character, for example, was based on a very much enhanced power of observation. There are many tales of blind people who have developed their other senses, especially that of touch, to partially compensate for their disability. Almost all of the senses are affected; some have remarkable powers of smell, others of taste, and others of hearing.

There is good evidence that if we have a particular dominance of one sense over others, then we tend to use words associated with that sense when we talk about observing things. For example, if you tended to use hearing more than other senses you might subconsciously use sound-related phrases:

- I like the sound of that idea.
- I hear what you say.
- It sounds to me as though
- Can I sound you out about. . .?

Visually dominated people will prefer phrases such as:

- I've got the picture.
- I see what you mean.
- I like the look of that.

People with a dominant sense of touch might use:

- Let me get to grips with this.
- It feels to me . . .
- I got in touch with them.

You may have even heard the phrase:

- Ooh! He was really tasty!

What's the point of all this? People who have a particularly dominant sense are likely to be more favourable to an idea presented in a way that appeals to that sense than they will to presentations using the other senses. For example, if you find that one of your team uses sound-related words more than others, next time you have to communicate with them don't send a written memo, but instead use the telephone. If it's a lengthy communication you might even send them a cassette tape and suggest that they listen to it in the car on their way to work the next day!

With a little thought the applications of such a technique are quite widespread. Certainly, if we find ourselves disagreeing with someone else in a meeting, it is worth asking ourselves whether we, or they, had observed the information accurately.

(b) Reaction

When we see something happen we experience an immediate reaction. Our reaction depends on a whole host of previous experiences dating back throughout our lives, but especially from the early years. People with 'strong' views usually have had many experiences which have tended to confirm these. For example, someone who has a strong dislike of dark rooms will probably have had some experience of a dark room, in the past, which was unpleasant. Reactions are the basis of most prejudices.

We cannot usually control these reactions. They happen and that's all there is to it. However, we can be aware of them and try to understand why we feel that way. On a longer-term basis we can be helped to understand why we have them. The basis of counselling is often to help an individual understand why they feel a particular way about an issue and then to decide for themselves whether they want to continue to do so or not. For example, a junior manager had recently been promoted. He saw himself as having status but very limited power. Before the promotion he had not been very widely respected by his peers or the people that reported to him. He was aware of this and had doubts as to why he had been 'promoted'. The new position although 'high profile' had no authority. Shortly after his promotion he began to use quite insulting language to describe the people 'below' him.

It was only after a particularly fraught meeting that one of the facilitators took him aside and confronted him with observations about his behaviour. After a long discussion with the facilitator, conducted over several days, the manager slowly began to understand that his behaviour was a reflection of his desire for positional power, i.e. having people respect and obey him because of his position. He could see that other people didn't have such a strong need and he began to look back over his schooldays to see how this might have developed. He identified a particularly distressing incident at primary school which he was sure had been the starting point of this need.

With this in mind he looked over his secondary school, university and business life with a very different perspective. His behaviour changed dramatically and at the same time he became far better 'tuned in' to other people's comments. He not only found that people responded far better to him at work, but he also developed far more confidence outside work too.

The process of helping other people like this is a tough one, and some professionals would say that it should be left to them. Unfortunately, few of us have access to such skilled help. It is critical to remember that throughout this process the facilitator would never have made a judgement. The decisions were entirely the responsibility of the manager. Most of us will never have to encounter anything like this, but we can try to recognise consistent reactions among our colleagues and use this knowledge to help them see things from our viewpoint. For example, two partners in a firm had very different views over borrowing strategies. One was in favour of expanding the firm by borrowing money, the other was strongly opposed to borrowing of any kind. As a result the business was not growing to the extent that the first wanted. The two began to argue about whether the business should grow at all. They were 'arguing' about the wrong issue. With the help of a facilitator, the second began to recognise his concerns about borrowing of any kind and could see that his own reactions were different from those of his partner. Although in this case they never resolved the difference, they did stop arguing about the wrong problem.

When we are reacting to something we may re-orientate ourselves to improve our observation, but we do not say anything and we won't show any signs of emotion. For instance, someone overhearing a comment may react by turning their head to improve the chances of hearing some more, but they won't raise their eyebrows or let out a gasp. Reactions are essentially inside ourselves.

(c) Judgement

Seeing something and reacting to it still do not affect the dialogue. Before we pass comment, or make any other kind of intervention (such as raising our eyebrows), we have to decide to do so. This decision may be conscious or subconscious.

One characteristic of people's personality is their tendency to make judgements. Confronted with the same situation some people are more likely to 'take a stance' than others. One outward expression of this is people who are very dogmatic, especially on subjects which are contentious. The Pro-hunting/Anti-hunting or the Pro-abortion/Anti-abortion lobbies are good examples. Supporters on either side of the argument should be capable of recognising that the issue is one on which opinion is divided and that no matter how strongly they feel there is probably someone who has an equal and opposite viewpoint. Nevertheless, anger begins to develop as the more judgemental members decide to vocalise, or in some other way demonstrate their views.

The opposite extreme are people who are strongly pragmatic. They will not usually intervene in a situation like this, recognising that they are very unlikely to influence the course of events.

(d) Intervention

OBSERVE: A member of the team says something. We hear it, we see their face as they say it, we feel the table shake as they thump it while speaking.

REACT: Our experience tells us that people who thump tables and go red in the face while shouting obscenities either have a strong view about something or are drunk!

JUDGE: Oh no! He's on his high horse again!

INTERVENE: What do we do or say? If we have thought through the implications of the ORJI cycle, have tried to understand our own reactions to the person, and have tried to see where misperceptions could have crept in, then what we say should have a positive effect. Its effect will be to create another ORJI cycle in other people around us and so on (see Figure 3.7).

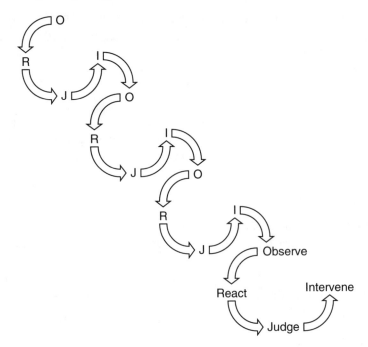

Figure 3.7   The ORJI cycle

GETTING THE 'RIGHT' RESULTS: ACTIVITIES

Activity 3.1: Team Roles

For any team that we work in it is useful to have an impression of the balance of roles that people are adopting. This activity provides a tool to enable you to do this. Figure 3.8 is a diagnostic chart that can be used to spot the common characteristics of members of any team. First look at the characteristics column and the contributions. Try to identify which role you would associate with each member of your management team. Take the members one by one. Having found good fits, check out your theory by looking at the common sayings. Are these the phrases that you would associate with the person that you are thinking of? For each member of the team, place a tick against any dominant team roles that you have identified using Figure 3.9 on page 74, then follow the instructions in this form to assess the balance of the team.

Role	Characteristics	Contributions	Major strengths	Allowable weaknesses	Common sayings
Plant (Clive Sinclair)	Clever, imaginative, unorthodox, serious minded, individual	Original solutions to tough problems, especially early in projects and if off-track	Imagination, intellect, knowledge	Independent, weak communicators, ignore protocol	What about...? / I don't have to justify myself to others
Resource investigator (Richard Branson)	Extrovert, communicative, curious, enthusiastic	Explore opportunities, develop contacts, and negotiate deals	Think on their feet, set up outside contacts, great source of energy	Lose interest unless constantly stimulated	I know someone who can.... Let me see what I can find
Coordinator (Lord Hanson), Desmond Lynam)	Calm, self-confident, mature, controlled, trusting	Motivating to work with, good at clarifying goals, work well in mixed teams	Welcome others' input without prejudging	Not usually the cleverest members of a team	So what you're saying is.... Has anyone anything to add? Let's keep the goal in sight
Shaper (Lady Thatcher, Brian Clough)	Highly motivated, challenging, agressive	Good managers, very motivating to work with, cut through politics	Thrive on confrontation, get teams to produce results	Headstrong, emotional, impatient and can offend, may impose pattern on group	No, you're wrong! The .... So what are we going to DO about it?
Monitor/ Evaluator (Ludovik Kennedy)	Sober, unemotional, objective, dry	Good at analysing problems, usually hold key strategic posts	Judgement, discretion	Dry, boring, poor motivator of people	There's always two sides ... Let's look out for ...
Team Worker (Michael Palin, Lynda Chalker)	Social, mild, perceptive, sensitive	Most supportive members, prevent people process problems, get maximum from all	Good listeners, well liked, non-threatening	Indecisive and avoid confrontation	Let's give ...'s idea a thought Would you like to add anything else?
Implementer (The Queen, Lord Runcie)	Dutiful, reliable, well organised, enjoy routine	Organises, turning ideas into actions	Hard working and practical, good organisational ability	Lack flexibility, resist unproven ideas, slow to respond	We can do so ... within the budget/ Given time we could ....
Completer/ Finisher (Nick Faldo)	Painstaking, orderly, conscientious. Appear clam but	Ideal for tasks needing attention to detail, high office	Fulfil promises and work to high standards	Worry unnecessarily, poor delegators	What about clause 23 on the third page? A stitch in time, etc.
Specialist (Geoff Boycott, Peter Shilton)	Professional, self-starter, dedicated	Indispensible where local information is crucial	Provide wide-ranging technical knowledge	Show little interest in others	I'll see what I can find out. We must keep up our standards

Figure 3.8 Team Roles diagnostic chart

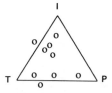

Name	PL	SH	RI	IMP	ME	CO	CF	TW	SP
TOTALS									

INSTRUCTIONS

1   Write the name of each team member in the left-hand column.
2   Record the dominant Team Roles for each person in the boxes.
3   Total the roles demonstrated within the team.

QUESTIONS

1   Is the team balanced or does it lack any strengths?
2   Are there any team excesses?
3   Are there any team weaknesses?

CONSEQUENCES

1   What are the likely consequences of the team composition on its ability to perform?
2   What can be done to address these?

Figure 3.9   Team Roles analysis chart

Activity 3.2: Applying the problem-solving process to a project

Figure 3.10 on page 76 shows a format to break down a recent project (which could be large or small) to see how it went through the basic problem-solving steps.

In the first column write alongside our PRIDE stage the phrases used on any training course that you have attended. You may find Table 3.1 on page 61 useful. In the second column record the tools and techniques that were used in this step. Figure 3.11 on page 77 shows a typical project and identifies the sort of tools and techniques that you may have used. The third column is to list the results of the particular step; what did it achieve? Finally, in the last column, make a note of the time that this step took to complete.

NAME OF PROJECT/PROBLEM:			
STAGE (or name that you have used before)	TOOLS and TECHNIQUES USED	OUTCOMES and RESULTS	TIME SPENT
PINPOINT			
RECORD			
INFORM			
DECIDE			
EFFECT			

Figure 3.10   Project analysis chart

NAME OF PROJECT/PROBLEM:		Developing our Quality System (to ISO9001)	

STAGE (or name that you have used before)	TOOLS and TECHNIQUES USED	OUTCOMES and RESULTS	TIME SPENT
PINPOINT	o METAPLAN o Process Flow Diagrams	o Agreed Scope of Application o Identified Key Processes	One Week
RECORD	o Brainstorming o (we also did the Alaskan Adventure Team Work Activity)	o Applied ISO9000 clauses to key processes o Agreed ISO level (9001 v 9002) o Identified Performance Measures o Responsibilities for Documentation	Two / Three Work-shops over a month
INFORM	o Working Groups (eg Accounts) prepare and make presentations o One-on-One Reviews o Control Charting	o Documented Working Practices o Assessment of present performance using measures from previous stage o Responsibility for procedure writing	Six work-shops over three months
DECIDE	o X-functional teams prepare and make presentations o Control Charts -> Deptl Quality Groups o Group Discussions	o Documented QMS Procedures o Priorities for Quality Improvement based on cost and measures o Plan for Company-wide Training	Four work-shops over three months
EFFECT	o Training Workshops o Visit by Certification Body o Control Charts	o All using procedures o Improvements being measured o Revision to QMS & Procedures and Working Practices	Several work-Shops over two months

Figure 3.11   Example of a completed project analysis chart

Activity 3.3: The dominant senses of your senior management team

Take a table like that shown in Figure 3.12 into a meeting of the senior management team. Whenever you hear one of the members use one of the phrases make a quick tally mark again the correct box. We have left a few spare lines for you to add new phrases as you spot them. Beware of metaphors and regional sayings which can cloud the issue. For example, 'He's really tasty!' is more likely to be heard with a Liverpudlian accent. Remember to explain what you are doing to your colleagues!

NAMES OF TEAM MEMBERS

VISION											
It looks to me ...											
The way I see it...											
AUDITORY											
I like the sound of it...											
It sounds to me...											
I hear what you say!											
KINAESTHETIC											
Let's get to grips with it											
Let's keep in touch											
I can't quite get a handle on this											
TASTE											
I like the flavour of...											
Ooh! He's really tasty!											
SMELL											
I can smell a rat!											
We'll sniff out a better deal!											
The smell of success											

Figure 3.12   Dominant senses analysis

Activity 3.4: The ORJI cycle

Look at each step in the ORJI sequence (see page 71). Consider the example of the red-faced person. What assumptions are being made about people who react in such a way? Where are they being made – at the observation, reaction, judgement or intervention step?

The next person you talk to will provide you with an opportunity to try using ORJI. It really doesn't matter who it is. Listen carefully. Listen for assumptions. Look at what they say and try to identify the steps before it.

Activity 3.5: The dynamics of a team

Using a plan of the people in a meeting, drawn on plain paper, record the people who make interventions. Begin by observing simply who is speaking – this is not as easy as it sounds. As your skills develop over a couple of meetings, build up your picture by trying to spot directed comments as opposed to general ones. Annotate the diagram with arrows.

Constantly look for patterns in the interactions among the group. Is one person dominating? Do two people tend to talk to one another rather than to the rest of the team? Does one person always address questions to another?

As you become more adept at spotting who is saying what and to whom, you will also become faster at marking up the diagram. Trained facilitators will add a further level of complexity by trying to assess the style of the comments that are made. One approach to this is to identify the 'ego' states of the individuals that are talking.[6] Three states are identified: Adult, Parent and Child. We are all familiar with the expression 'Talking down' to someone. This usually means that one person has adopted a stance of Parent and is expecting the recipient of their message to behave as a Child. The skilled facilitator spots these discrepancies of state and asks whether they are justified. What gives a senior manager the 'right' to talk to a shopfloor worker as a child, for example? By helping people to see how they are communicating, it is possible to help them to change their approach to a more constructive one that doesn't cause irritation and discomfort.

References

1 Foster M and R Dewhirst (1991) Facilitator Skills. *TQM Magazine*, September 1991, pp. 363–365. This interesting article about Pilkingtons is just one example of the different uses of this title. It is not the context that is used by organisations implementing Self-Directed Work Teams.

2 Belbin RM (1981) *Management Teams: Why they succeed or fail*, Heinemann, Oxford.

3 Blanchard K and R Lorber (1984) *Putting The One Minute Manager to Work*, Willow Books, New York.

4 Oppenheim AN (1966) *Questionnaire Design and Attitude Measurement*, Heinemann, London.

5 Wilson GB (1993) *Problem Solving and Decision Making*, Kogan Page, London.

6 Berne E (1975) *What Do You Say After You Say Hello?*, Corgi, London.

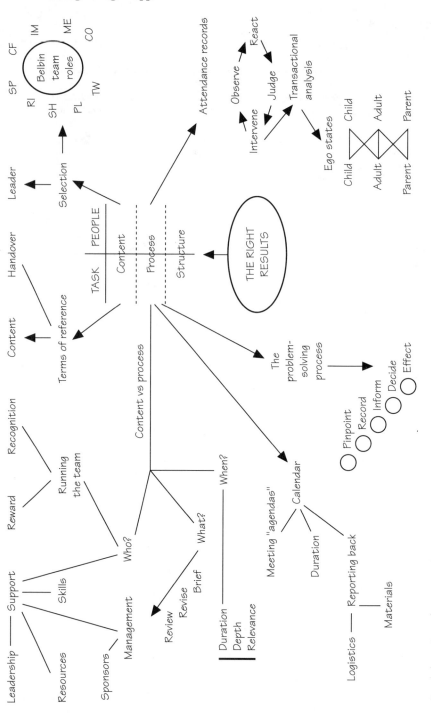

Summary Mindmap 3: Getting the 'Right' Results

The structure of the following chapters is similar. In each we explain the issues at stake, why they are important to the responsive organisation, and how they are addressed.

One or two short case studies follow. These look at specific organisations and how they have responded in the area under discussion.

The third part of each chapter looks at the key issues to be examined by the Audit teams. It poses questions about previous events or initiatives, about their effectiveness and how the organisation can build on them.

None of the questions posed will call for direct answers. Instead, they pose a variety of issues which the Audit team needs to explore. They are deliberately chosen to be relevant to any organisation. If your immediate reaction is to say that they are not, then discuss this within the team.

In some cases an Audit team will carry out all of the activities. In others it will only look at one or two in any detail. Some do overlap – though, again, there may be a benefit in performing each. The time taken by a team to complete each activity will vary. Not only the amount of resources available, but also the depth to which you pursue the topic will determine how long they take. It may be worth reviewing all the topics and then selecting one for more detailed research.

Some teams will tackle one topic and then make recommendations for follow-up activities. The rule is one of flexibility.

Chapter 4 is the longest chapter of the book. This is not because our enthusiasm was highest here! The subject of customer service is one of the most important *for immediate action*. It is also one of the commonest to be examined by Audit teams. For the teams looking at the other areas, it is worth reviewing the Service Audit, as there will probably be aspects that are also relevant to your own area.

4 SERVICE

WHY DO WE DESCRIBE THIS SECTION AS 'SERVICE'?

Most modern management 'thinkers' base their arguments on one simple assumption, namely that satisfied customers are good for business. Why do they think this is so? As we have already pointed out, one of these 'thinkers', Tom Peters, is well known for having said that during the 1950s and 1960s in North America it would have been impossible to 'screw up' a Fortune 500 company. Under certain market conditions this is certainly the case, or at least it must be, judging from the anecdotal evidence that greets us from every direction. You only have to look at some of the large monopolistic companies around the world, many of whom have a very poor reputation for customer satisfaction and yet who seem to thrive on it. Certainly in Britain until the late 1980s almost any company whose name began with 'British' either tried to change their internal culture (BP, BA and so on) or had to spend a fortune on positive PR. To be fair, many of these have made significant steps towards improved service *and* public perception, nevertheless, they still have many critics. This is not a book on economics. It does not take a great deal of imagination though to recognise the criteria and conditions in which a company can survive despite providing significantly poor levels of customer service. So why do the gurus point to the satisfied customer as the panacea for most organisations? Their arguments are based around three themes:

1. Satisfied customers themselves tend to bring back business.
2. Satisfied customers provide the best form of marketing through word-of-mouth recommendation.
3. Organisations reduce costs by servicing satisfied customers as opposed to customers that are dissatisfied.

Let us briefly look at these three in turn and see whether they are actually the solution to our organisation's problems. Consider repeat business. The argument goes, of course, that if a customer is satisfied they will come back and buy, again and again. Formulas have been derived, particularly in the areas of fast-moving consumer goods, which demonstrate the life-time value of customers.

Take, for example, a typical supermarket. Most of their individual customers will live in the vicinity of the supermarket for a period of about three years (with out-of-town stores the equation changes and many of their customers will literally last a life-time or at least be loyal from 10 to 12 years). If a typical household spends £50 on shopping in the course of a week then their monthly bill is £200, their annual bill is £2,400 and in ten years they have spent £24,000. Seen in that light their purchases at the supermarket are virtually the equivalent to those made in most car showrooms in the same period of time. So it is worthwhile satisfying those customers to get their repeat business.

The view of the car dealer may be less obvious. In a market where we are only serving about four to five per cent of our potential customers (despite all the additional trimmings that we may provide in the form of incentives to attend the store) we can 'afford' to lose quite a large number. For the garage, where admittedly we have not taken into account the after-sales service and sale of second-hand cars, the desire to provide exceptional service will remain low.

Supporting the arguments in favour of gaining repeat business are the age-old statistics that every dissatisfied customer will tell their friends and those friends will, in turn, be influenced by the one bad experience. This is a form of word-of-mouth 'de-recommendation', but word-of-mouth recommendation also works. The case for satisfied customers is that they will pass on, by word of mouth, their satisfaction thereby gaining trade. This might be a plausible idea in a small close-knit community, but for many organisations their customers rarely meet. 'Word of mouth' obviously extends to third-party recommendation but, as much of this is driven by PR specialists, the question remains is word-of-mouth recommendation really a reasonable argument for larger organisations?

An interesting third line of reasoning is the one based on the internal benefit of satisfied customers. Namely that to service a satisfied customer costs less than servicing a dissatisfied one. This is another way of looking at the cost of quality. Surprisingly few organisations have tried to assess their cost of service delivery even though it can provide the trigger for change. In their companion book to this one, Munro-Faure and Munro-Faure explain one mechanism by which the cost of quality can be assessed.[1] To ensure that their book was compatible with others they adopted the approach which is recommended by the British Standards Institution in BS6187. Unfortunately, in our experience this tends to underestimate the costs involved in delivering satisfactory service for your customers.

We shall briefly look at some of the issues at stake. Nowadays most consultants would recognise that there are six classes of cost of service delivery. The objective in any kind of improvement process is to reduce those costs that do not add value and to increase those costs that do add value. The six categories of cost of service are:

- prevention;
- control;
- internal failure;
- external failure;
- exceeding requirements; and
- lost opportunity.

In the traditional analysis only one element is seen as adding value, the *cost of prevention*. Prevention activities are essentially concerned with 'designing-in' quality before a product or service is created, generated, manufactured and delivered. It usually falls into two categories: the cost of good design (and all of the associated benefits with that) and the cost of good training (preparing the people who are going to deliver the product or service so that they can do so in a fault-free way).

Management teams often seem to lack confidence in their own organisation, staff and abilities and so as a result they build in a series of controls, ways of making sure that if a problem does occur, that it does not get shipped out or delivered to the customer. These *control mechanisms* are usually passive, in other words they are concerned with catching problems once they have occurred and not letting the problem demonstrate itself to the outside world. A lot of effort was made by organisations in the early 1980s to design systems that were fail safe – that showed straight away when a problem had arisen and prevented a product from proceeding down the production line without someone taking remedial action.

Nevertheless, much of our earlier control experience was based on the idea of designing controls around the final quality of products. Over the years tools and techniques have become increasingly more sophisticated, but none of them, regardless of the computer power that is employed to try to use them, is anything other than a non-value-added activity.

The third type of cost of service delivery is known as *internal failure*. This is incurred where an organisation discovers, probably through one of its inspection activities, that it has developed or produced a product or service which is in some way defective. Stopping the production process, recycling and reworking all incur costs. These costs accrue and form the category of internal failure.

If we look at an analysis of the effort spent by managers in organisations, we tend to find that most middle and junior managers spend the vast majority of their time in activities that are concerned with internal failure. In fact, for many organisations the specialist dealing with internal failure is also the company hero. One petrochemical company chief recounted over dinner one evening that the reason for his meteoric rise to power was his phenomenal ability to fight fires; as he pointed out many people could see him putting out serious fires, but no one had seen him set up the fires in the first place!

In percentage terms the costs escalate as we move from the internal prevention steps to internal failure and so to external failure. *External failure* is the cost incurred when the customer outside the organisation experiences the effects of poor service or products that we have delivered. Most analyses of this item tend to look, or have tended to look in the past, at the costs incurred by the company. For example, they include reworking, refunds, replacements, sometimes the costs of management time and of engineers' time in refitting, re-installing, etc.

Nowadays environmental auditing has developed and the fundamental practices of cost of quality audits have begun to change. One of the basic assumptions of audits is that we are only concerned with the internal costs, but the environmental lobby recognises that there is a very important element outside the organisation which needs to be taken into account. At a recent meeting of quality consultants there was widespread amusement at an environmental organisation that had carried out an audit on a small company based in Birmingham. The reason for the amusement was that one of the costs of the environmental pollution for the organisation was considered in terms of the detrimental effect on South American rain forests. Of course, this sounds obscure, but nonetheless it was significant.

The idea of a wider cost through delivery of poorer products is not new. Back in the 1950s Genichi Taguchi, a Japanese engineer, expounded his theory of the costs to society of moving away from a target value for any product or service. The equation he used was an expansion growth curve so that as the delivered quality moved away from the target value the more extreme impact of defects was felt by society. Taguchi's rationale was applied across a very wide range of applications and also across a great depth of scale from the costs of loss to society incurred by a small electronic component in, for example, a radio right the way up to the costs of poor quality in a production plant polluting the atmosphere. Surprisingly the expansion curve holds true in the few quantifiable cases that are well documented.

The British Standard for quality costs does not talk about the costs of *exceeding requirements*. Again, for many organisations this is badly under estimated. Nightmare stories abound in the quality arena of organisations which, in desperation, have adopted 100 per cent inspection as a means of ensuring that the quality of their product satisfies their customers. You only have to look at the many tonnes of paper that have been created under the guise of quality systems to recognise that somebody, somewhere along the line, has exceeded requirements. One organisation we were working with were amazed by having fewer forms rather than more. They could make their controls more visible thereby improving their effectiveness. They were very sceptical and it was only when we demonstrated it practically that they would believe us.

Exceeding requirements is an interesting cost. According to traditional quality theory, the cost of exceeding requirements should be reduced. After all, it adds no extra value and it tends to increase overheads. The counter argument, which has been most forcefully put forward by Tom Peters, is that it is legitimate to exceed the customer's expectations on the basis that you are creating a market advantage for yourself against your competitors. We shall look at this in more detail later on in this chapter.

Finally, the sixth category of cost of quality is that of *lost opportunity*. This is one of the hardest to assess and can be the most difficult for most organisations to tie down. We had an interesting case in point ourselves recently. As part of our work often involves running courses for organisa- tions we frequently require ring binders. Rather than buy the cheaper variety 'off the shelf', we prefer to have our own manufactured for us, this is surprisingly cheap for a good quality product. However, 18 months ago our supplier of some years standing delivered three batches in succession with a large number of defects among them. We had deliberately kept our stocks low and so their poor delivery caused us considerable inconvenience and additional costs. In the course of recovering from this situation we identified a local supplier who could produce to order, deliver the same products at virtually the same price, and because of the lack of travel involved was able to ensure that the damage *en route* was negligible. We were quite impressed by this newcomer.

Despite the fact that their organisation had had to recover the situation twice, our original supplier made no attempt to contact us in any way to apologise for their poor delivery. Only 18 months later did a new salesperson try to track down some of their lost customers. When we questioned the salesperson concerned we found an individual with a remarkable capacity for dealing with aggrieved customers, taking none of the flack personally.

Instead, he slowly and very courteously took us back over the track record of purchases from our organisation and at the end of a couple of conversations had pursuaded us to give his company one more try. On the basis of that track record he had actually calculated the amount of business that he believed his company had lost as a result of their mistake. In his estimation, over the 18-month period his organisation had lost in excess of £150,000 of business from similar incidents. As their overall turnover was only £1 million this was a very significant proportion.

So which of these costs are reduced when we create satisfied customers rather than dissatisfied customers? Obviously the costs of external failure, lost opportunity and exceeding requirements are all minimised, but perhaps the most significant is the cost of management time and control in monitoring their activities. An organisation with a significant proportion of dissatisfied customers tends to see more of its management time tied up in short-term tactical issues rather than longer-term strategic ones. This is not the role of a true manager and also tends to demotivate the members of staff.

Unfortunately, the evidence in favour of having satisfied customers tends to be anecdotal. In the late 1970s Tom Peters and Bob Waterman conducted a survey of 100 or so organisations. They based their sample in terms of long-term profitability and a number of other strictly financial considerations. Among the common characteristics they identified was a high degree of customer focus within the organisation. Although the initial sample had been based largely on performance data their subsequent work was almost entirely anecdotal.

A more recent and highly visible example of an organisation that has appeared to systematically 'rip off' its customers was that of the Ratner Jewellery Group. The lid was blown for the organisation by Gerald Ratner in a speech to the Institute of Directors. In the course of his speech he described his products as 'absolute crap' and demonstrated very effectively how a promotion that they were running amounted to very little in costs, but a great deal in PR value. Overnight, his position as one of the magnates in the jewellery industry in Britain was completely eroded. Within twelve months he had lost his position, many of the groups shops had closed and the public perception of the jewellery trade had been seriously affected.

Whether you believe that it is important for customers to be satisfied in today's market-place or not, it is important if the organisation is to respond to a changing marketplace and a changing world. We do need to know what our customers are looking for and endeavour to deliver at least the basic services that they expect. In earlier chapters we have looked at the mechanics of conducting an audit. In this chapter and the subsequent ones we are going to look at a variety of questions; questions that need to be asked and answers that need to be gathered to enable you to understand where you stand as an organisation. Specifically the outcomes of this Service assessment are sevenfold:

1. Who are the customers themselves?
2. What are those customers expecting?
3. What are our products and how do they live up to expectations?
4. What are we doing to ensure that they match?
5. How do we compare with our competitors?
6. What scales of performance should we be using in the future?
7. What targets and goals should we be setting ourselves?

When we talk of the 'response' of the organisation that response is one of Service. It is that 'Service' response that we are trying to capture in the title of Service for this chapter.

USING STANDARDS TO ACHIEVE GOOD SERVICE

One way of looking at service has been developed over recent years as our awareness has improved. At the simplest level there is the concept of quality and quality assurance. Most gurus have defined quality in some way or another. Whatever the definition you would expect, the common element to most of them is that quality involves delivering a product of service to an approved standard.

These standards vary. Most organisations delivering a manufactured product have standards which they conform to. Obviously the most elaborate components tend to have more specific demands, but equally there are many items which have become staples and for which the definition of the standard is created outside the organisation itself. A classic example of this is photocopier paper. Huge quantities of photocopier paper are sold around the world. While many people would be aware of the A4 standard for the paper size, they would also be aware that paper stocks will vary slightly in the size of the final trimmed page. A smaller proportion of those people will be familiar with the weight per square metre as a measure of the product. Fewer still would be aware of the variations in the paper, weave and so forth despite the fact that these are of increasing importance for the sophisticated printing methods within organisations.

In our experience the divide between internal awareness of technical standards and the customer's perception is probably greatest in the service sector. For example, surveys are frequently conducted of the effectiveness of overnight delivery services. What do we mean by 'overnight'? To some organisations 'overnight' means the product needs delivering the next day; to some it needs to be delivered by 5.00pm or the end of the working day; to others it means delivery the next morning; and for a smaller group it means delivery before 9.00am. Ask the customers and you are likely to find a very wide range of understanding of the service they are actually contracting for. Service at this level calls for clear goals, clearly spelt out standards and the right systems, equipment and people to deliver them. As we have said, this is the simplest level of service to deliver.

Developing the right systems is straightforward albeit often expensive for many organisations. The national quality standard BS5750 or its international equivalent ISO9000, attempts to provide a bench-mark for these organisations' systems. Increasingly sophisticated equipment and tools are being used by organisations to deliver a service level which perhaps in the past would not have been achievable. Progressively, these have become available to smaller organisations too.

The trend in the western world is towards organisations with fewer employees and a higher turnover per employee. In Britain in 1988 official statistics show that 20 per cent of commercial turnover was through companies with less than 200 employees. By 1992 this has risen to 56.8 per cent. At the moment society and industry have not begun to address the human skills needs for the growing smaller business sector. Nor have we appreciated the negative impacts of such dramatic and global downsizing.

One obvious example of these from a quality perspective is the fact that large organisations can employ staff with particularly high levels of specialist skills. The high levels of skills that they can bring should allow organisations to operate more effectively and more efficiently. Some authorities would dispute such evidence, or argue that the negative effects of being 'big' far outweigh the advantages.

If our organisation is to become responsive it needs constantly to reassess trends of this kind and respond accordingly. This should be far easier for businesses that have an established and local market, but for most companies this is not the case. One role of the Audit team is to take such a broad perspective, looking at major, often global, issues and the impact that they have on the services being delivered. This is a macro-economic focus.

FOCUSING ON THE CUSTOMER

The team, though, also has to look at a much narrower scale by focusing on existing customers. They begin to appreciate the breakdown of customers in terms of their geographical distribution, size of organisation, size of orders, frequency of those orders, times of delivery for different order points, and so on. For each of these criteria they look for imbalances in the services that are offered and those which are (or might be) expected by the customers.

Even quite large-scale discrepancies don't need a step change in thinking to develop solutions. For instance, a survey carried out by a Scottish University on behalf of a local Enterprise Council quickly identified that many smaller businesses in their area trade with central European countries. Most of these organisations had only a few staff. While the small number of senior members of staff who were engaged in active selling or in developing their business could understand and speak the languages involved, very few of their administrative staff could do so. In particular, the telephonist/ receptionist and order-taking staff had very few language skills. Since people with such linguistic abilities were probably out of the price range of the organisations concerned the local Enterprise Council set about providing a centralised referral point.

Using the power of modern telephone systems they were able to provide unique telephone numbers to a central exchange point so that European customers who were given a specific number could ring, be answered in their own language with the name of the company they were calling, and could have their immediate enquiry handled by an operator skilled in that particular language. The operator would remain available on-line while the call was transferred to the company concerned. This created a smooth transition for the customer from somebody speaking their own language (but perhaps lacking technical knowledge of the product), to somebody who understood the technical characteristics of the product (but didn't speak the language). In turn, this dramatically improved the trading records of those companies and, because the service was provided centrally, several of these organisations were able to break into further markets that had previously been out of reach because of their own lack of language skills. A similar development was inspired by a local council. This led to community-driven distribution and marketing activities for Cornish manufacturers, previously hampered by the distance from their potential markets.

Not all such solutions are so obvious and this is why it is so important not only to understand who our customers are, but also to really appreciate what they are expecting.

UNDERSTANDING THE CUSTOMER'S NEEDS

Most of us have taken part in surveys in the past where we have doubted why the survey was being carried out because of the nature of the questions which were asked. Probably the commonest cause of concern about customer surveys is that frequently they seem to be a marketing exercise for the company and not an information gathering process. But there are actually far more methods for listening to customers and gathering their expectations than the simple questionnaire. To begin with, for organisations that are delivering a technical service rather than a product, it is often perceived internally that the questionnaire is one of the few rigorous and quantitative methods of gathering this information. In fact there are whole areas of statistics that allow qualitative questions to be used in a form that allows us to determine their statistical significance. In the same way preferences, likes and dislikes can all be assessed in a quantitative way. It is vital that when the data is collected the information that is gathered from it is usable and useful to the organisation itself.

We are sceptical of the value of surveys carried out by external consultants as a way of providing ongoing assessment for organisations embarking on a programme of customer satisfaction. However, we do recognise that one survey conducted properly externally can equal many internal ones that have been conducted poorly for lack of resources, lack of support or lack of expertise.

Customer expectations by their nature are rarely measured or recorded with the same terminology used by the people in-house for a technical specification. One approach to overcome this discrepancy is the use of a tool known as QFD or Quality Function Deployment. QFD was a tool developed in the early 1970s by the Kobe Organisation in Japan, primarily at their shipyards. For an overview to the use of QFD you can read Munro-Faure and Munro-Faure[2] or for a more detailed review and explanation of how to use it, together with some of the pitfalls and tips for its effective application, consult Wilson.[3]

One element of the QFD process that can easily be used on its own is the development of a Matrix. Across the rows of the Matrix are the views and the feelings of the customers. In the columns of the Matrix are the technical responses used by the company to try to meet the needs of those customers. Involving the customer in this process gives them an opportunity to review how they perceive your performance.

There are many alternatives to QFD depending upon the product or service, some of which may be used to assess different products or services.

Frequently, when an organisation plans to extend its services or products beyond the scope that might reasonably be expected by customers historically, they make use of focus groups. Focus groups allow a team of people to develop their ideas through discussion with others. A properly trained facilitator can take the conversation several stages further than it would have gone had it been conducted individually or by a group of people on their own.

An alternative to the focus group approach is carried out by Japanese car manufacturers. Developing a new vehicle for the domestic market, they are in the habit of delivering a prototype to a railway station. They have their own engineers on the concourse to discuss the vehicle with passers-by. This has a double benefit. Firstly, it gains raw information directly from the customers to the engineers. Secondly, it gives the engineers an opportunity to develop their own thinking as they have to explain the features of the vehicle to the customers who have perhaps not come across them before.

USING BENCH-MARKING TO ASSESS YOUR COMPETITORS

Many organisations seem to believe that there will be a great deal of benefit from understanding far more about their competitors' business. This may be true for certain performance criteria and financial statistics. The information enables wider ranging strategic management issues to be discussed. From a product or service perspective there is less benefit from understanding the details of individual competitors' products.

For a period of about five years in the late 1980s a great deal of emphasis was placed on competitive bench-marking. The idea behind competitive bench-marking was to compare your organisation, product or service with those of your competitors, giving you a measure of how you perform. The first drawback to this approach is that is it arguable whether it should be the technical experts on the product or service (i.e. yourselves) who should be conducting the bench-mark. It may be better to use customers for whom some of the parameters you could measure might seem to be unimportant. The second drawback is that many of the organisations who undertook competitive bench-marking were already at the top of the league among their competitors. In some cases this can be seen to have cost them dearly. For example, one chemical company which regularly featured at the top of the lists for most customer criteria developed an extremely complacent internal culture which, in turn, has inhibited development over the last five to ten years. It is still not clear whether this has been fully appreciated by the senior management teams involved.

It is now widely appreciated that more effective bench-marking can be achieved when the comparisons are not made with competitors in your own market but with organisations who use similar processes as part of the delivery of their products or services in a different market. For example, suppose that you are a reasonably small company organising a series of conferences. One aspect of your organisation may be to provide a telephone response to bookings. Under the new approach to bench-marking, comparison would not be made with other conference organisers but to other organisations who take immediate-response telephone calls for bookings.

Depending on your organisation, where it is and how easily you can contact these other companies, the comparison might, for example, be made against a travel agency or a theatre ticket office or a railway booking system. The comparison would probably not stop at how you answered the telephone and processed the queries, but would probably penetrate further up the process by looking in more detail at the way in which information is used and reused. It would examine how information is stored, how access to it is provided, who routinely uses the information which is collated, and so on. This process of comparison can transcend boundaries. For instance, it is often much easier to organise such bench-marking activity with a company who could clearly not compete with you because of the difference in their geographic location. One major British steel company engaged in significant bench-marking activities with the Japanese Kobe Steel Works. The Japanese had no objection to this because they knew that they would never compete in similar markets directly, or certainly if they did, the time before they started to compete would be so great that hopefully the organisation in Britain carrying out this activity would have progressed many stages further.

Another type of barrier which is often crossed by such activities is the distinction between commercial and non-commercial operations. A petrochemical company routinely responding to orders from dealers for deliveries of fuel might compare itself against an immediate-response service such as the Ambulance Service or the Fire Brigade, which are concerned with negotiating similar traffic patterns in vehicles of a similar size on an immediate-response basis. If, on the other hand, they believe that an immediate response is not the issue, but the effective scheduling of calls is, then they should consider using a bench-mark against a courier organisation or against an organisation such as a newspaper distribution company. In both cases scheduling of calls is as important as the initial response times.

To date we have come across very few examples of the reverse process being applied where non-commercial organisations (particularly government bodies) bench-mark themselves against commercial activities. This is ironic as it is often these commercial organisations that can outbid a tender traditionally provided through an internal service. Two obvious examples might be the bench-marking of NHS Hospitals against private hospitals where very often the staff and end results are identical despite very different procedures, and yet one performs more effectively than the other against certain criteria suggesting that it is the systems and administration which cause any delays. A second situation might be the distribution of benefits by the Department of Social Security which might easily be bench-marked against the distribution process for bookmakers through betting shops.

The scope for bench-marking in this way is enormous and a great deal of immediate improvement can be gained by approaching the subject with an open mind. Meanwhile, the longer-term ones accrue from the much broader experience that people gain from investigating alternative processes. Another advantage of this approach is the development of scales of performance.

Having seen how alternative approaches can radically improve different characteristics of an operation's performance, it is possible to develop simple scales for performance measurement so that you can continuously monitor the improvement without having to constantly review or revisit the bench-marks which were originally established. One of the disadvantages which some organisations encountered during the late 1980s was that having made improvements they had to revisit their original bench-marks and carry out the activity again (because they had failed to establish appropriate scales for performance measurement).

The scales of performance which are used can vary tremendously. While in the 1980s most of these comparisons were based on the ranking of various suppliers and services, this is only really possible when organisations are making their comparisons against direct competitors. Once it is against part-processes, the important initial step is to obtain a realistic target. Thus, if a newspaper distribution company aims to take no more than four hours to distribute a newspaper to any part of the country from its printing point to the point of delivery, this sets the target for the petro-chemical company.

We came across one very interesting example of this being used in a High Street recently. The assistants from a shop with a specific amount of frontage were seated outside another shop of a similar frontage. Although they were in a completely different market they were selling products of roughly the same value. The manager was interested in comparing the number of visitors to the two shops, how they varied through the day, the number of casual visitors (leaving without a purchase), how long they remained in-store, and similar figures for those that simply window-shopped. When we spoke to him this was the germ of an idea. Since then we've seen his team experiment with alternative displays, an in-store coffee shop, and local promotions. In each case they bench-mark against the other store.

Case Study 5

Metropolitan Life

It's quite unusual for any organisation to stimulate a whole new area of science. This is particularly rare in the Service Sector. Perhaps to describe it as a new area of science is a little extreme, but certainly back in 1985 when the MetLife sponsored a research programme by Texas A&M University, few people would have predicted the value of the results which they produced.

In practical terms, MetLife derived a survey instrument which was based on service quality parameters, clearly established by the customers and prioritised to maximise their satisfaction. Since that time, MetLife has undergone a quality improvement process of its own.

Initially based around a concept of achieving personal quality, which was cascaded to all employees in the mid-1980s, this has subsequently developed into a programme of team-based activities, crossing functions and developing solutions to problems. The stimulus to this change process arose through the Texas A&M study, and a light-bulb of recognition which it created among the senior management team at MetLife. The concept which the research identified was that there were significant gaps – gaps of under-standing – between customers and the organisation.

Not only were there gaps between what was delivered and what was expected, but far more important, these gaps were perception-based. As such they need have no standing in reality. For example, many customers perceived that MetLife was slow in handling medical insurance claims. This was the customers' perception and was based on their expectations, and yet, had you asked any internal source, they would have told you that delivery was exceptionally good. In this case, the reason for the gap is simple. In many instances, doctors would hold claim forms for some days while they processed their own internal paperwork before forwarding the form to MetLife.

The Texas A&M model identified a number of potential gaps in any organisation, but especially in those which were providing and delivering pure services. The model itself has been enhanced and developed over the years. A simple representation of it is included in Figure 4.1.

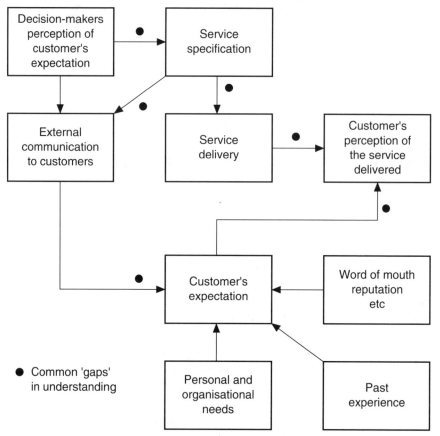

Figure 4.1   The service gap model (*After*: Zeithaml V, Parasuraman A and Berry L L (1990) *Delivering Quality Service – Balancing Customer Perceptions and Expectations*, The Free Press, New York.)

Case Study 6

ABB Asea Brown Boveri

ABB Asea Brown Boveri is the world's largest electrical engineering company – or rather, group of companies. Comprising more than a thousand individual organisations, it has 30,000 employees worldwide and an annual turnover in excess of $6 billion. In the late 1980s it was becoming evident that the organisation was operating as a loose collection of many separate companies rather than pulling with the weight of one giant. It was the difficulty of achieving cross-company communication that proved the trigger for the former President and CEO, Percy Barnevik, to implement a culture-change process. He recognised the importance of having a strong unifying vision to help the organisation overcome its cross-company barriers. He also recognised that a quality-driven process was potentially too vague for the pragmatic individuals in their organisation, and so the emphasis which he introduced was on added value rather than productivity or efficiency. As added value can only be measured by a customer, this made the process far more specific. Throughout the late 1980s and into the 1990s, the organisation set about re-examining the user needs and the customer needs of the products and services that they delivered. As a result, in each individual company, they had to redesign the services that they were delivering. Typical of the way in which this began was ABB Medidores in Argentina.

ABB Medidores began their customer-focus process by using QFD to assess the relative performance of their organisation against their competitors. The results opened their eyes to the diversity of views that customers often hold. In particular, it highlighted the fact that product quality was only one of several parameters on which they were being compared. As Percy Barnevik summed up: 'As customers change their way of doing business, they also change their needs and expectations regarding our contribution'.

The next stage in their improvement process was to implement task-forces targeting specific opportunities for improvement. Typical of these task-forces was one based at ABB Distribution in Vaesteras in Sweden. This task-force systematically reduced the order cycle time in the organisation by a factor of 90 per cent. As a result of the dramatic changes in the organisation structure that the task-force achieved, and the dramatic results which it produced, the organisation in Sweden has been restructured into ten profit-responsible, self-managing work-teams.

The lessons of ABB Medidores were very similar to those at ABB Relays in Florida. Based at Coral Springs, their improvement process began by a similar customer-perception exercise. Out of the initial steps in their QFD process, they identified 30 key measures – each one critical to customer satisfaction. This proved a pivotal discovery as Don Jans, their President, pointed out: 'If you can't measure it, you can't improve it'. The 30 measures include aspects of process quality, timeliness and responsiveness. Ranging from pre-order, right the way through to post-delivery, the 30 measures are displayed at the entrance to the plant on a large visual display and are routinely updated. They provide a tremendous incentive and reinforcement to all of the employees. As their improvement process has progressed, so ABB have entered into partnerships with similarly minded organisations. An excellent example of this was their award of a $70 million contract in November 1992 by the Tennessee Valley Authority (TVA). The contract involves the design and supply of two flue gas de-sulphurisation systems (FGD). The FGD systems, which work on a wet limestone oxidation process to remove 95 per cent of sulphur dioxide emissions, are to be installed at the Cumberland City Fossil Fuel Plant – a massive 2,650MW generating facility, which will commence commercial operation in 1995. The ABB/TVA partnership is a unique TQ-based one which revolves around shared goals, shared incentives and shared risks.

When Gerhard Schulmeyer succeeded Percy Barnevik as President and CEO in 1992, he re-emphasised the importance of added value to customers. As a result of recommendations from one of ABB's teams, Schulmeyer spearheaded a re-launch of their improvement process under the banner 'Ten-ups'. His rationale behind this was that if employees focus on working slightly harder, if the emphasis is on small-scale improvements, then the organisation would never achieve the step changes that it needed to remain competitive. As a result, the 'Ten-ups' process calls for a 50 per cent year-on-year minimum rate of improvement.

Typical again of the sorts of initiative that have been launched under this banner, the ABB Relays plant at Coral Springs worked with one customer to establish exactly what criteria they required to be met for the product and services which were being delivered to them. As a result the Coral Springs plant has been reorganised, firstly by process and secondly with independent task-forces gradually improving the delivery of each separate process. It is highly likely that these task-forces will emerge as self-managing teams within this organisation too.

THE SERVICE AUDIT

1. Vision

Throughout the 1980s and early 1990s we have been encouraged by a growing number of consultants and 'gurus' to develop a company vision. Has your organisation developed a vision? Examine it closely. Does it reflect customer service or is it a bold statement about corporate performance? Statements such as 'We will be the best' say a great deal about the sales performance of the organisation, and may imply some degree of customer satisfaction, but they tend to mean that monthly statements of sales values become more important than monthly statements of customer satisfaction. How was the vision statement developed? Was it produced by the top management team? Was it produced by just the most senior manager? Or was it developed by some form of group consensus, reflecting the overall views of the organisation? Or alternatively, was it a reflection of the historical values of the business?

If the vision was developed by a group then the chances are that it is more widely known throughout the organisation. But if it was developed by a small select group of people it is less likely to have been communicated. How widely known is your vision statement? Have you tried testing it out? Have you asked some of your employees whether they can repeat the vision statement and what their understanding of it is? Do you hear them recounting the vision to their friends and peers? Are there any examples of the vision being used in decision-making?

The Audit team need to establish the effectiveness of the vision, and develop plans to improve its view as a tool for problem-solving.

One of our colleagues, who worked in the Rover organisation in the early 1980s, pointed to a classic example of the vision statement really being understood and appreciated. The example which he gives was of a loud, noisy, working environment equipped with heavy, large, automated plant. One member of the shopfloor crew walked passed another member and noticed that the individual concerned was taking a short cut on a piece of work that he was doing. The first guy, walking past, tapped his colleague on the shoulder and simply pointed at the copy of the vision statement that was on display on the wall. The one who was taking the short cut stopped and did his job properly. There was no sign of hostility between the two; simply a recognition that one guy had had a temporary lapse.

Vision statements do not have to be communicated in words. There are lots of different ways in which they can be broadcast. How does your organisation broadcast its vision statement?

If customer service really is important do the employees know about it? For example, do they get to use your products? Frequently in organisations the product is something which cannot be used by employees, but, equally there are many situations where it can. How do you go about providing that facility? We know of two excellent examples, one of which we would endorse wholeheartedly, the other one we would have many reservations about. The first case was a coffee importer employing some 60 or so people at their head office in the centre of London. Their coffee machines were understandably charged with their own product. One of the first jobs in the morning for the earliest staff to arrive was to recharge the facilities, making sure that there was a fresh coffee smell in the environment as soon as people arrived at work. Unfortunately, the second example also used the sense of smell but in this case it was that of tobacco smoke. Here employees were given every encouragement to try the company's products. Whether this is ethical or not we do not know. We do know that the company is exceptionally successful.

Can you use your employees' other senses to empower them with one of customer service? Like the garage owner who serves early morning breakfast in the service bay of his facility where the loud and clear message is that customer service is about cleanliness, smartness and professionalism – characteristics which you cannot associate with a messy, oily environment, and poor housekeeping.

Messages can be communicated in all sorts of ways. One of us worked in an organisation which employed around about 400 people spread across a site of about a square mile. One aspect of the company's customer service was safety. They dealt with highly volatile petro-chemical components which could easily have led to a major disaster had they been ignited. The organisation was very proud of its safety record, a pride which stemmed from the man at the top. Nevertheless it still came as quite a surprise when one Thursday afternoon at around about 3.30pm the company tannoy system chimed and there was the site manager congratulating everybody on having achieved 2,000 working days without a time loss injury.

The Audit team will need to devise ways of helping the top team analyse the vision statement. Are there any contradictions in it? Is there anything there which counter-balances good customer service?

2. Top team commitment

Messages are communicated in hundreds of different ways. Take one company in the Information Technology industry. Despite all the wall plaques, plastic desk tidies, badges, posters, signs, and even a door mat that you rub your feet on declaring that customer service is the most important aspect of the company's performance, as you walk around the organisation it very quickly reveals its true colours. The only charts that you can see, the only performance measurements which are made, are of monthly sales. The sales people drive the fastest, flashiest cars while the 'mere' operations people, who produce the product and deliver it, drive around in cheaper, less well-equipped vehicles. It is very clear that the person at the top spends more time with the sales people than he ever does with the people in operations. This is a typical case of the philosophy of customer service taking second place to quick, fast bucks.

The Audit team will need to look at the top team. What do they do to demonstrate their commitment to customer satisfaction? Do they hold briefings and team briefings? Do they talk to individual customers? Do they man Customer Support desks? Do they sit at the other end of telephones on customer complaint calls? Do they follow-up lost customers? Do they follow-up customers at all? And do they do it in front of their employees or on the quiet? Can the top team agree what percentage of each member's time should be spent in direct contact with customers, and that includes every member of the top team? It is just as important for the accountant who might think that his function is entirely internal, to be actively involved in talking to customers. After all, it is the Accounts Department that possibly loses most of them. The team should look internally too. Is there evidence of the senior management team demonstrating a customer-focus towards their internal customers as well? Too often, one product line or one division in an organisation actively fights its competitors internally, trying to steal contracts or work from the true owner of them. Review the minutes from the last twelve months of management team meetings. How often did 'Customers' feature in them? How often was customer satisfaction referred to? Or was it simply the occasional customer complaint? We all know from statistics about customers not complaining that the few that manage to make it to the senior management team meeting must be the tip of a much larger iceberg.

3. Voice of the customer

We have already questioned how much time senior managers are spending in contact with their customers. What about people lower down the organisation? What is a reasonable amount of time for individuals to spend talking to customers? We would argue that at least five per cent of every employee's time should be spent in some kind of contact with the customers. But that is direct contact. How else do you obtain information about customers' views, perceptions, and relative importance of their expectations? Just how easy is it for somebody to contact you? Have you tried ringing in to your own organisation? You must have rung other companies and noticed how long it takes for the telephone to be answered. Is the same true of yours? And what happens with that internal telephone system when the individual rings in, gets diverted and then sits waiting. We came across a wonderful example in a Professional Membership organisation recently when one of us telephoned to try to get some information. The telephone number that we were put through to was not available; nobody answered. We heard the telephone click to another number and another number and another number. Eventually, after six transfers without any human intervention, the call was answered by the secretary to the Director General. Cynically we could not help wondering whether the telephone engineers had had more to do with that little aspect of customer satisfaction than the organisation itself. Look at what happens in your organisation. If the telephone does not get answered how do people leave messages? Does the switchboard collect them or not? How often do customers visit your site? Do they take the opportunity to feed back to your staff how they are performing? Do you encourage visits from your own staff out to customer sites? Recently one division of BP (British Petroleum) was keen to improve the level of input from its customers to its company. They offered to second their own managers to other organisations to offer help and support in the use of their products for prolonged periods of time, several days, at no cost to the customers.

How do you handle complaints? Who handles them? Whose responsibility is it to deal with a problem? Replay these two situations to your top team, or to anyone in your organisation for that matter, and see whereabouts they think you would rate on a scale between the two.

A week before Christmas, one of us, a reasonably keen jogger, was working away from home, writing. On unpacking he discovered that he had left two things behind. The tracksuit that he had brought with him did not have a pocket so he could not put the key that he would normally carry around his neck in a pocket. Secondly, he had left behind high-lighter pens which he thought would be pretty useful in his writing. Visiting the town later on that day he spotted a promotional gift being offered by the makers of high-lighting pens, Schwann Stabilo; packaged with the pens was a swing pouch. He bought the set and took them home with him. The following morning getting up for his run he popped the key into the swing pouch and set off. Within a matter of a few feet he heard a clink behind him as the key had dropped onto the road through a torn hole in the pouch. 'What a shame' he thought, 'that a company that could produce perfectly good, high quality marker pens should link its name with a badly produced promotional gift.' Returning to his cottage he sat down, put pen to paper and quickly jotted a note to the manufacturers of the pens enclosing the swing pouch and pointing out the fact that it had burst open the first time he had tried to use it.

He posted the letter for the evening collection at 5.30pm that afternoon. Only 36 hours later he received not only a replacement pouch but also another free gift consisting of a set of high-quality coloured pencils together with a straightforward, apologetic letter.

This is a simple example of customer responsiveness. Service does not just get constrained to the initial delivery of a product. It reflects all aspects of your business. For years the airlines have been familiar with the problem that coffee stains on the back of a seat cushion suggests that their engines are not properly maintained!

We all know the problems of marketing businesses. One of the commonest growing phenomena in recent years has been direct mail. The purchase and delivery of lists of names and addresses is a complex process. You can imagine our surprise therefore when one of us received a promotional coupon from an importer of gin. The address to which the coupon had been sent had last been used four years before. A miracle that the people who now occupied the house had forwarded the letter on, not realising that it was simply a piece of direct mail. By the time it had reached the new address the coupon was well beyond its expiry date. Accompanying the coupon was a letter claiming to come from the Managing Director of the particular company.

It is pretty irritating getting a voucher for something you would have quite enjoyed using, only to discover that the expiry date is late. But we felt a genuine concern that the organisation was wasting its money on its direct-mail activities by using address lists that were obviously so out of date. As the letter had come direct from the Managing Director, we thought we would respond by sending a simple note pointing out the problem. Not only was the note not answered by the Managing Director but it had been forwarded to some assistant in a Marketing Department in a completely different address. The assistant simply wrote to us thanking us for pointing out the fact that the voucher had expired and saying that there was a limit to the length of time that they could maintain a promotion. Anyone would have thought that we were after another voucher. But, not only had the letter been completely ignored, but the response did not arrive for three months!

Where is your organisation on that scale? Is it near the front end, 36 hours for an immediate response or is it at the opposite end, not only ignoring what the customer is asking for but when the customer tries to do you a favour, ignoring them for three months?! Don't worry though, even if your organisation is towards the extreme in the wrong direction you are in good company.

In the UK there are 25 organisations who are approved by the National Accreditation Council for Certification Bodies (NACCB). These are organisations who are allowed to carry out certification assessments for the British Standard BS5750. One activity our own organisation is involved in is helping companies to establish quality management systems. As we near the end of the development process of the system we have to contact appropriate NACCB-approved organisations to act as the assessors. We usually do this by checking to make sure that the scope within which they can assess encompasses our clients' activities and then recommend three or four companies for our clients to obtain competitive quotes from. Just into 1993 we decided to update our company files. We wrote to each of the 25 NACCB accredited bodies. Our letter very clearly explained that we were consultants, that we acted on behalf of clients, that we were updating our files, that we wanted two sets of their literature, one for our own use and one that we could pass on the first time that we had a client that was appropriate. We asked the companies to indicate their scale of charges and we asked them if there were any other services that they provided for consultants helping them to help their clients. We did not expect much but it would not be unrealistic for some kind of help and support to be provided by the assessors during the development stages of unusual systems. Possibly even a Freephone service for instant enquiries. We received responses from all 25 of the companies so they passed the first step. Unfortunately all but two of the organisations that we contacted completely ignored our letter. We received one copy of their standard literature with a standard mailing letter assuming that we were a company seeking accreditation. Most of them did not give us the information we had asked for. Their response times were remarkably variable, ranging from a matter of days for one organisation to over two months for another. None of them followed up their letters with any kind of telephone contact. One of them compounded the problem by sending us a follow-up letter asking when our system would be ready for certification! As if that was not bad enough, one of the 25 companies that we had contacted wrote back and actually informed us that they were not an NACCB certification body even though it was the NACCB that had given us their name and address!

How does your organisation compare? Are correspondence from customers and tentative enquiries handled by sales people? Are they handled by a secretary with a simple database system that requires no thought? Have your staff been trained to respond properly? What are considered reasonable times? And if that is the way you handle possible sales enquiries, how do you handle complaints?

4. Costs of customer service

We shall assume that the Audit team will be assessing the costs for the whole organisation. These will involve three elements: the price of people's time, the price of space, and the price of materials including consumables. Before looking at the costs themselves the team should agree on the absolute price of each of these items. They will probably need to call on a management accountant to obtain the figures as they may not have someone within the team itself.

For most traditional organisations there are several categories within each of these prices. The team should avoid overcomplicating the issue. Pricing people's time, for instance, should be based on the average cost of employing no more than three grades of person. Usually these will be managers, administrative staff, and 'Shopfloor' personnel. The pricing needs to be based on their complete package, including benefits such as private medical schemes, bonuses, pensions and cars, but should not include overtime or any element of internal recharging such as the Personnel Department or Training Department levies sometimes applied.

Similarly, the price of space should be calculated to include the costs of heating and lighting but not servicing such as cleaning. Again this should be broken down into logical types of area, such as factory, warehouse and offices.

Finally, the price of the consumables used by people in their normal activities in each area needs to be estimated. We include paper, pencils, etc., but not items used as part of the service. Thus in a factory, the raw materials do not count here; in a hospital syringes would not count; and in an office the computer network would not. The team shouldn't spend too long agreeing those items to include and those to exclude. Items not included here, because they are part of the service process will be included elsewhere.

Summarise the values agreed on a table like the one shown in Figure 4.2.

The team needs to decide on the timeslice that they are going to estimate. This will depend on the internal accounting practices and on the way in which the cost information is going to be applied. We usually find that either a month or a quarter should be used. This allows sufficient exceptional situations to be included to give a realistic picture.

Next the team needs to agree on a list of all of the parts of the business that are to be included in the assessment. This can be done by business process or by function. There ought to be someone in the team from each area. If there isn't then the team needs to consider inviting new members and possibly

Definition of Work Area / Bases for Calculations	Area 1: (eg Admin)	Area 2: (eg Production)	Area 3: (eg Warehouse)
Price of Manpower			
Price of Space			
Price of Materials			

Figure 4.2   Cost of service delivery: preliminary calculations

having anyone duplicating step down.

For each function or process, which we shall call 'areas' from now on, the team members need to calculate the cost of service delivery. This is usually done by individual team members or by pairs. It is a lot easier to do this by 'walking the job'.

For every human and for every item of inventory, they should ask 'what are they doing?'. For inventory (which is the easiest) we begin by asking 'what is it doing here?'. Using a form like the one shown in Figure 4.3 document the quantity and the space occupied in the column which describes what the inventory is being kept for.

Cost of Service Delivery: Time Activity Assessment							
	Prevent	Control / Inspect	Internal Failure	External Failure	Exceed Needs	Lost Oppor'y	Cost of Delivering Service
Area: Activity Description: Time: Value: Time Cost							
Area: Activity Description: Time: Value: Time Cost							
Area: Activity Description: Time: Value: Time Cost							
Area: Activity Description: Time: Value: Time Cost							
Area: Activity Description: Time: Value: Time Cost							
Total Time Available: Total Time Used: Time Unused: Cost:	Complete this section if this is the last page for a particular area						
TOTAL COSTS:							

Figure 4.3   Cost of service delivery: space and inventory assessment

We have to be rigorous and the team members will be constantly making judgements. For example, walking the job in a chemical plant, we find an area of about $4m^2$ on which are standing 20 drums of a cleansing agent. The members need to decide which category of cost of service delivery the drums should be calculated in. The sort of questions they need to consider are:

- What is a reasonable quantity to hold?
- How much do we use over a reasonable period of time?
- What is the minimum order quantity? Is this reasonable?

Suppose that they feel deliveries could be made once a fortnight, and that in that time they would use six drums. There are 14 drums in stock that don't need to be there. They therefore record six drums as a cost of delivering service. They decide why the excess drums are there. Someone might argue that they are there as a prevention measure, because the supplier is unreliable, or as a case of exceeding requirements. In either argument there has been an internal failure and the costs of holding the extra 14 drums should be recorded in this category.

In a different setting, say a car rental station, the team members may look at the shelves of the office and find one shelf with sufficient brochures for two months' usage. They may consider that this is reasonable and decide to class the costs of holding that stock under a cost of delivering service. One of their colleagues assessing the vehicle parking areas though might find 15 Ford Orions. They need to assess the likely demands for this class of vehicle, the replacement time if there is a run on one-way hires, and so on. In this case the predictability is harder and so local management information systems will be more important. If there are too many vehicles then their cost and the space that they occupy are an internal failure cost.

The service department of a computer company where warranty repairs are carried out represents entirely a cost of external failure. The machines have broken down within a short time of purchase and they have affected outside customers.

The second element for assessment is the time and effort of the people in the organisation. The team members need to decide what proportions of people's effort is being spent on activities that fall under the different categories. It is vital not to give the impression that this is a 'time and motion' analysis. No one is suggesting that people are not doing their job. The problem is in re-assessing whether the activities should need to be done in the first place. This information can be recorded on a chart like that shown in Figure 4.4.

Cost of Service Delivery: Space and Inventory Assessment							
	Prevent	Control / Inspect	Internal Failure	External Failure	Exceed Needs	Lost Oppor'y	Cost of Delivering Service
Item Description: Area Occupied: Cost: Value: Item Cost							
Item Description: Area Occupied: Cost: Value: Item Cost							
Item Description: Area Occupied: Cost: Value: Item Cost							
Item Description: Area Occupied: Cost: Value: Item Cost							
Item Description: Area Occupied: Cost: Value: Item Cost							
Total Area: Total Area Used: Area Unused: Cost:	Complete this section if this is the last page for a particular area						
TOTAL COSTS:							

Figure 4.4   Cost of service delivery: time activity assessment

Take employees on a production line. If the actual time it takes to complete the tasks that they are responsible for is, say five minutes per unit of production and they produce nine units in an hour then for every 60 minutes only 45 should be needed. The 33 per cent extra are not a cost of delivering service, but must be a result of prevention, control, internal failure or exceeding requirements. With most individuals it is usually easy to identify activities that they are doing that prevent problems from arising – from reading instructions or work schedules, or appending notes to other colleagues further down the line. Let's suppose that this takes five minutes in every sixty. There will be some time spent sorting out problems as they occur, say five minutes on internal failure, and let us suppose that they spend five minutes completing a statistical control chart recorded as a cost of control.

It is rarely worth taking every individual and assessing the split of their time. Instead look at people carrying out identical or similar tasks and apportion their time pro rata. In the case of our computer service department almost all the people's time may be spent on external failure, but they may also put aside some time to prepare fault reports for Production and for Design. The first of these is still external failure but the second might be described as prevention.

At the chemical factory three fork-lift truck drivers were engaged to shift drums between stores. One of these stores was defined by the team members as a cost of internal failure because it was simply holding stock that had been over-ordered. The drivers' time was therefore split according to the amount of effort spent moving these stores. Elsewhere in the same plant, stocks of finished goods were held. This was so that orders could be met at short notice for a critical customer. The team were under a lot of pressure internally to describe this as a cost of delivering service. But they recognised that not only did it take up a lot of space, and most of the stock was there for a considerably longer period than it took to make, but several people were involved in managing the area. They decided that this was a case of exceeding requirements which didn't add any value for the customer.

For people on the front-line there is usually strong agreement about activities that are worthwhile (prevention and of delivering service), about those that are necessary (control), and those that are frustrating (failures and exceeding requirements). For managers there is often far more dispute over the classification of activities.

Figure 4.5 shows a list of twenty typical 'management' activities. Decide for yourself where you would categorise the costs, then look at the completed copy (Figure 4.6) to see where we would expect them to be. We have

Cost of Service Delivery: Management Activity Analysis							
Apportion the costs appropriately	Prevent	Control / Inspect	Internal Failure	External Failure	Exceed Needs	Lost Oppor'y	Cost of Delivering Service
Dealing with customer complaints							
Reading Trade Press							
Talking to Suppliers Representatives							
Cancelling Engagements for pressure of work							
Meeting to review loss of a client							
Holding planning meetings							
Replacing a demotivated employee who left							
Impromptu meetings							
Too many management meetings							
Overrun Management meetings							
Proof Reading Memos							
Correcting Invoices							
Authorising Expenditure							
Written replies to internal memos							
Setting up task forces to tackle problems							
Chasing up time sheets							
Recovery after a customer complaint							
Backing up a PC Hard Disk							
Reworking Annual Budgets							
Disciplinary Interviews							

Figure 4.5   Cost of service delivery: management activity analysis

Cost of Service Delivery: Management Activity Analysis							
Apportion the costs appropriately	Prevent	Control / Inspect	Internal Failure	External Failure	Exceed Needs	Lost Oppor'y	Cost of Delivering Service
Dealing with customer complaints				✓			
Reading Trade Press	?				?		
Talking to Suppliers Representatives	?	?					?
Cancelling Engagements for pressure of work				✓			
Meeting to review loss of a client	?	?		?		?	
Holding planning meetings	?	?					?
Replacing a demotivated employee who left		?	?	?		?	
Impromptu meetings		?	?				?
Too many management meetings		?	?		?	?	
Overrun Management meetings		?	?		?	?	
Proof Reading Memos		✓					
Correcting Invoices			✓				
Authorising Expenditure		✓					
Written replies to internal memos		?			?		?
Setting up task forces to tackle problems			✓				
Chasing up time sheets		✓					
Recovery after a customer complaint				?		?	
Backing up a PC Hard Disk	✓						
Reworking Annual Budgets			✓				
Disciplinary Interviews		?	?				

Figure 4.6   Cost of service delivery: management activity analysis (answer)

used a question mark to show where we think there could be some room for debate about the category.

In a traditional organisation, the team will quickly find that most of the time spent by 'managers' is in control activities.

Once the team have completed their assessments for each area they need to meet to reconcile these. It is important that double accounting has not occurred. There will also be some discussion about the categories that people have used. Obviously, for a large organisation the analysis could run to several pages. It is important to strike a balance between usable information and excessive information.

5. Customer focus initiatives

Most customer focus initiatives begin with some kind of outward communication process telling the rest of the people in the organisation about the basic messages of customer service. We have already looked at the way in which you obtain information about the customers' views and the customers' requirements. Now look at the way in which you communicate them.

What have you done in the past to focus your employees on customer service? Activities range from wishful thinking to major customer focus initiatives. What has your organisation's investment been in the past? How many people were affected? Of the people that were affected how many of them still remain? Did you have goals that you were working towards and were they quantifiable? Is it worth reviewing them now to see if those measures have been maintained or have been lost? Initiatives of this kind should produce immediate tangible results. Indeed, some organisations which provide training and consultancy in this area guarantee that you will recover the cost of their fees within a matter of weeks if not days. What sort of activities have you been involved in? How well did they perform at the time? Are they still performing and what have the benefits been that you have obtained from them? As we have seen in section 4 the cost of most activities can be tied down in real currency. Take Motorola, for example, who have had independent external auditors assess their training function and have established that for every dollar that they invest they get \$33 in return.

6. Communicating the voice of the customer

Take a typical month's, or quarter's, internal communications, by which we mean memos, magazines, newsletters, news sheets, team briefings, team meeting agendas and so on. Look at the whole organisation if you can. How many of those meetings and those internal communications have information about customers and especially about what the customers are looking for?

For most organisations the amount of information disseminated in this way is fractional. Usually less than one per cent of the information involved concerns customers. So if it is not being communicated that way, how is the customer's voice being heard throughout the organisation and especially for those people who are off-line (people in specific functions that do not normally come into contact with customers)?

Where a product is quite complex it can often be very illuminating to ask the employees in the organisation to rank the importance of various features of the product and to compare those with the customers' preferences. Frequently the discrepancies are huge. What can you do to overcome this? When new products are developed or new services designed are customer requirements reflected in the design process? Do customers test the product? We have already mentioned the example of a Japanese automotive company that routinely takes mock-ups of its new vehicles, places them on railway concourses and stands staff around to discuss the features of the vehicle with the passers-by. When a new product is launched are its features explained to your staff? Do they understand why certain aspects have been built in? This can be just as valuable with an intangible product, such as a service item, as it can be with a tangible one. One Building Society, for example, whenever it changes the portfolio of products that it offers, sends a simple short description to all of its staff explaining what the reasons were for the change, and the relevant benefits for each of the products. Of course it is done like a selling document so that the staff can persuade people from an informed stance rather than from ignorance.

Track two or three new products. Try to find out at what stages customer feedback was obtained and how those products were developed. Similarly, track a few failed products. Look at ones which have been on the books for a very short period of time and then removed. Why did they fail? What sort of customer feedback was obtained, both before they were designed and after they were launched? Is this type of analysis carried out routinely? Shouldn't it be?

7. Guarantees

Most firms offer a guarantee on their products even though technically, in the UK, the shop from which a consumer buys is responsible for replacement of a product. Even then most manufacturers will refund or replace whatever you have bought that is defective.

Do you guarantee your products? If so, how easy is it for people to claim on their warranty? When something goes wrong, how do you use that information? Is it collected? Is it collated? Who is responsible for that collection process? Is the customer just simply accepted, given a refund and then ignored, or are they followed up by somebody? Not just someone trying to ingratiate themselves with the customer and retain them, but somebody who genuinely wants to learn how to improve the product for the future. Is the guarantee a 'refund or a replace' or a 'replace-plus one' guarantee?

Timothy Firnstahl is the Chief Executive of an unusual chain of restaurants entitled 'Satisfaction Guaranteed Eateries' based in Seattle. Some years ago Firnstahl introduced a total quality, culture change process in his organisation. He went through a variety of learning curves as he did so, discovering the hard way that you could not threaten employees to do a better job – that you had to progressively coach and empower them to do so. One of the features of his approach to his product is that satisfaction really is guaranteed. Every employee is constantly being reminded of the importance of responding to a customer, and if a customer shows any indication of being unhappy with the product that they have received or the service of an employee, then any member of the team has the responsibility and is expected to give not only a refund but a 'refund-plus'.

How does your organisation handle guarantees? Are customers treated like criminals for trying to claim against it? Do you have arbitrary cut-offs?

We have been amazed in recent years by some IT companies, and in particular software developers, who insist on less than 12 months' guarantee for their product. Most users of software don't discover many of its features until they have been using it for some years. So it is hardly surprising that once they have done so they will begin to discover the occasional bug. It is those higher level bugs which are going to be the hardest to spot anyway. So when the customer does the courtesy of providing you with some expert user information, that will save you many hours of decoding and bug fixing when you next issue a release, don't they deserve a little more courtesy than to be told that it is three months since they purchased the product so they are not even entitled to a free upgrade? As we have seen in section 4, some companies seem to treat warranty claims or at least the labour costs associated with them as just another source of additional income.

8. Barriers

It is a very rare case for an employee to come to work wanting to do a bad job. Equally it is a very rare case for a commercial organisation to want to have customers who are not satisfied. Despite this, many organisations place enormous barriers in the way of good customer service. What is a typical transaction for your organisation? If you find it difficult to answer that question go to your sales ledger. Which are the largest volume customers? Which are the most repetitive transactions? Take two or three examples and track them through the process. Think of all the departments in your organisation and the way in which they interface with the customer as the customer's transaction is handled. This means extending up the chain towards the sales people and marketing people and down the chain towards distribution and logistics. Now repeat the exercise with some of your unusual customers. The 'one-offs' are often handled very differently by companies – sometimes far better, sometimes far worse.

One way of carrying out this activity is to develop a flow chart or map of the process. We usually find it is best to draw up the flow chart and then to superimpose this on a map of your site or location. Then review the flow chart. Look at each of the cases where information has to flow from one group of people to another. How is that flow managed? How do you monitor its effectiveness? Often, transferring information from one department to another is an excellent excuse for a time delay and because priorities are different in the two parts of the organisation, a customer can be left waiting. Of course the situation is even worse when the two department head's are competing with one another for a position in the pecking order. Here non-cooperation can spread remarkably quickly throughout the department.

While we are looking internally, for each of the people on the flow chart, examine the impact of incentive schemes – situations where, in theory, good performance is rewarded by an exceptional pay or reward system. Then look carefully again, are these incentive schemes effective? What are people's views of them? Survey them, ask the people what they think. Unfortunately, incentive schemes often represent a very small proportion of an individual's income and they cease to be effective as an incentive to do anything. In fact, in a number of organisations where these incentive payments are made on a half yearly basis, for as much as two months after the payment has been made productivity actually drops. The reason? Because people were dis-satisfied with their payment!

Frequently sales people's incentives are an active disincentive to the rest

of the organisation. This can be overt, where there is widespread con-
demnation of the fact that these individuals are being rewarded for their
performance whereas others are not. Alternatively, they can be covert,
where the incentive has the effect of causing a log jam, often at the end of the
month. As the sales people are under pressure to generate income, they
cease to have any regard for the rest of the people in the organisation and
their ability to service those orders.

A simple, recent example of this type of disincentive was the Hoover
company. As part of its promotional activity Hoover offered purchasers of
its products over £100 in value free airline tickets to the USA. The offer was
exceptional and the company benefited tremendously from the growth in
sales. However, demand out-stripped supply not only for Hoover's products
but also for the airline tickets. The impact was severe and retrograde and
while the impact on people outside the organisation has received much
attention, that inside will have been serious too. Review those policies that
affect the relationship between the customer and your company. For each of
the interfaces what exactly happens? Is the customer expected to conform to
your rules or do you conform to the customer's rules? Frequently organisations drift into a foolish state where their concern to prevent abuse or fraud
actively hampers the customer.

While you are reviewing the relationship with the customer think too of
suppliers. The purchasing division of some organisations has an amazingly
bad reputation, setting themselves up as a high and mighty, judge and jury.
In a wonderful encounter recently we heard of a simple invoice submitted to
a company for some work which had been very successfully completed and
received. The organisation had sent its supplier so much paperwork to
complete for the order process that it had taken almost as long to read the
order as it had to complete the work. You can imagine the supplier's
amazement when their Office Account's Manager was contacted by telephone and informed, in no uncertain terms, that the next time they submitted an invoice they had better make sure that they did not mark the
envelope 'Mr Brown' but instead 'For the attention of Mr Brown'!

Who creates rules like that? And how much are they costing the organisation? Can we really be responsive and effective when we are confronted with
petty rules of this kind? Review the flow chart. Wherever it could be said 'It
is our policy to do X, look critically. If doing X is something that the
customer would like then that is fine. If it is something that the customer
must have, then obviously it is essential. But what about those policies that
the customer doesn't really need?

It is our policy to take credit references. It is our policy only to accept written orders. It is our policy to charge a handling fee for returns. It is our policy to issue credits only when we have examined the goods and ensured that a genuine defect has occurred. It is our policy not to disclose staff members' names. It is our policy only to accept orders on an official order form. We do not accept orders by fax. Anyone caught travelling on this train without a ticket will be prosecuted. Delivery is only free with credit card orders. Orders must be received by four o'clock for next day dispatch. All letters must contain the internal mailing address. We do not operate a central switch board, please dial the person you wish to speak to direct. To help you obtain service more speedily please press the star on your telephone.

Do you have a customer contact point? Is it easy for customers to access it, like Texaco's 0800 number? Are the customers' aware of it? Does it feature on the packaging of your product or on the wrapping for their service? Are people actively encouraged to use it or left to find it for themselves? Is it easy for them to use or is it a sealed box?

For years now we have been fascinated by customer complaints and customer comment systems in large airports. For many years, London Gatwick airport had a comment card box conveniently positioned in the quietest part of the airport terminal. Wall mounted, well out of reach of any smaller customers. The box was painted to blend in with the walls and despite instructions on it to complete one of the attached cards and post it, cards were rarely to be found anywhere near the box. We are delighted to say that in their new North Terminal this is no longer the case. The boxes are at waist height allowing customers of any age to complete a comment card. Comment cards are themselves in copious supply right by the side of the box and hopefully, before the summer holiday season the organisation will have thought to put some pens and pencils ready for customers' to use. A common concern, of course, is the theft of the pencils which is why banks so conveniently attach theirs by a chain. Usually designed only for right-handed customers the chain is rarely long enough for a left-hander to complete their transactions. And what is the bank saying about its customers? 'We trust you so much that you won't walk off with the pen'? Compare this with other organisations who willingly give you their pens, is there something we do not know about bank customers?

It is remarkable how insensitive organisations can be to their customers, and it is only by a systematic and painstaking re-examination that we can often get to the bottom of some of these problems. But, having all of the right systems in place and having removed all of the departmental and inter-departmental barriers, having scrapped pointless policies and the disincentive schemes, there is still one fundamental which has to be right.

What is your commitment to training? Using your flow chart how many of the staff who have contact with customers have been taught how to deal with customers? Do your switch board operators know how to deal with someone at the end of a telephone line? Or do they simply use their switch board in a mechanistic way? Have the fitters in the garage been taught how to respond properly when a customer asks a question? Have your accounts people had any inter-personal skills training?

Carefully review your training provisions. You will probably be quite amazed at how few of the training courses people attend have anything to do with customers. Of course, there is a need for more technical training and for basic managerial skills or problem-solving skills training. But what should the proportions be? Has anybody established these? Is there a policy on them or a strategy for them? Frequently in conversations with Personnel Directors, we discovered that the person determining the provision of courses is usually somebody in the Personnel Department, and rarely anything to do with the individuals and their needs. Is the training conducted in-house or outside? If it is outside what steps do you take to make sure that it meets the standards that you need, and how do you make sure that the experiences of the training are relevant to your own organisation?

9. Measures

How do you know whether you are doing a good job? Review the data that is collected in the organisation. Look at it carefully to see how it was established. Is it relevant? Does it match customer expectations? Take one or two examples and see whether indices which have been recorded by you as acceptable were actually acceptable to the customer. Does the data that you are collecting accurately reflect the customer's perception of the same circumstances? For instance, one petro-chemical company assured us that customers' orders were responded to within 24 hours or 48 hours if the customer expressed no urgency. In practice, when we spoke to the customers the perception was completely different. As far as they were concerned they had to contact the company nearly ten days before they wanted a delivery and often they would have to call more than once.

How do you use the results from these measures? How widely are they communicated? Are there targets set for performance or trigger points for improvement activity to begin? Have you established the levels of natural variation in a process so that you do not over-react or under-react. Where targets exist do they reflect 'best-in-world' practice or just 'best-in-your-class' practice? Do the people carrying out the work share these results? Do they understand the meaning of them? Have they been given instruction on how to interpret them? Do they have any control over them at all?

10. Internal customers

We have already hinted about the problems of an internal customer relationship when we started talking about barriers. Unfortunately, human nature being what it is, it is often very difficult to identify examples of non-cooperation or delays which occur between departments when only the internal customer is being considered. However, what you can look for are agreed standards. Has the purchasing department agreed a standard for delivery with the operations group? Does the service team have an agreed standard with the front reception desk? Is there an agreed standard for house-keeping?

Again, using the flow chart, review each of the consecutive steps where one group of people hands over to another. For each relationship consider whether there are agreed standards that have been documented and that people are actively monitoring and working towards. What is the current level of performance? Has it been bench-marked? Is it an acceptable standard for your organisation, for the industry, or against world-class performance.

11. Information exchanges

When we began reviewing measurement we implied that it was important to bench-mark against other organisations. This bench-marking activity involves an exchange of information. Again, with your flow chart as the tool, identify each of the stages for which external information has been obtained or is constantly obtained. Identify how this happens. How often does it happen? Who is responsible for it? Is the information being used for comparison coming from a competitor in your own industry or from an excellent performer in the particular process that you are looking at?

Although key processes should be bench-marked against other organisations, probably in different industries, there is a great deal to be gained from a review of your own market. How are you performing? Do you know whether your competitors are also bench-marking against outside organisations? So much can be gained from bench-marking, it is such a simple tool to use and it is one which can be great fun for many people – especially for front-line workers who often do not get the opportunity to leave the site.

We had one wonderful experience with a steel company in South Wales. A small group of warehousemen bench-marked themselves against a banana importer. At first sight there should be very little to compare between the two. In practice, both dealt with perishable goods in similar quantities. The size of units was broadly comparable. Distribution was equally comparable and turnover of product was remarkably similar. Having seen how the banana importers were handling their products the warehousemen went back with a renewed vigour to improve the handling of their own. Not only did they discover savings through reducing the amount of damage to goods in stock but they also reduced the volumes of inventory and amount of warehouse space required by a significant proportion. All of these reductions represented major savings to the organisation.

References

1 Munro-Faure and Munro-Faure (1992) *Implementing Total Quality Management*, FT Pitman, London.
2 Ibid.
3 Wilson GB (1993) *On Route to Perfection*, IFS Publications, Bedford.

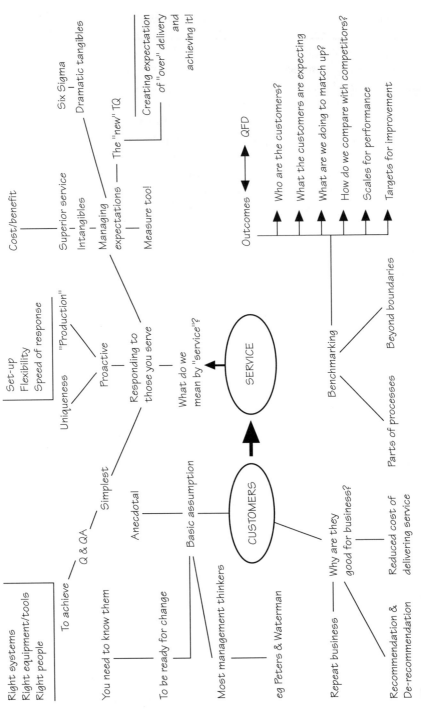

Summary Mindmap 4: Service

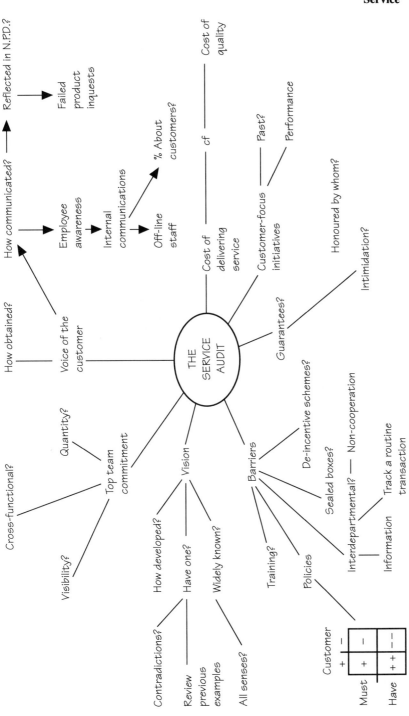

Service Audit Mindmap

5 IDEAS

THE INDIVIDUAL START-UP

There is a simple story of two school children being educated in a British school in Katmandu. Their parents were colonial administrators and the children regularly cycled to and from school, passing through the colourful bazaars of the Katmandu market. Representing a significant level of affluence in the area, the two children were frequently accosted by the people in the market stalls offering their wares. The story goes that one day they were approached by a woman selling soap. She was positioned immediately opposite another soap seller but, her approach was radically different. Instead of just asking the children to buy soap from her she explained the differences between her products and asked the children questions about the ways in which they washed, their preferences, the scents they preferred and so on. The children were so impressed by the woman's obvious interest in them that they bought some of the soap from her. A few weeks later they came through the same street in the bazaar only to realise that there was only the one woman left selling soap. Her competitor had gone out of business. As they approached, the woman again began a long series of questions asking them about their preferences for the soaps that they had tried and explaining how her soaps had changed.

Although it may be difficult to demonstrate rigorously, it is widely believed that a high degree of innovation is essential to obtain a strategic advantage over your competitors.

TRADITIONAL DIVISIONS

Many modern organisations began as an individual start-up, where one individual with a vision and a product developed a business revolving around themselves. They bought in additional support where they needed it, either for production or administration. As these traditional organisations began to mature so they would take on more and more new products. These products would be developed, not within the administrative sections or any other parts of the organisation, but mainly within separate specialist departments. These are usually known as R & D – Research and Development.

TEAM-BASED START-UPS

For years this situation has persisted. Then, in the early 1970s, we began to see a change in the approach that organisations were using. When they started up, particularly in the IT field, it would be increasingly common for an organisation to develop around a nucleus, a small team, often of five or so people, all of whom were involved in the innovative process of developing a new product. Often these organisations had proved to have relatively limited life spans. As the small team developed its own interest and each individual within it developed themselves, so the group eventually began to break up. Again commonly in the IT field (though often found elsewhere too), these individuals have gone on to spawn new small teams, on a new innovative start-up process.

THE MATURING ORGANISATION

As we have often seen, skills at the start-up are not necessarily those that you require to manage a complex and growing business. However, as we progressed through the 1970s and into the 1980s it became increasingly obvious to organisations that they could no longer be complacent about the source of new ideas and new products that they were going to launch. Whereas in the 1950s and 1960s a product life span would often have been as long as five, ten, fifteen or possibly longer years, as we moved into the 1980s product life spans were often less than 12 months, and this of course was particularly true of the emerging technologies. Thus an organisation could no longer rely upon one or two individuals to provide all of the new inspiration, particularly in an organisation which had thrived on its first wave of development. Equally, those organisations which had begun with a team-based start-up could no longer grow and develop without having further positive inputs of new ideas.

Even today, smaller companies as they mature begin to instil a sense of functionality, which usually means an R & D department has to be created albeit only manned by one or two people. In this case R & D is often a misnomer. It has little to do with new products or new research. It is usually concerned with tweaking and adjusting existing products and product ranges, or alternatively developing new ones directly off the back of an existing portfolio.

As we entered the 1980s management experts around the world began to recognise the fundamental way in which research and development was carried out. They saw that whether we were concerned with new product development or enhancing existing products, it was vital to have a clear flow of communication with customers, and for this communication to take place at all levels in the organisation. Systems of culture change were developed concerned with introducing new ways of working in a traditional organisation. These were very similar to their Total Quality counterparts where the culture change was towards one of improved customer satisfaction. In the case of the so called 'creative' organisation, they were also aiming to achieve the goal of delivering to customers exactly what they expected. As these organisations introduced teams into the traditional culture, they usually began with the senior managers, identifying key issues to be investigated. Often these key issues, because of their nature, spanned several departments or functions. The first category of these team type activities in mature organisations was known as Task Forces.

As people became used to the idea of working in teams rather than working alone, so the emphasis began to shift. In some organisations this was to take what had previously been large-scale cross-functional activities down a level or two into the individual functions. Nevertheless, they still worked on problems assigned to them by the management team. In other organisations the interim stage was for teams made up of individuals from different areas to tackle problems and issues that they themselves had identified. The final stage in this evolutionary process is for the teams themselves to spawn spontaneously, to tackle a problem which is of their own particular interest and is therefore more likely to be restricted to a within-department issue. By the time this type of merging and networking and then disbanding has become part of the culture, significant changes will have made headway under the TQ or a similar banner.

For organisations seeking to introduce a learning culture or one in which creativity is the key, the same sorts of team-based activity are necessary. One such company is Motorola. Over the last few years they have progressively encouraged their employees to take a more active role in innovation. To date some 40 per cent of Motorola's employees world-wide have taken part in one of their customer satisfaction improvement teams. These teams are charged with the very important task of identifying innovative ways of improving the satisfaction given to their customers.

THE CONSTANTLY CHANGING CREATIVE STRUCTURE

The fifth type of environment in which innovation becomes a key issue is for the maturing company, probably developed as a team-based start-up where the whole organisation still tries to maintain that highly creative culture. To date, relatively few organisations could be pigeon-holed in this way. But increasingly, commentators are pointing to this as the new model, the new style of organisation which will be of increasing importance as we move into the 21st century. In these organisations, unless you continued to contribute new ideas, new creativity, new approaches, as an individual, your career would be numbered! So what is the environment we are trying to create?

THE IMPORTANCE OF TEAMS

The first key aspect of the new culture of innovation, as we have already implied, is that it is based on teams, rather than the 'loner' approach. In the past, many books have been written about the role of the individual in developing new products and processes within organisations. Today, we recognise that if we remove the controls from our own employees we can achieve far higher levels of innovative and creative thought. Clearly though, if we are going to remove the controls we do not want to create an internal structureless anarchy (something which many individuals find frightening about the true Total Quality culture). In this case we make use of what is known as group process, or the power of the team, to make sure that individuals with maverick ideas are not allowed to dominate the organisation.

By creating teams, either temporarily or permanently, and then removing the constraints acting upon them, we are able to consciously encourage our employees to take a greater responsibility, a greater authority, and more ownership for their own individual activities. In this way, as they recognise opportunities for improvement and development, they will take the initiative and put these into place. Unless you have seen it demonstrated, the power of the team as an arbiter is one of the most fascinating processes in a modern organisation, and yet it is probably one of the hardest to believe. However, if we are going to free these individuals by removing the controls upon them, and reorganising them into teams, we have to ask what is the role of their managers?

THE ROLE OF THE MANAGER

In the traditional organisation, where individuals were allowed to operate without a great deal of peer group influence, the role of the manager was usually to act as a 'controller-cop' making sure that these individuals did not get out of hand. Nowadays, as the teams begin to take over, the role of the manager has changed. No longer policing, the manager needs a new set of skills – those of a developer of people. Almost inevitably this also means that fewer managers are required. In some exceptionally large organisations, many tens of thousands of managers have been made redundant. One example of this has been British Telecom organisation which, as it evolved through the 1980s, made radical improvements in terms of creativity, effectiveness and efficiency. While managers were still required to help as trainers and developers of the people who were previously working for them, many were no longer required. British Telecom reduced its managerial numbers by several thousand in one year.

We shall look in more detail at some of the changes which the adoption of a team-based structure forces upon an organisation in the chapter on administration.

Recognising the strategic importance of innovation to our organisation and acknowledging that this has to be across the whole organisation and not isolated in a specialist division, we begin to change the structure of our business. We have changed the role of our managers and we have changed the role of our employees who work within the teams. But where do these teams get their new ideas from?

THE SOURCES OF INNOVATION

It has been said that many new ideas are in fact re-worked old ones. Of course it is true that this is often the case. Similarly, many innovative ideas are simply older ideas applied to new situations. If this is the case, the team only really has to look around itself to identify possible opportunities. But being equipped with a few bright ideas does not mean to say that they have developed a solution.

In this situation the teams need to have the facility to carry out their own experiments. These experiments are bound to cause some kind of disruption, but, again, this can be managed in a constructive way. Lucas Diesel, for example, trained almost every employee in the simple techniques of experimental design so that whenever they were confronted with an opportunity to make an improvement they could test it rigorously before they actually put it into place. By teaching them a particularly lean form of experimentation, known as Taguchi's techniques, it was possible for these employees to make changes authoritatively, swiftly and with minimum waste. The impact was enormous and the fortunes of Lucas Diesel have grown accordingly.

Operating as a team in a liberated environment and with the right sorts of skills in experimental design and so on, employees can begin to make a significant change to existing products. Their attention can be focused on more consistent inputs and improving the quality of selection of products and suppliers. They can reduce the time taken for handovers. They can encourage greater added value for the product lines. Their skills can be concentrated on changing the product-process flow itself so that they are able to combine steps or to parallel track, and certainly to remove or reduce excess activities. They usually do this by determining key measures for the particular process that they are looking at and exploring alternative technologies.

Almost every organisation that has tried this recognises that, had they involved their employees earlier, they would have had a far greater return on their investment. But involvement in innovation does not have to be restricted to the people within the organisation. There is no reason why outsiders (in particular customers or suppliers) should not be involved as part of the innovative process. In chapter 4 we looked at some of the ways in which an organisation can develop customer listening devices within itself.

Coupled with the information received from sales people, it is possible for teams of employees within the organisation to develop major new product lines as well as improving existing ones. One Birmingham steel works, for example, involved in wire-drawing activities, sent out its maintenance engineers to visit customers and suppliers alike. The team of engineers reported back with a number of possible ways in which they could add value to the product, improving its usefulness to their customers and at the same time reducing the variability of the product itself.

CHARACTERISTICS OF THE INNOVATIVE CULTURE

This is all part of the innovative culture but how do we achieve it? The recommendations of the gurus are again consistent. Rule number one is to recognise that older people are not less creative but they are likely to find it harder to change in the culture to which they have become accustomed. For this reason organisations tend to encourage the younger people in the company to take a more innovative approach first. Such organisations become less interested in structure. Indeed, one Director commented to us that if he sees a junior manager taking up a new promotion and then issuing a new organisation structure, he knows that that individual won't last long in his business. As he said, 'tinkering with the way in which people report to one another has little or no benefit to our business'.

It is vital in this process to get customer input. It is equally important to organise people into small teams. The teams have to be given the tools and techniques to experiment and encouragement to 'suck it and see'. As some people have described it the approach becomes one of 'Ready – Fire – Aim'. Try out something, if it does not work, enhance it, modify it and prove it. Those companies that have succeeded in changing their culture have almost always done so by integrating the people who are off-line into teams of people who are on-line. For example, a team of people investigating a wrapping operation might well include somebody from accounts or somebody from purchasing. One highly successful improvement team which we came across in an organisation had investigated the causes of poor quality being introduced in their initial production process, a cleaning house operation. Here, large drums of wire were dumped into caustic soda and then into an acid bath and finally rinsed off. This was a way of removing scale and rust from the outer part of the product. Improvement teams had been initiated for years trying to tackle this particular issue. Frequently they had been limited by their own perception of how far the organisation could be made to change. What was recognised was that they lacked somebody who could not only act as a champion for them, but could also provide them with the clout, the financial argument in favour of radical solutions. In a master-stroke the quality improvement group appointed the Finance Manager as their adviser. Under his care and supervision they developed some of the most radical solutions and then put them into place, having put their argument in front of the Board of Directors. The company saw the investment returned time and time again.

Not all experiments are going to be successful. Indeed, if you use some of the most efficient experimental techniques, you can guarantee that there will be some raw product produced which is of virtually no commercial value. So how do you handle waste products? How do you handle the disruption of experiments? How do you handle failure in the organisation when an experiment which was expected to be successful has delivered unexpected results? The management process is vital for the success of the culture change. If people perceive that they have tried the new way and been rejected by their managers, then clearly they are not going to adopt it again.

This is why the whole process has to be managed in a serious way, and this is also why evidence in the form of the Audit can be so important to achieving a trigger for change. The senior managers in the organisation have a vital role to play in creating a large vision, a picture of what the alternatives are, and some evidence of their confidence in people to enable the change to happen.

One organisation that has changed dramatically in recent years is Motorola. We have already mentioned the very large numbers of employees in Motorola who take part in their Customer Satisfaction teams. Just one of the ways in which this organisation manages its innovation process is to have created a form of competition between these teams to encourage them to think big and at the same time to provide recognition for their efforts. The competition is open to all teams, and about half of them take part. It begins with a local round within their own plant or utility, then there are regional competitions, international competitions and finally a global competition. At each stage a panel of judges assesses the effectiveness of the group's solution, the way in which they achieved it, the way in which they have learnt from it, and furthermore, the way in which they have helped other people to learn from their experiences. As Motorola say, there is no point in having a solution to a problem which then has to be re-invented elsewhere. The award system is one way of communicating some of the solutions that have been developed.

As a management team it is important that you will have thought through how you are going to react when disappointment or unusual results are achieved as well as how you will recognise achievements and successes.

Case Study 7

Lucas Diesel Systems

The name of Lucas is known world-wide. Whether you live in Britain, in India or anywhere else for that matter, the symbol of the Lucas organisation is almost instantly recognised. Some years ago, the organisation instituted an ongoing programme to improve its performance in engineering and manufacturing to internationally bench-marked levels.

Early in 1986, Lucas Diesel Systems identified the next step in this process as being the introduction of experimental design. It was vital for all engineering and manufacturing activities and all quality improvement projects to be based on sound findings. After careful selection the organisation identified Taguchi's techniques as the most effective means of achieving this.

In May of that year a seminar was conducted with Genichi Taguchi. As a result of the enthusiasm the seminar created among the senior management team, it was decided to introduce the techniques to a much wider audience within Lucas.

A steering group was formed in June of that year. The role of the group was to establish a thorough and deep penetration of the organisation with the concepts and approaches to experimental design proposed by Dr Taguchi. By July they had commissioned their first training course. About 30 individuals attended the course and, as a prerequisite for joining, they had to select a suitable project to carry out after the course had been completed. As Jack Fryer, the Managing Director of Lucas Diesel Systems, explains: 'These early projects proved to be of critical importance in launching the methodology in the company'.

The selection of the projects proved vital. Firstly, they had to represent real problems rather than hypothetical situations. Secondly, they had to aim for quick results. In most situations these two would have conflicted. Nevertheless, some of the problems that they tackled had been well known for many years, and it had been widely accepted that they would take some time to generate results. Of the initial thirty projects, some completed in less than one month, others in twelve months.

The steering group recognised that it was important to provide an infrastructure to support the introduction of the methodology. This was particularly important in such a large organisation as Lucas. Meeting bi-monthly, the steering group, which comprised senior engineering and manufacturing managers from across the company, managed the introduction of the method for two years. After the first two months, a user group was formed which also met bi-monthly and provided a forum for people using the techniques to exchange their experiences and share problems. At any one meeting about 30 engineers would attend.

After the first course (which had been held in July 1986), a small group of engineers were appointed as 'Taguchi gurus'. The four people concerned were seconded to the project full-time. In addition to the basic training course they received advanced training from America and then took on responsibility not only for supporting ongoing projects but also for training new practitioners, managing a database of projects and running a large number of awareness seminars.

With the encouragement of the steering group, these gurus went on to publish a Taguchi newsletter containing information on projects, software products to support the analysis of the techniques, training courses, and so on. By September they had created their own in-house training programme.

This had three tiers of training. At the most straightforward level for general awareness they produced a twenty-minute video giving a general introduction to the method and allowing everyone to share some understanding of the results that were achieved, and to appreciate the importance of collaborating in the experiments. Although primarily directed at the operators, this course proved very popular with managers as well, and it was decided to develop an open-learning programme aimed both at managers and other individuals who did not require a detailed knowledge of the method but whose support for experiments was vital. With these two programmes providing support for initiatives in the field, a three-day course was developed known as the practitioner course. One ingredient of the three-day course was a full day devoted to practical experiments.

By October, results produced by Lucas experiments were being reported nationally at conferences. Though initially intended to last for two years, the steering group decided by November that it would split from the user group. In January 1987, the advanced training had been provided for the in-house gurus, and in February, a second externally provided training course was delivered. By April 1987, Lucas was ready to hold a full symposium of its own cases. This coincided with the launch of the complete training programme. By October 1987, Lucas had had further papers published in international symposia and in the following month, held their second full-group symposium. By February 1988, they had carried out so much work and had developed such expertise internally that they were ready to devolve the technique to their customers. They held a seminar specifically intended for the customers of the organisation. Throughout this period they had been developing a database of relevant case studies, so that individuals could learn from previous experience. In April this was launched as a knowledge-based system making use of the latest technology in artificial intelligence. By June 1988, they had moved from the realm of specialist symposia, provided mainly for people with an interest in Taguchi, to open symposia organised for the motor manufacturer's trade. As of late 1988, over 3,000 engineers had received awareness training, 500 had been fully trained as practitioners in the technique, more than 100 significant projects had been initiated and for most of the ones that had been completed significant benefits had been seen in quality, cost and reduction of schedules.

Jack Fryer is keen to point out that introducing a technique like this alone cannot achieve results. It is important that the environment is right, that there is an infra-structure which supports the process, in particular where results may be less successful. It is very important that there should be a senior champion and, in his view, vital that projects should be involved early in the process so that the technique is no longer one of a hypothetical nature but really practical. As he observes, the technique links in very well to the other quality improvement tools such as SPC, QFD, and so on. All of these have a role to play in any organisation's transition to flexibility and responsiveness.

Case Study 8

AMP

It takes a remarkable kind of resilience to enter a national quality award believing that you are one of the best – only to lose. Yet that is just the situation that faced AMP in 1988. Nobody could dispute the financial success of AMP, one of the USA's largest manufacturers of electrical components and specialising in the niche of electrical and electronic connectors. They were founded in 1951 and publicly listed in 1956. Since that listing they have grown 15 per cent per annum at a compound rate! Based in Harrisburg, Pennsylvania, they employ over 22,000 people and have an annual turnover in excess of $2.5 billion. In 1983, recognising the trend towards improved quality in their marketplace, AMP launched an ambitious quality improvement programme.

An intensive audit of customers established 59 critical success factors and the company set itself the goal of achieving a tenfold improvement in each within five years. Few people would have believed that this was possible, particularly in an industry which was rife with competition. But a tenfold improvement was the target, and a tenfold improvement was the result. By 1988, AMP had achieved average incoming acceptance levels well in excess of 98 per cent and more than 70 per cent of their customers reported that they were achieving a 100 per cent level. In the same five-year period, their on-time deliveries had risen from 65 per cent to 90 per cent – a figure which has continued to grow until in 1992 they were achieving in excess of 95 per cent. Between 1983 and 1988, their cost of quality was halved. In 1988, they re-emphasised their improvement programme goal of another tenfold improvement. Thus it was that with such a record of success in 1988, they applied for the national quality award, known as the 'Baldrige Award' named by Ronald Reagan after his Secretary of State for Commerce who had died in office.

The application process for the Award is elaborate and consists of questionnaires, survey information and substantial on-site visits. It must have come as quite a surprise when AMP were told by the examiners that they had failed to achieve the Award. The reason given was that the environment in their organisation did not involve employees sufficiently.

Today of course, more and more organisations have recognised the critical role that employee empowerment has in any quality improvement process. But in 1988, it was only the far-sighted few that genuinely appreciated the level and extent of involvement that had to take place and the nature of the changes that were necessary to allow it to happen. It was nearly 18 months later, in February 1990, that AMP launched its ambitious new 'Plan for Excellence'. They remained as committed as ever to the goals of achieving the Baldrige Award, and geared their Plan for Excellence to the criteria that are used in the assessment for the Award.

The investments that they are making are dramatic. AMP have always been highly committed to the training and development of their employees. Indeed, before they attempted the Award in 1988, they had an awe-inspiring record for the extent of involvement and development of employees in basic problem-solving skills. By 1992, 10,000 of their 22,000 employees had been trained in problem-solving skills, 11,000 had been trained in value-added manufacturing, and 3,000 engineers and supervisors had attended a programme of 28 sophisticated technical courses. The goal of this training and development investment is to dramatically boost innovation in the organisation and, coupled with a number of marketing initiatives, to encourage earlier involvement of the organisation in their customers' process of new products developments. In this way they are able to achieve dramatic improvements in product quality and reductions of cost for their key customers. Typical of this early involvement process was the approach by Boeing in the late 1980s to help them develop 'smart' connectors for aerospace applications. The resulting products are likely to dominate the aerospace market for years to come.

The key aspect that had been missed and which the Baldrige Award examiners were highlighting, was the fact that training and development are only of benefit if the employees genuinely have an opportunity to apply the skills that they have had developed. In most organisations this works in one of two ways: either internally (by helping the employees to become reorganised and to focus on improvement within the organisation) or externally (by getting the employees in the workforce closer to the customer and their needs and specific requirements). AMP has addressed both. In 1991, coinciding with their 50th anniversary celebrations, AMP held a 'Resource Fair'. Attended by several thousand employees, this event was intended to boost inter-departmental communication. The event was very similar to one which was organised some five years before at British

Airways. In BA's case, they had initiated their quality improvement process by an awareness-raising workshop entitled 'Putting People First'. This had been highly successful but it was felt, at the time, that there was a need to help individuals relate more directly to their internal customers, and as a result the second phase of their programme was entitled 'Customers First'. It consisted of away-days, held throughout the organisation's operations, where groups of employees drawn from a variety of backgrounds worked together and were presented with reviews of the activities from many other departments.

At the AMP Resource Fair, groups of employees put together exhibitions and demonstrations of the work that they did. Employees toured the exhibitions with their families looking at, and learning from, the experience of their colleagues. This Fair was so successful that various attempts have been made to try to repeat it with similar learning experiences. For example, in June 1992, four sales engineers visited AMP's Pennsylvania-based manufacturing plants and prepared outdoor barbecue lunches for the workers on all three shifts. Once the lunch was over, the engineers took roughly fifteen minutes to introduce themselves, the territories that they covered and the customers that they worked with, and then introduced the end-products that the plant's devices were being fitted into. In each case they brought along samples, took them apart and demonstrated to the workforce how the AMP components were used. The events, so radically different from those that most employees would ever experience, were extremely popular.

The second aspect necessary to allow employees to take a greater role in the development and running of the operation, is a re-organisation into self-managing teams. Although AMP only embarked on this process twelve months ago, they have already established 500 product-focused or project-orientated employee-teams.

It is important in any of these initiatives not to lose sight of the vision of the organisation. Although the road has clearly had its learning points, Harold McInnes, Chairman and CEO of AMP, reinforces: 'All of these continuing programmes have total customer satisfaction as their goal. During the past decade they have produced enormous leaps in quality'.

THE IDEAS AUDIT

It is surprising how entrenched views can be about the sources of innovation within an organisation. It is also surprising how little people know about the development of their own product or product lines.

1. Market and organisation survey

A very good starting point for an audit of innovation in an organisation is to look firstly at the industry, then at the company, and then function by function throughout the business. Over quite a long historical time scale it is worth plotting (often graphically), how the industry has developed through the years. Indicate where new initiatives took place. Indicate where major milestones in the history of the industry have occurred: when new fields have been opened up, when new technology has been provided, where distribution channels have opened, even where new motorways have been created, if this is relevant to your products or services. Show what has happened to competitors in the past. When new regulations and statutory requirements have come into play, show where subsidiaries have opened or where foreign offices have been created. As you begin to develop this picture it becomes very obvious where the sources of new ideas have come from. Such a historical record can become quite a useful document.

Arco, the old Atlantic Richfield Oil Company, carried out a similar survey and developed a fascinating graphical representation of the changes in their industry from its very earliest days. Today you will find a copy of that historical document displayed prominently on the walls of most of their offices.

2. Physical layout

There is a wealth of evidence that the most effective way to get a group of people to be creative is to give them plenty of space. Similarly, those organisations that report consistently good results, and achieve highly innovative solutions to problems, claim that they do so in an environment that is not only large and open but also relatively spartan. Large quantities of personal memorabilia are unlikely to reflect an individual who is focusing on innovative solutions, but rather, one who is deriving a great deal of interest and benefit from home comforts! We would hesitate to suggest that an open plan environment is right for these types of groups. They usually need somewhere where they are less distracted and can isolate themselves. Many organisations report that it is more effective to send people to a hotel for a few days than it is to keep them in their normal working space. It is for exactly this reason, namely that distractions are minimised.

In the longer term, however, the physical layout has a significant effect on people's likelihood of making chance encounters. Some of the most striking innovations have occurred through chance encounters between individuals from different disciplines. Much of today's more academic research is recognised as occurring across disciplines. As part of the review the Audit team should look at the type of environment that people are operating in. Does the organisation contain a high proportion of people who are in relatively cluttered, highly individual offices? Are they in open and largely clear spaces? Monitor accurately how many chance encounters people can make with individuals from other areas of their work. For example, if you have got the manufacturing people in a completely different site to the research and development people there is very little likelihood of cross fertilisation of ideas.

The Audit team should take this issue seriously. It reflects itself in the way in which we organise our functions. If the business is separated into Accounts, Purchasing, R & D, Manufacturing, Personnel and so on, there is very little likelihood of teams of people collaborating to assist the customer. This in turn increases barriers between parts of the organisation and leads to a very high likelihood that customers will not only be unsatisfied but that the organisation will be unresponsive.

3. Younger Staff

What does the company do to encourage those younger members of staff who are least likely to have been moulded with the organisational stamp? To what extent do junior members have job mobility? How is their location varied from week to week? What responsibilities are they given? Are they really being stretched? Do they operate in peer group teams? Or are they put into teams with large numbers of existing personnel? All of these factors can be measured accurately and quantitatively. The Audit team needs to establish what sort of changes to those measures should happen, give a time scale and explain how they should be achieved.

One city sanitation department took all of its new workforce (who joined each month) and made them man their own vehicle, thus the vehicle became known as the 'Class of?' (whichever month its crew had joined in) giving the group tremendous identity and leading to far greater productivity than was achieved with ordinary balances of older and newer workers. Even though there was an element of fumbling in the dark at the outset, collection rates were greater, frequency of collection was higher, vehicles were better maintained, members of the public reported fewer bad attitude problems and overtime costs were reduced.

4. Management involvement

What is the role of managers in your organisation? How are they involved in the active encouragement of innovation and creativity? A common term which we hear in organisations is that of 'sponsor'. It is often difficult to understand exactly what this role involves.

In some cases it is to champion the ideas that a group of employees have perhaps developed and to take them forward to higher levels. There are real problems with this particular route. It usually means that those higher levels are considered a dominion outside the scope of the employees themselves, which is certainly not rewarding and is frequently demotivating too.

On the other hand, sponsors can act as a barrier crusher, people who actively encourage the team as they push forward the frontiers in search of a solution. Certainly the role of the manager is to encourage at every opportunity.

As part of the Audit, consider a few examples of innovative solutions already being developed to solve problems within your organisation. Interview the team leader or the facilitator, establish what was the role of managers in the meetings and in encouraging the group to progress. How frequently were they involved?

In one organisation that we worked with, two teams were working on problems simultaneously. In the case of one team, although they had a 'sponsor' the person played his role very much at arm's length, usually enquiring of the team leader how they were doing just before the next management meeting. In the second instance, when we spoke to the team leader it became very obvious that their sponsor was virtually a member of the team, except that he did not come along to any of the meetings. As the team leader explained, almost every day he would have some kind of contact with the manager concerned. This would either be in the form of a simple enquiry as to how they were doing, or relaying some information back to them that he had heard on the grapevine. He even sent them copies of articles or items that he thought might be of interest to them. We pushed the team leader as we were trying to see whether he found this an intrusion or encouragement. He was emphatic it was encouragement: not only was the manager sending him snippets of information, but if he thought it was particularly relevant he would save him the trouble by copying them himself and sending seven or eight copies, one for each member of the team. But on every occasion he marked it very clearly: 'Only hand these out if you think it is relevant'.

When the teams neared completion of their projects it was very obvious that the first team with the arm's length sponsor had broadly met their objectives. They had, though, been less adventurous in the solutions that they had developed. The second team had not only tackled the problem that they had originally been briefed to tackle, but they had also extended this brief further, addressing a number of other key issues. The solutions that they had developed, although no more expensive, were far more adventurous with many other positive side-effects.

At the management meeting at which both teams presented their findings, one group were clearly nervous, the other group were very confident of their position, and of course they were able to be because they had so much encouragement and involvement by the manager himself.

Thus, although we are setting up teams of people to carry out innovative work, it does not mean that managers do not have a role, quite the contrary.

5. Recognition and reward

Another issue which is often debated at this stage is whether or not teams should be recognised and rewarded for their activities. Very briefly the distinction between the two is straightforward: recognition involves giving almost any person, or the whole team as a group, a wider public audience. This is provided either for their idea or more generally for their involvement.

Recognition very often ranges from giving people a simple badge, inclusion of their names and a brief summary of the project in a newsletter, having them make presentations to other members of staff, and possibly to visitors too, or occasionally wider audiences still. Recognition *can* include reward.

Reward is where there is some kind of financial or similar incentive to individuals to take part. Although the two can be linked, most authorities recognise that rewarding a group for their involvement is potentially undermining. What you don't want to do is to create an environment in which people contribute – but only for a price. It should be seen as part of the natural working process. That said, in any organisation, an outstanding contribution would be recognised with some form of financial return. Often the discussion about recognition and reward can be a very useful one to hold at senior management level.

One steel company based in South Wales had such a debate. Eventually they settled on the idea of giving each member of the participating teams a painting. The paintings were commissioned from a member of the shopfloor who was a keen amateur painter. As they required a very large number in order to meet the needs of several teams this was probably the first major commission that this individual had had. Not only did it transform his life, even allowing him to become a semi-professional artist, but the paintings themselves had a tremendous intrinsic value to the individuals who received them. Within a couple of years the success of the artist had meant that the paintings had taken on a real financial value as well. Of course opportunities like this are pretty unique, but it is well worth exploring them within your organisation.

Part of the Audit process should be to look at possible ways of recognition and reward for involvement in ideas and innovation, and to put forward recommendations for approaches that would be acceptable to the vast majority of the employees.

6. Feedback

We have made several references to the senior management team and their role. One of the common criticisms that organisations receive of their innovation programmes, is that teams making recommendations wait a very long time, either for feedback or for decisions, or both. The problem is simple, in most cases an enormous delay seems to occur between the team making the recommendation and it either receiving some kind of feedback, or a decision being made to go ahead with the investment that is required. This is usually interpreted by the teams as an indication of either lack of commitment by the senior managers or alternatively that the validity of their information is being questioned.

The approach that the Audit team may take in this could follow one of two routes. Firstly, they can examine existing teams and find out what length of time it takes for their recommendations to be accepted. Alternatively, it can be quite useful to have comparative figures so that teams become less concerned when the delays are genuine. In this case the Audit team can take existing decisions and look back to find out when the original recommendation was made.

In doing this we are not justifying the lengths and times that are involved and if this does become a significant issue, then the Audit team can make recommendations of ways in which the time delay can be reduced. In some cases delays arise because the wrong people are invited to presentations. In others it is because internal bureaucracy gets in the way, while in others still there is a holding company that has to be involved for projects over a certain value. In the latter case, couldn't a member of the holding company be involved in the presentation? Or alternatively, even in the team itself?

7. New product development

If we are serious about being responsive to our customers' requirements we have to act quickly with all new product development, but that is not an excuse to dump rubbish on to the market. The role of the Audit team is to look at the existing pattern of new product development. Who is involved? Why are they involved? What are the delays? What are the timings? What are the costs involved? What environment is used to create new products? Who are the people involved, including sponsors and managers? Track back the new products that have been devised and developed over the last five or ten years. Where was their origin? How long did they take to become marketable products? What were the lengths of time at each stage of their development? What levels of quality problems were associated with the products once they were launched? How many times was launching delayed?

New product development is not the exclusive domain of marketing people. What does the organisation do to encourage other people within it to put forward their proposals? After all, many new product ideas do not originate within the company alone, but instead, in the domestic lives of employees.

A similar phenomenon is found in advertising agencies where many new ideas are generated away from the office. How long does it take for an idea reaching its prototype stage to be introduced to customers? Were customers involved in developing it? Were customers involved in suggesting it? Were customers not involved until the basic prototype had been produced?

The experience of the early Japanese car industry was that most customers were seen by the technologists as being behind the times, and therefore incapable of perceiving the sorts of improvements and modifications that they are recommending. They could then justify spending long periods of time developing a product to prototype stage before presenting it to their customers. Over recent years the Japanese car industry has taken an amazing proportion of foreign markets. It has achieved this very often with products that were exposed to the customers even before they had reached the drawing-board stage. They have broken their traditional problem.

Test marketing is well established in the software industry. Indeed, for some years it was a standing joke that often products would be demonstrated on launch, several months before they had even been tested. Some of the larger software companies were caught out, with cables under demonstration tables running from what was supposedly a small personal computer to a mini-computer hidden in a back room or under the stage. Nevertheless, the software industry does engage in beta-testing which is their own equivalent of test markets. Whatever your products, do you display the results of these test market activities where everyone can see them? In the Audit team look at how this information is communicated, how effectively does it reach your employees? Does it only go to nearby managers – to those intimately involved in the project itself? Or is it widely disseminated throughout the organisation? Are there fears that commercial secrecy must be maintained? If so, what is the foundation of these problems?

8. Use of information systems

Head-hunters and recruitment consultants will tell you that you will never be given a job unless you tell someone you are looking for one. In exactly the same way, if you are trying to achieve a change in culture, you will never change the culture unless you tell people about it. If that culture involves much greater involvement of everyone in the development of ideas and creativity, then it is vital that you have an effective way of spreading the knowledge, spreading the successes to the rest of the people in the organisation and learning from the failures. How does your organisation go about this?

Approaches vary tremendously from one business to another. Smaller organisations tend to evolve around notice boards. At Wootton Jeffreys, for example, a medium-sized specialist consultancy practice concerned with highway and transport issues, quality information is routinely distributed around the organisation through the use of strategically placed notice boards. However, because of their size and the nature of their accommodation it would not be practical to have separate notice boards for every subject so, instead, all quality notices are printed on the same distinctive pink paper. Other organisations, where the notice board is a less significant factor, may use alternatives such as newsletters.

We came across one Midlands-based company which produced the paper place-settings in the canteen. Up-to-the-minute information could be run off as late as ten o'clock in the morning and still be on the place settings by the first shift at lunch time. The organisation used this very effectively to relate safety, quality, performance, productivity and innovation concepts to all of their employees.

Some companies recognise that if people are given information at work they probably won't read it and they probably won't take it home, so they get round this by sending it to their home addresses. Others use signs, electronic or otherwise; some businesses even use flags. One organisation displayed product recall information beneath its safety signs at the entrance to the factory. One leading car manufacturer took advertising time at the local cinema to appeal to some of the younger members of its workforce.

A growing number of commercial multi-nationals, including BMW, use satellite transmissions. At a regular interval either weekly or monthly, a programme is put together professionally by a television production company working on behalf of the organisation. The programmes are video-taped, taken to the company headquarters, broadcast by satellite to regional headquarters around the world where they are either re-broadcast or video-taped and then distributed to the local dealers. Most of this activity takes place over the weekend and then on Monday morning when the local workforce arrives, they sit down with a cup of coffee and watch the latest corporate video. These programmes can never be full of ritzy, glitzy, highly sophisticated advertising material. If they did people would become bored very quickly. Instead they are full of useful information, directly relevant to each of the activities that they are engaged in.

One supermarket chain plays across the tannoy system in its local super-markets, a tape prepared at headquarters, while the shelves are being filled on Thursday evening. The programme is put together as an entertaining blend of news and popular music, directly replacing the one which is normally broadcast while customers are on site.

Esso, the petro-chemical company, experimented for a while with improving the safety of its tanker drivers by fitting in every cab a cassette deck and distributing monthly cassettes of driving tips, music and general company information.

All of these are acceptable routes to spread the word about successful experiments. As you might expect, the more high-tech organisations often adopt more high-tech solutions. Many computer software companies have developed sophisticated network-based databases, occasionally linked to electronic-mail systems.

Review for your own organisation what means are used to disseminate the ideas and progress of team activities. These approaches are also all part of the recognition system.

It is often easy for us to forget that sophisticated 'information systems' of this kind have often been in use for many years. Many sales-based organisa-tions, especially those in the fast-moving consumer goods (FMCG) industries, which rely upon extensive networks of representatives around the country, hold quarterly, half yearly or annual prize-givings and award ceremonies for the best sales people. Why not replace these with a corporate prize-giving ceremony but for teams of people who have contributed the best ideas and innovations.

9. Company-wide innovators' week

If your organisation does not already have a track record for innovation, one approach, which can be well worth exploring, is a company-wide innovators' week. In a systematic way over the course of the week, every employee is assigned to a small team (usually of four, five or six people). Working to a structure the teams are given an opportunity to develop their own idea to tackle a particular problem.

Coordinated across the company to make sure that there is little or no duplication of these ideas, the teams are given the opportunity over the course of the week to develop their idea, to explore it, to obtain and understand more detailed information about it and to establish a solution to the problem that they have posed. Alongside these team-based activities, individual ones are also organised.

Postcards are distributed and every individual who identifies the solution to a problem and puts it into place records the fact on the card and submits it to a central point. The cards may be pinned up, enlarged, broadcast, or in some way held up as examples to the rest of their colleagues. Over the course of the week an enormous amount of enthusiasm can be engendered. Even small organisations can hire a pantechnicon with a video cinema inside it and show examples of creative thinking and creative organisations. They might use the pantechnicon as a way of demonstrating or displaying the solutions to problems that people have developed over the course of the week. Rewards can be simple, ranging from a mug or a cup, up to quite sophisticated schemes. One organisation, for example, gave each team a budget of £100. They were simply told to spend it wisely, but equally they were told that any profit that they generated through the use of the idea would be split 50/50 with them. Although most of the teams were satisfied to have returned the same value back, two teams in particular raised several thousands of pounds for themselves. The only condition was that their accounts had to stand up to some kind of scrutiny.

The Audit team might like to think about the practicality of running such an event. In order to encourage the management team to select it or to adopt it, they will need to provide evidence. They can begin to do so by analysing the returns that have come from similar, smaller teams in the past.

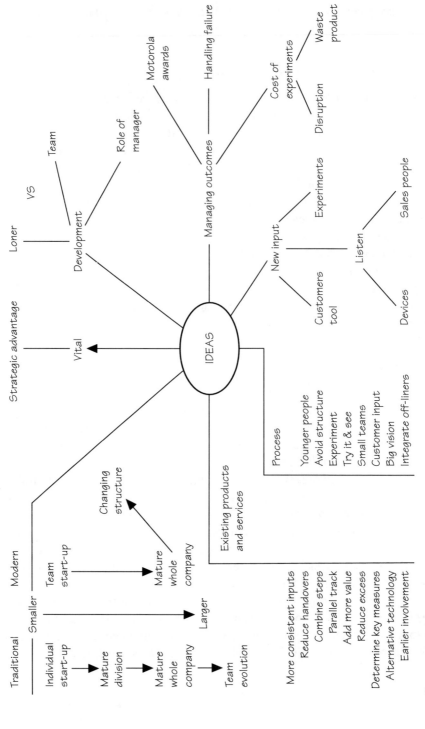

Summary Mindmap 5: Ideas

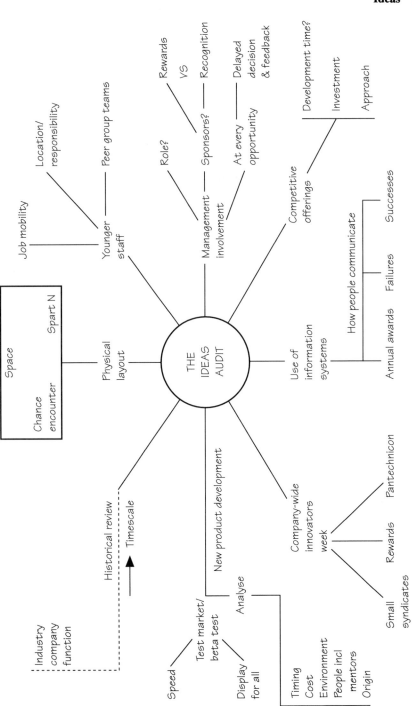

Ideas Audit Mindmap

6 PEOPLE

Most of us are familiar with modern day organisation structures which usually resemble a hierarchy – often in the form of a pyramid. The person 'at the top' usually has a management team that reports in to them. The members of the management team are generally appointed because they, in turn, head different functions. Each functional head would probably have their own management team, and so the hierarchy breaks down layer by layer.

We owe much of this hierarchical structure to the original theories proposed by Taylor at the start of this century. They have been used ever since with very little concern for their effectiveness. It was Taylor who felt that individuals should be given large numbers of small scale, small duration repetitive tasks to perform and many manufacturing industries have continued to adopt and follow this approach. The level of variety in some people's working lives is therefore quite remarkably narrow.

THE NEW STRUCTURE OF ORGANISATIONS

For years now there have been diagrams floating around organisations with spoof alternative structures on them. Now imagine a genuine alternative, put your mind back to the days of those Busby Berkeley movies – the ones where a score or more of 'bathing beauties' would carry out a synchronized swimming exercise. Filmed from above the appearance was that of a kaleidoscope with, firstly, all of the people pointing head first towards one another, then perhaps breaking off, legs moving, arms moving, until they formed a different shape, this time broken into three or four smaller clusters. Then slowly moving together again until they formed another shape and so on. Imagine for a minute that each of those bodies in the swimming pool represents a small unit, probably between five and twelve people in your organisation. Each one is a team. More or less intact they align with other teams in different ways according to the demands of the work on them and the type of task that they are undertaking. These teams are now to be found in many hundreds of organisations, scattered throughout the world, though primarily in North America and Japan.

Although there were naturally a few pioneers, no one really seems to know exactly where this concept emerged from. It appears to have been invented in many different places at roughly the same time and in particular began to take off around about the middle to late 1980s. The teams themselves may be called a variety of different things, but the two consistent approaches which emerge are either called 'self-directed teams' or 'self-managing teams'. The common features to these teams are that they are a formal organisational unit. Except in very rare circumstances, this group of people will work together for most of the time. They will not be further split up, unlike a traditional department or section. They are a formal group. This contrasts with many traditional organisations who have informal structures; small teams which may be pulled together at different times. These groups remain together throughout.

As we have said, self-managing teams will usually number between six and twelve individuals though in most cases the smaller end of this scale is the commonest. Usually they will have been designed to take responsibility for the whole of a particular aspect of work. In many cases they work together throughout the day, though in some organisations they may be isolated and have review meetings held periodically. These can range from five minutes a day to two hours a month, though in most cases there is a daily meeting lasting only a few minutes. Periodically, longer-term problem-solving meetings will be held separately. In organisations where shift-working is important, teams may cross over shifts so that some members will work for one shift and other members for another. These so called 'cross-shift' teams will often overlap their time by a few minutes so that there is a formal handover. Alternatively the cycle times in the shift pattern are arranged so that part of the group will overlap for part of the time with their predecessor and successor shifts.

THE NATURE OF TEAMS IN ORGANISATIONS

In some cases teams like this have been introduced in green field sites. However, in the majority they have been part of an ongoing process of culture change, developing from the TQ movement. As such it is easy to see them as a natural extension of the teams that were introduced for problem-solving activities.

In the late 1960s many organisations were in the process of implementing quality circles. One of the commonest failings of quality circles was the lack of support that was provided for the individuals in them. They were either not trained or the time that they gave was under-valued by the rest of the people in the organisation. Often too, the members of the team were not properly trained to work as members of a team. They were used to working alone and they found it difficult to work in a group.

However, the concept was similar. For most organisations implementing quality circles, the initial step was for the management team to identify certain problems which needed to be addressed. The scale of benefits that were offered meant that these problems were usually large issues, often spanning between several functions. In the terminology that evolved at the time these groups, working across functions on a problem selected by the management team, would be called a 'Task Force'. As the Task Forces began to deliver positive results so the organisation began to switch to a different shape of team. The switch could occur in one of two directions. Either the Task Forces would make way for a different type of team, still working on management-selected problems but within an individual function – in which case they were often called Departmental Quality Groups or, alternatively, the individuals in a particular area would choose their own problems to tackle. Because most of these problems were related to poor communication, they tended to remain cross-functional. In this case the groups were called Quality Improvement Teams or QITs.

Eventually these organisations saw a transition of their improvement groups towards quality circles. A quality circle consists of a group of people from the same area of work tackling problems which they have chosen to resolve. The modern day self-managing or self-directed team is a natural extension of these quality circles, though they have only evolved from quality circles in relatively few cases. In most situations they have been adopted from scratch.

THE RESPONSIBILITIES OF TEAMS

These teams take responsibility for a complete part of the 'whole' work. In the majority of cases, they 'own' a product, but this is not always the case, particularly in service organisations where they may handle a portfolio of products. The team takes over full responsibility for all aspects of the planning, control and improvement of the products or services within their area. As such they will be responsible for purchasing decisions, for scheduling of work, for liaison with suppliers, for budgeting activities, disciplinary activities and all review-related actions such as hiring and firing, training and appraisals. Obviously you do not take a group of people from the shopfloor and expect them to instantly take on board all decision-making.

In practice most work teams do not consist of just a group of people 'off' the shopfloor. Similarly, the level of responsibility which has been taken up in different organisations varies, though all of those activities that we have described will become the responsibility of the work team ultimately. In some organisations that have not been progressing down this route for as long as others, only the purchasing, scheduling and liaison with suppliers would have been handed over totally to the group.

The transition process typically takes about six years. In most cases it is not long before budgeting becomes part of the responsibility of the work team. They may achieve this by having specific training in how to budget and how to balance both internal and external accounting and auditing processes. Alternatively it may be through the co-option of a member of the purchasing or accounting departments, which will by now have been disassembled.

Teams soon take on responsibility for discipline where one member behaves in such a way as to cause the rest of the team to either suffer directly or to be placed in some kind of threat. Disciplinary actions usually arise from either a safety-related problem or one caused through poor working habits. Organisations with work teams are obviously subject to exactly the same statutory requirements as any other organisation. In the area of discipline these are often very precisely defined and this is just one indication of the way in which an organisation which adopts work teams has to completely re-structure and re-think many of its operating practices. For example, in the case of the disciplinary issue, approaches vary tremendously. The Lake Superior Paper company, who adopted this approach several years ago, have retained a formally structured disciplinary process. In the past it would have been conducted by managers, on a progressively escalating scale up to the point where it involved a panel drawn from the Personnel Department and the senior management team. This process has now been re-written and instead a small panel comprising representatives of the team that the individual comes from together with representatives from other teams and an independent arbiter, form the ultimate referral point. The structure is based loosely around the original concept of warnings and written warnings.

Other organisations often adopt an approach which is more concerned with helping the individual to learn better working habits. One petrochemical company, confronted by an employee who was regularly performing a task in a way which was clearly not safe, left the discipline to the work team in which he was operating. The team decided to get him to prepare a video depicting the correct way of performing the task safely. They then got him to use this as a training aid for other units working in the same area. Had this been done by a senior manager it would probably have been seen to have been patronising, almost like a scene from school. However, because in this case it was his peers who were asking him to perform this task, and he was given suitable training and help in how to prepare the video and then in how to carry out training himself, the individual was able to improve his own skills and accepted that it was not so much a punishment as a development process for himself. The whole process was considerably more constructive than that which would have been achieved in a normal disciplinary system. As teams become more established they introduce their own processes of review through the skills of goal setting, providing feedback and raising performance. They increasingly take over responsibility for training, hiring and firing.

It would seem that one of the milestones in introducing self-managing teams is the introduction of negative and constructive feedback. Initially it proves difficult for peer groups to provide this, though with perseverance most organisations recognise that it is far more effective.

CHANGING THE STRUCTURE OF THE ORGANISATION

As the teams become established so the requirements for support functions change. Most organisations who have introduced self-managing work teams report three phases in the development of the relationship with the support functions, among which they usually count training, finance, maintenance, quality control and so on. The first phase is a focal shift. In many traditional organisations there is a serious conflict as to who is responsible to whom in the relationship between the support functions and the main line production.

The first shift therefore is for the support functions to begin to see the main line as representing the principal customer. No longer is a maintenance schedule organised to suit the maintenance department (as still happens in some organisations). Instead it is the product team that calls the shots.

The second phase is for the team to enter into formal liaisons with the support departments. In this way a member of the support team becomes part of the self-managing work team on a part-time basis. Eventually, in most of these organisations, the support functions become integrated fully with the self-managing work teams, and the support departments are closed down.

THE BENEFITS OF SELF-MANAGING TEAMS

There is a transfer of skills from the support functions, who often perceive themselves as specialists, to the members of the team and vice versa, with members of the team introducing the support functions to some of the alternative pressures of providing an online facility. So why should such arrangements be so successful and why should they be so popular?

To a senior manager bought up in the traditional mould, self-managing work teams would appear to be an anachronism. After all, the loss of control and the transfer of responsibility to people who have previously been seen as incapable of handling it must represent a serious threat.

One of the first questions which is often asked by people as they begin to introduce self-managing work teams is: 'What will the unions think of it?' In practice, virtually all union movements fully support the concept of self-managing work-teams. Where problems do exist, it is usually due to the poor implementation process.

The benefits to the organisation are straightforward. Firstly, there are significantly reduced operating costs. Most organisations find that the majority of their managers are no longer required. This does not mean that they down-grade jobs, but the responsibility which would perhaps have been held by one person paid a considerable salary is now shared among a team with a considerable saving in on-costs! The second benefit to most organisations comes from a dramatic improvement in communication. The impact of functional barriers on internal communication is usually quite extreme. With the self-managing work team these functional barriers are removed, so communication dramatically improves. As many quality problems, and certainly many productivity problems, are directly related to poor communication, teams can produce fundamental results almost immediately. The third benefit to the organisation and the one which is indeed critical to the responsive organisation is an improvement in flexibility. It has been widely demonstrated that as an individual is given more and more responsibility and expected to demonstrate more skills, so they reach a point, a plateau, beyond which they find it difficult to stretch. This represents a limiting factor on their flexibility. With a team the proportionate level of increased skill against flexibility is much higher. So a team is able to be more flexible pro rata than an individual can ever be. Related to this is the fact that group process within a team acts as a constraint, one which would not operate on an individual. Thus the overriding fear, which most middle and senior managers have of self-managing work teams, namely that of industrial anarchism, is completely unfounded and in reality quite the reverse is likely to be true. Although teams increase flexibility they will also become more conservative, often adopting less extensive solutions to problems while ensuring a satisfactory solution. This obviously further reduces the operating costs. For instance, an individual confronted with a need for more accessible information might put forward a case for a computer-based database with all the development and support costs involved. The team might adopt a simpler wall chart at a much lower cost. When individuals are surveyed and asked for the benefits that they perceive have been obtained from working in a self-managing team, usually the first thing to be mentioned is the improved variety and greater understanding that they have of the work process that they are involved in.

THE CHANGING NATURE OF JOBS

As a team begins to develop so the individuals within it will take on broader and broader roles. Clearly this has an impact both on job titles and job descriptions. In many traditional organisations the job title brings with it considerable 'positional power'. It has long been recognised that it is possible to motivate individuals by raising their status through the job title without necessarily improving their rewards.

Many organisations that embark on self-managing teams provide an initial transition of job title for the members of the team. This can help to overcome resistance in the traditional organisation initially, but it is unlikely to have a long-term benefit. Equally, in many of these organisations immediate attempts are made to try to keep job descriptions in line with the roles that people are undertaking. In practice these attempts are usually dropped within about twelve to eighteen months as it becomes very obvious that individuals are capable of far greater flexibility than a job description can allow.

Self-managing teams are intimately connected with multi-skilling. The advice that most successful organisations give after implementing self-managing work teams is to avoid making multi-skilling a mandatory process. Many of the negative impacts of multi-skilling arise from this mandatory approach. Taking on new skills impacts the organisation in many ways. Usually it is difficult to develop a successful scheme. A skill-related pay, and the training which is necessary, is often difficult to balance and provide in an equal fashion. Individuals who would have undertaken significant training in a new skill area find that the skills they have adapted and adopted are unused or uncalled for. Where the development of multiple skills is part of the normal growth process of an individual in a team, it is far more likely to be successful.

One way in which organisations try to achieve this is through a formal job rotation. Individuals in one team identify opportunities for themselves in other teams and when a vacancy becomes available they apply. Although there doesn't appear to be an obvious reason for it in many of these organisations, as the team have taken over responsibility for hiring and firing, so they will make the individual from another team apply in the same way as they would outside applicants. This is often seen by the team as a more rigorous approach and ensures a better quality answer rather than one which has been biased by preconceptions. This is just another ramification of the improved control which comes from self-managing work teams as opposed to individuals.

ALTERNATIVE REWARD SYSTEMS

Obviously as individuals take on more and more responsibility, they expect to be rewarded for it. Almost all self-managing work teams are associated with a revision of the reward systems operated by the organisation. These reward systems usually consist of two elements: a base pay and some kind of additional factor. The additional factors fall in to one of two types: they are usually either skills-related or, alternatively, some kind of bonus arrangement. We have already pointed out that in the earliest stages skills-related systems are going to have difficulties as a result of logistically organising a fair system for every individual. Skills themselves also vary dramatically. It is possible for individuals to improve their depth of knowledge of a subject, their breadth of knowledge of a subject and their vertical knowledge of a production or service delivery process. As many organisations have implemented self-managing work teams so they have recognised that the key difference in the skills required by the individuals in teams, when compared with the previous system, is an improved level of analytical reasoning. This is something which is often associated with a degree-level or undergraduate training. Whether this is reasonable or not is not really clear. Certainly many of the organisations which have been down this route for some years are beginning to provide degree-level training in-house for many of their employees, with one or two having made it their stated objective that within a few years they will operate with an entirely graduate work force which will have developed in-house. Clearly, balancing the differences between depth of skill, breadth skills, vertical skill and analytical reasoning to provide equality of rewards is extremely difficult.

The alternative, a bonus-related system is preferred by most self-managing work teams. Not only is it far easier to monitor, it is also far more effective at rewarding group performance rather than individual performance. As individual reward is often seen as one of the serious down sides of a traditional system, bonus-related elements which the group have control over are usually seen as a far greater motivator.

Case Study 9

American Airlines

Most organisations have had their fair share of industrial disputes. The case, only a short while ago, in which American Airlines were accused of discrimination against fat people proves that even some of the best organisations cannot escape from this problem! But American Airlines have been committed to the development of their employees for many years. Although many other organisations joined the 'Quality of Work-Life' movement in the early 1960s, it wasn't really until 1983 that the Chairman of American Airlines, Robert Crandall, launched their Quality of Work-Life Programme. Crandall has developed a reputation as a highly commercial and astute business man, but nevertheless one who is particularly fair and trusting. For a decade now, he has been more than committed to a process of progressive empowerment within American Airlines. The visibility of his vision is clear and he creates many opportunities to demonstrate it to the workforce. Just one example was his tour in 1988, when he addressed all 18,400 employees of American Airlines within the USA. This was a task that in many other organisations would have been delegated to another manager.

As Crandall has observed, the airline industry has its foundation in the military. In the early 1980s the priority was to shift from a discipline-based structure to one of trust and mutual respect. The quality of work-life movement provided the forum for this. For many organisations however, since the 1980s, the quality of work-life movement has diminished in priority. At American Airlines this is not the case. As Anne McNamara,

Senior Vice-President of Administration and General Counsel has said: 'We can't return to the days when management made all the decisions and other employees carried them out'. For many organisations implementing team working, a new role is created for individuals with particularly well-developed process skills to act as facilitators to working teams. Initially they will be specialists, though eventually they become the example for the new style of management. This shift in understanding usually requires a step change on behalf of the senior management team too and the recognition that a style of leadership which has been adopted for many decades before is no longer appropriate. As we explain elsewhere in this book, this recognition can be exceptionally painful for many people in the organisation.

As its Quality of Work-Life Programme developed into the 1990s, American Airlines implemented a new phase entitled 'Committing to Leadership', representing an investment of nearly $15m. Throughout the 1990s, American Airlines sent every one of its 14,000 middle managers and supervisors for a week long intensive programme of training in process skills, covering such topics as participation, empowerment, involvement, team working, problem-solving and internal communications.

The Quality of Work-Life Programme had already proved highly successful, with many critical success factors having been identified, measured and improvements clearly demonstrated. For example, the number of passenger complaints received by American Airlines fell from 1.2 per hundred thousand passengers in June 1989 to only 0.46 per hundred thousand passengers in 1990. This level, representing 38 complaints in 12 million passengers, is very close to that of Six Sigma, which organisations such as Xerox and Motorola are striving to achieve at the moment.

By equipping their managers with a completely different skill set, American Airlines are hoping to kick-start their improvement process in much the same way as other organisations have successfully done. To provide an incentive and a new environment for these people to apply their skills, in 1991 Robert Crandall launched a series of automation initiatives. Whereas many other organisations have implemented automation as a way of doing away with human involvement (either to reduce errors or to remove overheads), in American Airlines' case they are providing the right tools for jobs that have become progressively more sophisticated in recent years. For example, the development of artificial intelligence systems at their Dallas Fort Worth Airport Systems Operations Control, has increased productivity by the loading agents by virtually 40 per cent. In another case, at their maintenance base in Tulsa where 5,000 maintenance engineers are employed, American Airlines has invested in robots which are retrieving parts from stores and delivering them to the maintenance engineers where they work. In this way the organisation has saved nearly an hour per shift per engineer, while at the same time raising morale.

THE PEOPLE AUDIT

1. Devolution of authority

One of the earliest stumbling blocks for most change processes is a lack of understanding and awareness on the part of the senior management team of the changes that are involved. Never has this been more important than in the case of establishing devolved authority through self-managing teams. The Audit team needs to establish very clearly the extent of the exposure of the senior management team to practical examples of the new culture. This may have occurred through tapes, videos, books, away days, seminars, conferences, and so on. For some organisations this kind of activity is encouraged generally, but in many others it is a rare exception, often reserved for the most senior manager. The first step therefore can be to develop a programme of 'exposure' activities for this senior management team.

There is an enormous temptation in most organisations to try to rush ahead without taking this step. Equipped with a picture of the activities that have gone on before, the Audit team should prepare a recommended programme for the senior managers. It is unlikely that this step will take much less than one year, although of course it may parallel track with other activities including audits.

The danger of a senior manager running ahead with the process is that they will fail to capture the minds and hearts of the other managers in the group, and even though they may feel that their position is almost unassailable, it is surprising how it can be undermined through a loss of face when the rest of the senior managers perceive that they are being threatened by a loss of control.

Most organisations that have implemented self-managing teams are very proud of their achievements and are usually happy to allow visiting managers into their works.

If, in this organisation, the senior managers perceived that they have already devolved considerable levels of authority, the Audit team should test out this perception by surveying the attitudes of the staff and the employees throughout the business. It would be pointless though, at this stage, to test everyone so a small pilot sample would be taken and, along with other awareness issues, they would be asked to assess the level of authority that has been devolved.

2. Previous initiatives

The Audit team should assess the current organisational structure and look at any previous initiatives that have been carried out in an attempt to shift the culture of the organisation. This assessment should not be taken light-heartedly, for there are usually considerable lessons to be learnt from previous exercises. In each case, study the process that was followed, the stages at which various people were exposed to the change and how effectively each step worked. Interview the key players and examine the costings. Which activities were perceived as giving value for money and which were a waste of time? Has the current organisational structure been changed to accommodate previous initiatives? Examine the current culture. Is there a strong vision shared by all in the organisation? To what extent can people on the shopfloor relate to it? Have they had it explained to them and has anyone helped them make it apply to their own particular activities? To what extent are people reflected in the company culture? Would it support the devolution of authority or would it contradict it?

The Audit team needs to establish its own lines of enquiry that it considers reflect the culture. In some cases they may look at how goals are set and how rewards are given. In others they may look at the induction process and the way in which individuals are trained to tackle their work. They may look at the monthly management reports to see which subjects are used to monitor progress. They will almost certainly take a sample of the employees in the organisation at various levels and, either through direct interviewing or by means of a questionnaire, they will assess the terms and words that are used by people to describe the corporate culture. We shall look at this in the next chapter but the team should also look for evidence of respect and disrespect shown to employees.

3. Employee attitude

In many organisations the main activity used to assess the readiness of the people in the organisation for the change process is a survey of employees. This usually considers two aspects of the change. Firstly, the awareness of the employees of the new culture which is being created and secondly, their attitudes. Through the careful development of a questionnaire it is possible to use this survey as an initial stimulus to change in the organisation. By providing information associated with each question it is possible to raise awareness, provided that the bulk of the people responding are able to read the information given.

What evidence is there of employee attitudes and involvement from previous initiatives and to what extent are they involved indirectly? For example, is there a suggestion scheme? How effective is it? How else do suggestions get made? How often do they get made? What is the pattern of suggestion delivery? Do most tend to come from one person or from one area? Were suggestions usually made to obtain budgetary approval or are they part of the development process of a solution? In other words, does a team of people then get together to apply the result?

4. Existing teams

To what extent are teams a part of the regular organisation today? Does the physical layout of the organisation encourage people to work in teams? The Audit team needs to assess the nature of existing jobs. The three key factors which they should be looking at are: firstly, the opportunities to provide groups of people with responsibility for a whole process; secondly, they should be looking for the opportunity to balance the utilisation of skills across that job; and thirdly, they should be looking for sufficient complexity in the work that is being carried out so that there are opportunities for team members to take a greater responsibility for this operation.

Many of the activities which they will be expected to undertake as a team have previously been carried out by people outside the immediate working area, including supervisors, managers and members of other functions. Clearly the Audit team needs to be sensitive in the way in which it tackles this task. In organisations where there is a lack of trust, or the bitter after-taste of time-and-motion studies, a careful process of consultation and explanation has to go on beforehand.

The change towards self-managing work teams is unlikely to be suggested in these environments unless there has been a change of the senior management team. The Audit group needs to assess the impact of this change and whether there is still a residual bad feeling, or potential bad feeling, from the previous group.

As part of their assessment it may be appropriate for them to recognise suitable awareness-raising activities to be carried out for the shopfloor workforce. In several cases this has involved wholesale transport of entire groups of people to see alternative working practices in different organisations, in much the same way as has been arranged for the senior management team. For example, at Allied Steel and Wire, a major UK steel business, more than a period of some three years was spent, during which time many members of the workforce (at all levels in the organisation) were sent as part of a bench-marking exercise to visit the Kobe Steel works in Japan. In this way people were exposed to alternative working practices for a long period of time before the suggestion was made that the organisation itself should shift. Although there were a few well-informed individuals who were perhaps aware of the trend which was about to develop, for most people the shift towards self-managing teams was a natural continuation of a process and was not thought through and planned beforehand.

5. Union activities

As we have said earlier, one of the first questions that we are usually asked when introducing self-managing teams into an organisation is how the union will react. In a survey of several hundred organisations in the USA it was found that the unions had been wholly supportive of the change to self-managing work teams. In a little over half the cases most of the development and planning work had gone ahead with members of the union, and in a small number of cases it had been the union's initiative in the first place.

Provided that the process of implementation is carried out in a constructive way and is well planned there should be little or no threat to any individual in the organisation. Most employees find the whole process rewarding and often find themselves developing beyond their own personal expectations. As we have said, the group that is hardest hit is probably the middle management team, for whom the transition of focus is considerable. Nevertheless, in most organisations the middle management group report that the benefits far out-weighed the short-term disadvantages and stress.

The initial thought in many peoples' minds is that it is the middle management team who will most likely to be made redundant. If an organisation is competing in a marketplace which is saturated and where competition is largely on price, this fear is understandable. Unfortunately one of the primary triggers to change of this kind can often be the threat that is perceived from competitors and so the environment is often exactly that!

Surprisingly, as a result of introducing teams, the numbers of individuals who need to be 'laid off' is usually far lower than had originally been predicted. The reason for this is that as the organisation begins to become more responsive and the dialogue with customers increases so the possible opportunities in which to add value to product lines dramatically increases. This means that not only does the organisation not have to lay off anywhere near as many people as it had originally planned, but also the turnover per employee increases. For example, as the wire works in Birmingham (which we mentioned earlier) began its change process, it sent a team of maintenance fitters to visit a number of their customers' sites. Had they not done so it would have been the group of maintenance fitters who would have been most likely to have left the organisation, as the majority of their skills would have been absorbed into the normal working team. As a result of their visits, however, the fitters put forward a significant number of business plans for enhancements to the product lines. This allowed the organisation to dramatically increase the value which it was adding to its products, not only for existing customers but also by expanding into other customer bases and markets. The fitters had not only saved their own jobs, but also those of many of their colleagues who became involved in teams servicing these new product lines.

Similar examples exist in many of the organisations that have implemented self-directed work teams. The common experience of most of these organisations is that members or representatives of the union should be involved throughout the process of discussion and especially in planning stages, as their insight into the way in which their colleagues work usually proves invaluable.

From time to time, in small organisation's implementing teams, the individual who has become the union representative may find themselves stretched to cope with the possibility of such dramatic change. In this case, discussions with representatives of the national organisation and the involvement of both local and national representatives can be well worthwhile.

To summarise, the Audit team needs to establish union perspectives and should involve union representatives in its work. However, all unions in our experience are in favour of this type of empowered team, the only constraints being an agreement up front about the changes which will be made in the negotiation and representation activities of the union.

6. Technology

The Audit team needs to assess the flexibility of the existing technology. There are two elements here. Firstly, production activities and the associated equipment and service provision activities need to be examined for the potential to reorganise. In some businesses the constraints that act on the environment make it almost impossible to reorganise the work layout. In others, given the will to do so, massive relocation of equipment can be achieved in remarkably small periods of time. The clue as always is the involvement of the right people.

The timing of the Audit will determine the scope and extent of this type of review. If the administration review has already taken place then many of the decisions which might otherwise have to be made about the grouping of activities and the flexibility of existing technology will have already been decided and actions will have already been taken to improve the situation.

The second area of technology that the Audit team needs to examine is one of information systems. Many businesses have developed with information systems that are really only intended to serve the management team or specific functions. The first change that needs to be made is an increase in the amount of company-wide information relating goals (both for the organisation and for individual product lines) to the work that is carried out by the individual teams. If the technology does not exist to provide this information then it will be difficult for the teams to be able to monitor their improvements and their progress. This in turn will undermine the initiative.

This does not mean that massive investment has to be made in high-technology systems, as access usually exists although it has not been made use of, or alternatively, communication lines can be adjusted. An interim stage for many organisations is to make sure that paper-based reports are produced which contain only the information which the specific team requires in order to make its decisions. Over time the team's thirst for information will increase and the necessary investment in technology can be made in a planned way.

The Audit needs to consider not only the technology in the form of hardware and software, but also the design and format of reports and information. If we are expecting a group of people who have never had to work with tables of statistics and data it may be appropriate to present the information in a different format.

7. Support function

The Audit team needs to look at the distribution of skills, attitudes and make-up of the support functions. How are they structured? Where are they located? What backgrounds do the people within the functions have? How should they be incorporated into the self-managing teams? Are their skills highly specialised and how long do they take to acquire? To what extent are their activities automated? Have the people in the support functions had experience of the main business activities? What are their attitudes to the change process? To what extent have they been exposed to the alternative working practices that are being introduced? Do they perceive any barriers to introducing the change process, with particular regard to their own specialist function? For example, there may be constraints that they are aware of from a legal, health and safety, or financial respects. Alternatively, they may know of barriers imposed by a parent company with whom they have more direct contact than other people in the organisation.

The Audit team again needs to be looking at the level of exposure that these groups have had to alternative practices and to develop plans to make them aware of the potential. For example, the Audit team should look at previous changes which have taken place within each support function to look at ways in which they have attempted to become more internally customer-focused, or the way in which they have introduced new technology. Some support functions have already spent a considerable length of time discussing and attempting to reorganise to maximise the customer focus of their function within the organisation. In this case, the experiences and learning points which were achieved need to be reviewed so that mistakes are not made twice.

8. Stability of markets

As we have already said, one of the common triggers to introducing self-managing work teams is a growing awareness that the marketplace has changed and that the organisation is under a new and different type of threat. While this desire to be responsive is vital, the process of implementation inevitably involves a considerable amount of learning and, if the marketplace is so volatile that there is no stability at all, it will be very difficult for the organisation to undergo a progressive change. The Audit team may need to examine the stability of the company and its markets to assess changes that are going on in competitors, and to consider different forms of competition, especially where the market has remained relatively closed for a long period of time. The benefit of this review can be to set an immediate time scale for the change process and especially for the immediate changes that are going to be necessary. Where they perceive that the marketplace is highly unstable and do not envisage a plateauing of this activity, the organisation needs to act quickly.

In the case of the wireworks which we described earlier, most of the organisational changes occurred over an annual close-down period of two weeks. Whereas normally employees would have been asked to take their holiday during this period of time in August, the senior management team decided that it would provide the ideal opportunity for a complete reorganisation, as much of the existing factory layout had to be changed. New computer systems were installed, shift patterns were changed and a significant amount of basic working practice training needed to be carried out. The two-week period was exceptionally busy for most people. The months leading up to this activity had become progressively gloomier and gloomier, with redundancies followed by threatened redundancies and with the obvious closure of a number of local competitors. The reorganisation turned out to be a highly motivating experience for most of the people involved. The massive effort was rewarded by the senior management team with a summer party on the final weekend before the plant operated again. This, in turn, generated media attention and stimulated a number of new customers. Although there were obviously a large number of 'teething' difficulties and many of the longer-term issues still had to be resolved, the company had kick-started itself into a completely different culture and environment. The two-week activity built new levels of trust throughout the organisation and broke down many of the existing entrenched opinions and attitudes.

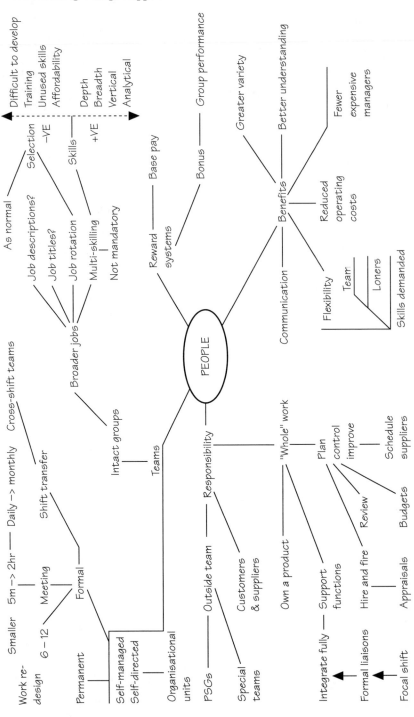

Summary Mindmap 6: People

THE PEOPLE AUDIT

- Nature of jobs
  - Physical layout
  - Sufficient complexity
  - Skills utilisation
  - Potential "whole" work
  - Goals related
- Existing teams
- Technology
  - Flexibility
  - Company-wide
  - Information systems
    - @ Grass roots
- Stability of
  - Markets
  - Company
- Adequate support functions
  - Attitude?
- Previous initiatives
  - Lessons
  - Relevence
- Current structure
- Senior management awareness
- Devolution of authority
  - "Their" perception tool
    - Supporting culture
    - Evidence
      - Respect
      - Disrespect
- Exposure elsewhere
- Union activites
  - Local
  - National
- Employees
  - Managers are too!
  - Awareness/attitude
  - History of suggestions?
  - Ownership/share

People Audit Mindmap

7 LEADERSHIP

There are three key aspects to the leadership process within organisations as they embark on the introduction of self-managing work teams.

- the role of individuals within the organisation;
- managing the reactions to change; and
- achieving a change in behaviour.

THE ROLE OF INDIVIDUALS

Whereas before there may have been several tiers in the hierarchy, leadership now polarises in three forms. In small organisations, typically up to 200–250 employees, there will be only one senior manager. This may be the owner, the Chief Executive or the Chief Operating Officer reporting to a Board of Directors. It is the role of this group of people or individual to establish the very clear purpose of the organisation. It is their job, as we have said, to provide the 'vision'. Of course they also need to live and breathe it.

We have emphasised the importance of a clear vision throughout this book. It is universally accepted that without some time being taken to develop and formulate this, any attempt to change culture is likely to be unsuccessful. It is important to stress though that vision does not mean a 'vision statement'. The latter may be used to summarise the vision or to communicate it to a wider audience. But the vision itself will probably remain locked in the minds of the senior managers.

Even in quite large organisations, below the senior management team there are rarely more than two other layers. The first would be Group Leaders and the second, Team Leaders. Group Leaders share a role in the development of strategy. Their other duty, though, is the development of the Team Leaders. In some organisations the role of the Group Leader is more important than in others and it is difficult to identify a pattern in this. Generally they will look after a small number of teams. They adopt a stance of serving the teams, often in the form of an administrator, ensuring that activities are coordinated and resources are optimally used. At the same time they will be working with the leaders of the teams to make sure that they are comfortable with their own development role.

The Group Leaders do not attempt to remove any of the ownership of processes from the teams themselves. In our experience difficulties within teams may be voiced as a perception that the senior managers are less prepared to commit to change than they would verbally have us believe. These problems usually have their origins in a Group Leader who is in turn finding it difficult to relinquish control. In some organisations the Group Leader has a very fluid role; some will be made far more use of than others, depending on the approach that they adopt and the way in which they work with the teams. It is usually best for these relationships to define themselves. Once they are established the senior managers can review them without establishing a precedent for retaining the position.

Thus the teams may benefit a great deal with one Group Leader but if that Group Leader is not available, they may not suffer. Group Leaders are, without exception, outside the teams. The day-to-day development of the team is the responsibility of its own Team Leader. This position replaces that of the foreman or supervisor in most organisations. The emphasis is different in that the Team Leader remains with the team throughout, is responsible for one team only and is not sharing their time with other functions.

We often find that organisations which have implemented self-managing teams have chosen the Team Leaders mainly from the supervisors and foremen, with the initial selection being carried out by the senior management team. Approaches to this selection process differ tremendously. In some cases individuals are subject to a battery of personality tests and profiles, in others they may attend an assessment centre or take part in outward-bound-type courses. The views on the effectiveness of this approach differ tremendously. Experiences in North America suggest that it is best if the Team Leaders can include individuals from the shopfloor, as there are often many very highly motivated individuals who will respond to the new opportunity and environment although they may not have thrived in the traditional system, which would have led to their promotion as a foreman or supervisor.

Roughly half the organisations that have so far embarked on self-managing work teams have set the tenure period for Team Leaders to a reasonable length of time, such as three years. There is a clear understanding that the role is of a limited duration. Generally, the shorter the duration of the contract or the tenure of this position, the more likely the policies and approaches which will be adopted by the Team Leader will be short-term.

Who chooses the Team Leader varies tremendously. Initially most organisations rely upon a management team decision. A smaller number will use the Group Leaders to select the Team Leaders. However, most organisations progressively move towards the team selection of their own leaders. Questions are often raised about the evaluation of the performance of Team Leaders. What happens if we make a bad decision and the wrong person is appointed? How do we handle discipline of that individual? And so on. The key is a well-established evaluation process that is clear to both parties. Again, the range of organisations' responses to this approach is tremendous. While some have complete self-evaluation, others evaluate by the team, and some through a third party (such as a Counsellor or the Group Leader), while in others no evaluation takes place at all. Most of the organisations that have progressed down this route recognise that it is important that the performance evaluation of the Team Leaders should not be linked to their reward. In traditional organisations where this is the case a significant defensive reaction can be built up to any kind of feedback. As the Team Leaders are learning on behalf of the organisation it is important that feedback should be immediate and direct, and linking it to a reward system leads to unnecessary defensiveness. Most Team Leaders are nevertheless rewarded differently to the other members of the team. Usually this takes the form of a simple pay differential, though a few organisations shy away from this as they argue that the motivation of the Team Leaders should be a desire to perform better and work with the team, rather than for the financial reward.

Whatever their role in the organisation, whether it is as the most senior managers, as Group Leaders or Team Leaders, and indeed as team members, everyone has a responsibility for the behaviour that they use and the way in which it leads others. We have already looked at the changing role of the manager and how in simple terms their responsibility changes from that of 'controller-cop' to a 'developer of people'. This calls for a form of adaptive leadership. For a manager who has previously been rewarded and recognised as succeeding in the traditional mould, changing the ground rules can have a dramatic effect on their self-confidence. As Robert Hass, the CEO of Levi Strauss, has said: 'It has been difficult for me to accept the fact that I don't have to be the smartest guy on the block . . . in reality the more you establish parameters and encourage people to take initiatives within those boundaries, the more you multiply your own effectiveness by the effectiveness of other people'. Ralph Stayer, who is Chief Executive of Johnsonville Foods, one of the pioneers in the self-managing work team forum, put it: 'The very things that bought me success – my centralised control, my aggressive behaviour, my authoritarian business practices – were creating the environment that made me so unhappy. If I wanted to improve results, I had to increase their (employees') involvement in the business.'

THE ROLE OF MANAGERS AS DEVELOPERS OF PEOPLE

In the previous chapter we looked at the pace with which the transfer of duties can be expected to happen and described a scenario where the transfer occurred almost immediately. As we have said, this is far from common. In most organisations the transition process takes as long as five or six years. The new role of the manager can be summarised in three parts. There will be certain residual skills that they have, very often those for which they were originally selected, which give them a position as 'expert'. This, often technical, expertise is vital to the operation of the business and various teams will probably need to call on them when they first confront difficulties in these areas. The second role is that of administrator. We don't mean by this a pen-pusher, but someone with a central role whose job it is to coordinate activities and efforts in different discrete areas. For this reason many organisations call this new management role that of 'Coordinator'. The third job is that of coach. Table 7.1 (based on Wellins RS, Byham WC and Wilson JM (1991) *Empowered Teams*. Jossey-Bass, Oxford) summarises the percentage of time that most managers will spend in these activities. In many organisations the role of coach is a difficult one to relate to, and to understand it properly it helps to understand some modern thinking about the development of individuals.

Table 7.1 Proportion of time spent by managers

	Traditional	Self-managing
Coaching	10	60
Budget	14	10
Monitor	–	15
Special projects	15	15
Production	35	–
Troubleshooting	10	–
Directing	16	–

After: Wellins RS, Byham WC and Wilson JM (1991)
Empowered Teams. Jossey-Bass, Oxford.

Most traditional organisations do not distinguish between training and development. Training can often be provided off-site; it usually involves the transfer of some skills or knowledge. Knowledge-based training can be carried out in a classroom with books or manuals to supplement the lectures or talks which are given. Where an element of skills transfer is involved individuals on the course will usually receive or carry out exercises related to the course content. When you analyse the content of many courses it is often possible to see that the amount of skills transfer is minimal, so it is hardly surprising that when the individuals return to work they find it difficult to apply the information that they have collected. As a result, within a matter of a few days, they will have forgotten the content of the course and resumed the behaviour that they were using beforehand.

As organisations begin to implement a culture change, usually one of total quality, they often appoint a small number of people as facilitators. At the time they are often acting under the guidance of external consultants and the true role of the facilitators may not have been explained fully. A facilitator is usually trained in the skills of process consulting; probably the closest subject akin to this, which most people have had some experience of, is counselling. Whereas a teacher or trainer usually sets about imparting information by stating it clearly, very much as a traditional teacher would, the facilitator works in a different way. Using a responsive blend of open questions and careful timing, they help individuals to draw out of themselves, ideas and knowledge that they have already assimilated in some other way. This style of behaviour (carefully timed open questioning) is the role model for the new coach. It involves helping individuals to develop their understanding and skills in a particular area, only when they are ready to do so, and not by force-feeding them. Change consultants, when they begin to introduce facilitators into an organisation, are attempting to change the type of management style that dominates in the organisation by creating new role models. The idea behind this is that the success of these facilitators is witnessed in the organisation, not only by people below them but also by individuals who would be more senior. In this way, the less assertive style of working becomes more acceptable, without a loss of face on the part of other managers. The development of an individual is not achieved only in this open and supportive environment. This environment is appropriate only in certain circumstances, but it is usually so poorly developed in most organisations that emphasis only needs to be placed on it and not on other styles of training and development.

STYLES OF LEADERSHIP

Many modern management practices are based around the work of Paul Hersey and Ken Blanchard. While analysing a very wide number of different leadership situations, ranging from the military through commercial and business environments to those of the caring services, they identified four common styles of leadership. Their model, known as situational leadership, has formed the basis of management training in recent years. Although many of their ideas were similar to those that had preceded them, Hersey and Blanchard found that models of leadership style which had been used in the past were too complex for people to follow without prolonged periods of training in the model itself. Their approach was much simpler. They recognised that an individual's capability with a particular set of skills was related to two elements: firstly, their knowledge of those skills themselves, and secondly, their confidence in using them. Taking these as the axis of a graph and considering only two extremes on each scale, one where knowledge was limited and one where knowledge was reasonable, and on the other axis where confidence was lacking or confidence was reasonable, they came up with a four-part model which is illustrated in Figure 7.1.

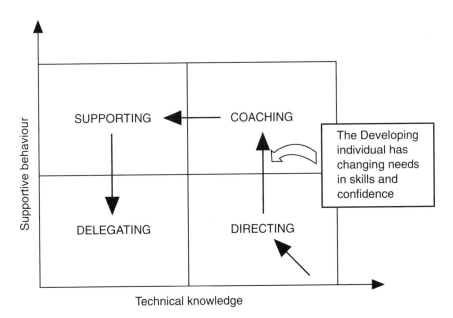

Figure 7.1   Four leadership styles

Initially, when they are asked to perform a new skill, most people lack knowledge of that skill. Their confidence, though, is not necessarily lost. They may well have been performing particularly well already at a different task or set of skills. Thus, the immediate issue to the developer is not one of improving their confidence but instead, one of improving their knowledge. For this reason the first style of leadership which is necessary is one of 'direction', telling people clearly exactly what is expected of them and how they should go about delivering it. Of course directing does not have to be carried out in a lecture-room style but there will be more emphasis on transferring the knowledge of someone who has already done the job to the individual who has not.

Once an individual has acquired some of the understanding of the job or task in hand so they will need to begin to apply it. It is when they begin to apply it that their confidence may be eroded. Having been performing at a particularly high level in other skills, the new set may prove difficult for them to adapt to, and this in turn can undermine their confidence. The role of the leader here is not to continue to provide more information, but to begin to develop and support the individual by reinforcing positively when they do things well and constructively when things don't work out the way they had expected. Nevertheless, it is still likely that there will be some subtleties of the new skill or technique that they are trying to use that they will not have properly acquired and for this reason the developer will be giving some more detailed instruction. The closest analogy that Hersey and Blanchard could identify to this style of leadership, one where confidence is being built up in a supportive manner but at the same time expertise is also being transferred, was that of a sports coach.

Most athletes have a personal 'coach' and this individual takes on two roles; one of identifying ways in which their skill can be improved and the other in developing their confidence in their own ability. In some cases the coach can take on the role of a surrogate parent and in certain circumstances the organisation has to guard against this becoming too predominant. At work it is unlikely to be a problem. As the individual begins to demonstrate that they have acquired all of the skills necessary to do the job they will still need their confidence boosting, and they will need to know that, should anything go wrong, there is someone who is not going to be critical of them to whom they can turn. This third style of leadership is known as 'supporting' and it can be provided not only by the Team Leader but also by other members of the team.

Eventually the individual will reach a condition where they have all the knowledge and skills that they need to carry out the task and they are perfectly confident in their ability to do so. Under these circumstances the style of leadership is one of 'delegation'. Again we have to be careful of a misunderstanding of the term as some managers perceive delegation to be the equivalent of 'dumping'.

The objective throughout this process is to lead others to lead themselves. Throughout, you have to have realistic expectations of what an individual can undertake at this stage in their development, and it may well be that you will go through a small loop of this kind many times with an individual as they progressively take on more and more demanding skills. In the same way, for the managers who are going through a transition process themselves, they will have to learn to cope with each of the stages in the model and how they behave with their team members. Thus, for the successful Team Leader and Group Leader, familiarity with and confidence in all four styles of situational leadership is vital.

REACTIONS TO CHANGE

Anyone who is encountering change goes through a series of stages as they come to terms with the new environment, or the change that has happened around them. One useful application of Hersey and Blanchard's model which is often taught to managers as they prepare for their new role is that of the 'grieving' process. This was originally described as the stages that an individual will go through when they have lost a close relative. In practice it applies to almost any circumstance where an accepted environment has been changed. The initial reaction to a loss of this kind is one of disbelief. Frequently you will hear in organisations individuals who will say just that, 'I don't believe it', when they first come across the new ideas and new concepts. The strength of their reaction varies from the highly vocal to the more passive, such as, 'It will never happen'. At this stage the individuals are groping, looking for more detailed information, for a better picture of what will happen, and how in particular they will be affected. To the senior management team introducing such change it is important that they maintain a 'directive' stance, giving as much information as they can and admitting where they don't have the answers.

Although they will still not have fully accepted the changes which are going to happen, many individuals will then go through a phase of high emotion. We have seen individuals in organisations break down in tears at these times, although more often in public there would be a display of open anger or aggression. In fact, at one memorable seminar we found ourselves acting as a referee in between two sparring supervisors. One was prepared to accept the change and the other was not. When this frustration is not released at work it will often be taken home and, we have spoken to many spouses who have described their other half breaking down at home when they would not dream of doing so at work. These displays of open emotion can be managed, though sadly the level of resource that is necessary is often prohibitive for the smaller organisation. At British Telecom, as they began the change process which they forced upon the organisation by removing some ten thousand middle managers, an entire department of confidential counselling was provided to support the individuals who were going through this emotional reaction.

In the case of the organisation which we described earlier where the change process was bought about very speedily during a seasonal stop-down, much of the initial emotional reaction was vented in the early few days of the stop-down, but because of the high level of energy which was required to make the necessary physical changes, the emotion was translated into a more useful form. The third phase in this reaction process is one of low energy acceptance. It is at this point that individuals have accepted the changes that are going to happen, but they feel drained by the emotions and disinclined to take any steps of practical action. While at the emotional stage they would have responded to coaching; in this low energy acceptance stage they need their confidence rebuilding and the appropriate leadership style will be one of supporting. Using coaching, which would involve repeating the messages that the change is occurring, is more likely to frustrate them and keep the emotional levels too high. Eventually, as the individuals begin to redevelop their confidence, they recognise that they can do things and begin to respond to the new environment. Thus they move from a low energy stage to a high energy adaptation stage. At this point the managers of the change process can adopt a 'hands off' delegating style.

In designing new methods of implementing culture change it is vital that these stages of the development of individuals should be actively managed. One of the downfalls of the Total Quality culture has been that for many organisations the advisers that they have turned to have lacked a knowledge of even the basic reactions of individuals to a culture change process. As a result the skills that have been used and the activities which have been encouraged have often conflicted with the natural reactions of the people in the organisation. The result is that the TQ process has become undermined. This is particularly the case where organisations have perceived that Total Quality is simply a case of implementing new systems and changing the tools and techniques that people use.

Confronted with circumstances like this it is important for the senior managers to take time out to review their vision and again to visit organisations beyond their own to assess the scope of the change which is involved. In their own way they are recycling to a directing style for themselves.

Case Study 10

Levi Strauss

The popular image of many organisations is often a reflection of their internal culture. Certainly few people of the generation under fifty in Europe, and older in the States, have difficulty in identifying with the product of Levi Strauss Associates. But identifying with a product is only part of the public image of Levi Strauss. Each year, *Fortune Magazine* surveys roughly 8,000 chief executives and senior Managers in organisations throughout the USA. The survey that they publish is known under the title 'Most Admired Companies'. Consistently, Levi Strauss will appear within the top ten of the five hundred or so companies represented.

With such a popular product, it's surprising how little effort is made by Levis to publicise their organisational strengths. Common to all the organisations that we have described, has been a strength of vision held by the most senior managers in the organisation – whatever their position or title. As an example of this visionary leadership, one need look no further than Robert Hass, the Chief Executive of Levi Strauss. Now in his fifties, in the late 1980s he was looking critically at his own position in the organisation and began questioning whether the lessons of leadership and management that he had learnt were adequate in the changing environment. Reflecting the growing trend he summarised his vision of the future: 'In a more volatile and dynamic business environment the controls have to be conceptual. It is the ideas that control, not some manager with authority'.

Hass has frequently resorted to the use of employee surveys and audits as a way of determining popular opinion about management issues, such as job-sharing, alternative employment conditions, the representation of women and of minority groups. Hass's model for the new organisation is based around self-managing work teams. As he puts it: 'I see us moving towards a team-oriented multi-skilled environment in which the team takes on many of the supervisors' and trainers' tasks'.

Levi's approach to introducing these team-based activities and creating greater ownership for key business processes has been driven from a people-perspective. Unlike other organisations which spend considerable amounts of time and energy in improving technology and developing complex systems, Levi Strauss Associates tackled the issue by helping every employee understand how people work. Typical of the initiatives that Hass uses to create common goals is 'Leadership Week'. As part of their training and development programme, in Leadership Week, a member of the top team of management, together with a trainer and a group of about twenty employees, will be removed to an hotel or some other location far from work. Through a series of carefully constructed activities, the trainer will help the top team manager and the employees understand how barriers can arise at work and establish why people work the way they do.

For many managers in organisations that have been traditionally hierarchical, there is a tendency to perceive that the more senior you are the more you should know. Hass is quick to recognise this, not only among his employees but also for himself. He says: 'It has been difficult for me to accept the fact that I don't have to be the smartest guy on the block'.

As we have seen elsewhere in this book when looking at the ORJI cycle, the emphasis in this new model of leadership is not on understanding more than an individual, but in carefully responding in any form of two-way communication. One application of this, that emerges often in Leadership Week is the importance of reacting properly when things go wrong. Lynne Southard is a middle manager with Levi Strauss. She was confronted with a typical decision. An employee reporting to her as a member of the team, had made a serious miscalculation about the quantities of raw materials required for one of the company's products. As a result, they ran out of stocks, had to buy at higher prices, caused serious production delays and inconvenienced their customers.

You might pause for a moment and consider what would happen to such an individual in your own organisation. The Strauss approach is perhaps different, as Southard explains: 'We sat down and found out what went wrong and how to prevent it in the future. Unlike in the old days there was no blaming and finger pointing'.

Case Study 11

Goodyear

In 1984, Robert Mercer, then Chairman of Goodyear Tyres, shocked the tyre industry by announcing a new manufacturing policy for Goodyear.

Dubbed 'First Class or Scrap', their new approach countered common industrial practice. Traditionally, tyre manufacturers have segregated tyres with cosmetic blemishes so that they can be reworked or sold as seconds. Mercer's concept was that the organisation should only aim to produce first-class products. If they failed to do so, then the product should be scrapped. In this way, he forced executives to count the cost of poor quality and to recognise these costs in reworking.

In re-defining his policy, he was creating the starting point of a major U-turn in Goodyear's culture. The organisation had always placed great emphasis on the input from customers about their product and service. For many years they had conducted intensive and extensive customer service audits. Indeed, in 1986 and 1987, they were heralded by the American Management Association as being the leading exponent of consumer testing. In 1987, for example, they conducted eight surveys. Each one involved an individual interview with a customer. Over the course of those surveys, they interviewed more than 150,000 customers and users of their products.

Mercer's successor as Chairman, Tom Barratt, continued the initiative and launched others of his own. Fundamental to all of these was the need to re-think the fundamental practices of the organisation. As Barratt explained in 1990: 'Today, we are looking at the entire corporation and asking for far more than getting a little better. We are asking people to re-think their jobs'. The changes that have resulted have been extensive. Typical of these is the plant at Lawton in Oklahoma, where 164 teams, with a cross section of skills, have been created, replacing the traditional hierarchical organisation structure. These teams are based around business centres and in turn represent product-line organisations. As a direct result of this re-organisation, the Lawton plant operates with 35 per cent fewer managers, and productivity is double that of other Goodyear plants.

Self-managing teams have become a part of the Goodyear management structure, but it is important to remember that they do not replace the need for problem-solving groups, which may be permanently in place or pulled together when the need arises. The difference is that in a culture where self-managing teams have become established, it is more likely for individuals to pull together a team when they recognise the need, rather than wait for a management directive to go ahead.

One such example is at the Goodyear Stow, Ohio, mould plant. Tyre production is essentially a moulding operation and so the development of new moulds is an expensive yet critical part of the process. A small group of operators at Stow recognised the fact that the organisation was currently out-sourcing parts for the moulding operation. They believed that they would have greater control over the quality of, and greater cost responsibility for the moulding operation if the work was conducted internally. A group of 14 operators of the machines collaborated together to develop a specification. They presented their economic case to the Board of Management, and as a result were given the go-ahead to carry out a more elaborate study. Using a simple quality tool consisting of key-specifications in a matrix, they identified five potential manufacturers of the appropriate equipment. They visited a number of these machines in use and as a result put forward a purchasing case for a particular system. Within a matter of months of installation it was returning savings in excess of $0.5 million per annum.

The global recession has had an impact upon many organisations and almost any organisation which is directly dependent upon the automotive industry for the vast majority of its sales is bound to have been affected by the downturn in the business use of vehicles. It's hardly surprising therefore that between 1988 and 1992 Goodyear's share prices began to tumble. Eventually a senior management shake-up took place and Stanley Gault, the former retired CEO of Rubbermaid, was appointed to the board of Goodyear. As a superb example of visible leadership, you need look no further than Gault. Within two weeks of his appointment he had spoken personally to over 3,000 employees of Goodyear. (Incidentally, he does not like the word 'employees' and therefore very quickly re-dubbed the workforce of the organisation 'associates'.) Under his leadership he combined a number of existing quality programmes and then began to look for new ways of involving associates in the day-to-day management of the business. As a result of the input that he received throughout his first two weeks and a number of audit-type activities carried out, he established a number of ways of improving the involvement of the associates. Among these were a union and company joint process of collaboration for factory improvement; monthly presentations around the world by teams to share ideas and results and an ideas-generating suggestion scheme. In the brief period since his appointment, more than 2,000 teams have been established around the world. It is these groups that make their presentations each month.

The teams have been introduced to empower any associate to take whatever action is necessary to improve the satisfaction of their customers. But Gault recognised that not all individuals will take part in teams, and therefore the suggestion scheme was developed to run in parallel. Already 45,000 associates world-wide have been introduced to its practice and stand to gain as they contribute new ideas for the organisation.

THE LEADERSHIP AUDIT

1. Time

Most of us are remarkably poor judges of the way in which we spend our time and the first stage of most leadership analyses is to assess the activities of the senior management team as they currently stand. The results of such an exercise are usually so illuminating that the senior management team will almost always ask for the same analysis to be carried out for a representative sample across the organisation. As ever, the important aspect is that we are not carrying out a time-and-motion study but we are interested in finding out how people prioritise the activities that they engage in. The object of this analysis is to see how much time is being spent throughout the organisation on leadership activities.

As can be seen from the Table 7.1 earlier in this chapter, traditional organisations tend to spend very little time on leadership by comparison with an organisation that has implemented self-managing teams. The current activity analysis gives the senior managers opportunity to re-prioritise some of the activities that they are engaged in at the moment. Not only does this have an immediate impact by improving the amount of leadership time that they are able to devote to the rest of the organisation; it is also creating a precedent for change and a role model for change in themselves before the middle managers are confronted.

2. Approach

The second area that the Audit team needs to consider covers the internal and external visible signs of leadership within the organisation. We are concerned with introducing a new culture, one in which individuals at all levels of the organisation are encouraged to take more responsibility and more authority while working as members of self-managing teams.

It is obviously going to be much harder to achieve this transition if the symptoms of leadership within the organisation are negative, carrying subtle or not so subtle messages about the perceived status of individuals in the hierarchy of the organisation. The role of the Audit team is to identify as many of these as possible and to develop plans to remove them. They need to look at memos, the words that are used on them, the ways in which different areas in the organisation are described. Where personal names are given to members of the senior management team but only generic names given to groups of workers in memoranda and internal communications. These are all indications of the relative status of people.

Areas of the plant, factory or working area, where there are signs displayed, may not indicate fairness. For example, one senior manager had a sign at the end of his corridor very clearly saying 'Private'. As the corridor was never walked in by outside visitors, or members of the public, it was very difficult to see who the sign was intended to be directed at other than members of the shop-floor. In this case nobody knew how long the sign had been there as most of the senior managers hadn't noticed it! It is remarkable the number of organisations which claim to have been undergoing a culture change process for many years and yet for whom such visible signs of status have never been purged. Among the other classic symbols are reserved car parking spaces, separate toilet facilities and staff-versus-shopfloor canteens.

For an example of visible leadership creating a clear vision of the new culture in one of these areas we need look no further than a senior manager at Xerox, Ren Zaphiropolous. Arriving at his new position for the first time one Monday morning he saw that the car parking spaces were labelled for individual senior managers so that they could always park close to the entrance of the building. Walking into his office he instructed his new secretary to put in a person to person telephone call to the business-desks and newsdesks of the local radio and television companies, together with the editors of the local newspapers. He then asked her to contact the Maintenance Department and to send for the Senior Maintenance Engineer to see him in his office immediately. When the engineer arrived he was given cash out of Ren's pocket and told to go to the nearest hardware store to buy some new wide paint brushes and a large quantity of black paint. While he was doing the shopping Ren spoke to the various media representatives as they came through on his telephone. At eleven o'clock that morning an impromptu press conference was held in the car park. Ren, wearing shop-floor overalls proceeded to get on his hands and knees and paint out the reserved markings in the car park, while the media journalists and television crews recorded the event for posterity. Although this is an extreme example it indicates the strength of vision that needs to be held and the importance of backing it up with tangible actions and not allowing such blatant examples that contradict it to go unaddressed.

Most organisations have a few subtle signs of this kind and a very large number have some not so subtle ones too. Segregated canteens are an obvious example, though to us, perhaps one of the worst is the case of an organisation that claimed to have been moving towards self-managing teams for nearly a decade. On leaving their site we visited the toilets. Entering through a single door which matched all the others on the corridor we were immediately confronted by two more. One was panelled and had the word

'Staff' on it. The other was a Formica covered door with 'Others' written on it!

Often such signs of discrimination become clearly visible externally as well, and if the organisation is serious about its transition it has to rid itself of these too. Examples might be: press releases where photographs only bear the names of the senior managers; company reports where the senior managers are named but individuals in photographs of the plant are not; separate entrances marked Staff and Management; press reports of 'Staff' teams playing 'shopfloor' teams at sports; inappropriately named prizes such as the 'Management Challenge Cup': differential treatment on retirement; and clearly separated social functions. All of these are external symbols of the leadership style within the organisation.

The Audit team will probably also look at some of the internal systems to establish whether they too have bias associated with them. A common discrimination which is applied is whether individuals have a degree or not. This frequently leads to a culture in the organisation, usually described as 'them and us', though with many other guises such as 'professional' versus 'staff' or 'staff versus shopfloor'. In the organisation which is seriously moving towards self-managing teams every effort will be taken to purge the internal culture of this kind of distortion.

3. Controls

As we have said, one of the commonest anxieties for most managers in this sort of change process is the fear of loss of control. The Audit team therefore needs to examine how control is currently maintained. Most organisations use a system of paper records or forms to maintain control. The Audit needs to look at these forms and to establish which ones are actually relevant to the organisation and which are superfluous controls. The most effective way of doing this is to look at the consequences of *not* completing the document. A form which is a genuine control will be directly related to the process and without it the production or service delivery process will cease. Forms that have been introduced as controls over other people, usually do not have a direct relationship to the process and frequently call for several signatures to verify authority. The assessment team needs to look at each of the routinely completed forms within the organisation and identify where they are going to and from. They need to question where they were created and if they relate to rules or procedures, who created those rules and procedures. It is surprising how often in large organisations, authority levels are created on the basis of some historical precedent, and yet when you investigate, it is impossible to identify where they came from, why the levels were set at the levels they were, and who is responsible for policing them. Some of the most effective examples have been set up in such a way that they create a self-policing loop where no one can establish who was responsible for the form in the first place – but different individuals are responsible for policing the system! One organisation with three outlying units had a purchasing procedure that specified limits of authority for various levels of the management team. The people policing the system were the local purchasing units and yet, because it had been handed from one person to the next, nobody knew where the system had originated from. It was only as a result of the leadership team's activities that it was shown that the different units had different systems, with quite different levels of authority in each!

Another type of documentary control of this kind is the reports that are generated routinely by organisations. Often, these started as a paper-based report, and have subsequently been computerised, giving them a renewed respectability as a result of the high-tech output. The perception is that because the information is being consolidated in black and white, on paper, it can be looked at, checked and verified, and people in parts of the organisation that have bucked the system will be identified.

Of course, the simple test is whether anybody receives and reads the reports. One quite remarkable accounting company, with many thousands of employees, routinely issued each week to each of its directors and partners, a list of each of the consultants and accountants showing various performance statistics related to the individual. No standards were set for individual's performance – they were not counselled or given any guidance for appraisal – nor were goals set in any of the parameters that were reported. Most of the directors and partners received the information and discreetly either filed it or threw it away. The people who were producing the information didn't know why because it was a task that had been assigned to them on handover from another member of staff.

The Audit team needs to look at these reports to establish where they are going, why they are generated, and whether they are effective as controls or not. They should also assess the amount of time that is spent in people-contact, that is the time spent with the leader in direct contact with their team. Finally, under this area, the assessment team should look at the number of situations where procedures and authorities should be dispensed with and instead best practices introduced, removing some of the authoritarian nature of the existing rules.

4. Shared information

A very common discussion point among senior managers is the extent to which they should be sharing information further down the organisation. Opinions can become quite marked in this area and the vehemence of the arguments put forward can sometimes seem quite strong. Usually, the statements go something like this:

'We should share more information with members of the workforce, so that they can do their jobs more effectively'.

'I don't agree – that's quite dangerous. They might share the information with other people, and it won't be long before one of our competitors gets to see it. And let's face it, they could do a lot if they knew some of the information that's floating around here'.

There are two fairly fundamental flaws with this argument. The first one is that if you cannot trust your workforce with the information that you give them, why did you make such a lousy job of recruiting them in the first place? Secondly, have you ever heard of a serious leak of information coming from anybody other than someone at the top of the organisation, and frankly, in many organisations, the senior managers are the ones who are more likely to have contact with competitors and competitor organisations.

The role of the Audit team is to look at the information needs of most of the people in the organisation and to establish the extent to which the information that they receive is adequate for them to do their jobs. Depending on the emphasis placed upon this in their brief, the assessment teams range from asking the simple question: 'Do you have enough information to help you make day-to-day decisions?', through to a detailed needs assessment as part of a first stage in a structured systems analysis.

5. Leadership skills

If leadership skills are so critical to the organisation and the transformation of its culture, then it is important to understand what investment has been made in the past and how well this has been received. The first stage in the assessment is usually to identify who the people are that are providing leadership within the organisation. We are not talking about incidental leaders – people who form key players perhaps in small work groups – but those individuals who have a specific responsibility for providing leadership. The team will begin by identifying these people and then establish what training they have received, when they received it, what style of training it was, and how effectively they think it was provided. They may carry out an assessment asking those individuals to establish how important they consider their leadership role is, and they could test this by asking the perceived customers of the process how valuable they find it. There are usually huge discrepancies in views, with most managers perceiving that they spend far more time helping to lead their workforce than the workforce are able to demonstrate. We shall never forget visiting an organisation which had spent a very great deal of effort and time in introducing statistical process control to most of their employees. On touring the shopfloor, we found one operator sitting beside a machine which was virtually wall-papered with control charts. He patiently explained each of the control charts with the exception of two. When we pushed him, he explained that the two remaining charts were an average and range display for the amount of time that his supervisor spent on the shopfloor!

If the organisation has already begun implementing teams, then the Audit team can look at the resources that have been provided to support these groups, assess its effectiveness and make recommendations for additional support, if it is appropriate. At the same time, if facilitators have been introduced, it will be valuable to test the perceived role of these people within the organisation.

6. Reactions to change

The Leadership Audit team needs to look at the organisation and decide whereabouts it may fit in the scale of reactions to change. If the organisation has not confronted change before in a similar fashion to that which is being proposed, then it is likely to react differently to one that has been exposed to various changes in recent years. The team needs to look at the various causes of change throughout the organisation's recent history. What were the reactions to those changes? How did they manifest themselves? Were there immediate strikes? Or were there very high levels of up-take of initiatives? What were the characteristics of those who were managed well and those who were managed poorly? Which aspects do people remember? Who was involved in implementing the change process? For how long were the impacts of the changes that were introduced experienced by the organisation?

Equipped with this knowledge, the group should prepare plans for the introduction of change within the organisation in such a way that the reactions can be pro-actively managed. This doesn't mean simply regurgitating books on the management of change. Nor does it call for unsubstantiated suggestions. If most parts of the organisation are still using materials that were introduced some time ago, then it indicates that the change process associated with them was successful. It is these positive experiences that the group should be collecting and using to plan the new introduction.

7. Development activities

We've explained that in the new, responsive organisation there is a significant shift of emphasis on who is responsible for the training and development of individuals. One of the fundamental shifts in this is that no longer is a training department responsible for the development of people. Instead it's the responsibility of the individual manager and again, not just to second people for training courses, but to take an active role in helping them use the information that they have gathered. The Audit team needs to establish the current practices for development. Who is involved in delivering training? Who is involved in following up training? Is there any formal process by which managers help individuals put into practice the skills that they have acquired? Does the process work? Does the organisation have any barriers to the application of this knowledge, such as a rigorous internal cost code system for time use, which prevents managers from spending time on staff development? How much time and money is being spent on training activities? This includes, of course, not only the cost of delivering training through the training department if there is one, but also through the use of outside consultants. Many of their projects and assignments will involve formal training activities.

Also include people sent on external courses. What is the balance of these courses? Are they concerned with transferring specific information about a particular job or a particular new development such as new European Community directives or new VAT regulations? Are they concerned with the development of skills and are those skills specific job-related skills or are they concerned with more lateral development? How does the organisation go about assessing needs for training? Is there a formal process or is it *ad hoc*? Are managers trained in the needs analysis process? To what extent have counselling skills been taught in the organisation. Does management promotion reflect the ability to develop individuals? Is there a formal programme of development for individuals? How does this get customised to the specific needs of those people? Does the corporate development route overtake the individual's specific needs? The role of the Audit team is firstly to make an assessment of current practices and then to make recommendations for preparing the organisation to introduce self-managing work teams. This can often call for a significant amount of activity in developing and training managers before the transition occurs. Equipped with a clear picture of the existing level of development and the new vision for the organisation, a professional training department or management college will prepare a programme that is specifically geared to the needs of the organisation, together with effective ways of monitoring its success.

8. Individuals

Two simple exercises can be carried out by almost any individual in the organisation outside the Audit team. The value of these exercises is to try to establish exactly how committed you are to the delivery of leadership as opposed to other normal management activities. Despite their simplicity, most people will find that if they carry them out effectively, they gain a tremendous insight into their own priorities and the way in which they should perhaps be shifted.

The first is to look at your own behaviour over a reasonable period of time such as fortnight or a month. Keep an accurate diary or time-log for this period. You're not expected to become a pedantic monitor of use of time, but a simple log for a couple of weeks can reveal distinct patterns in your behaviour over that time.

The second activity is even simpler. Using a cheap dictaphone or pocket cassette recorder, discreetly monitor your own behaviour when you are in the company of other people for whom you might be considered to have responsibility for their development. Later, on your own, replay the tapes. Analyse what you say. Have you taken the role of doctor and patient, listening and then prescribing a course of treatment? Have you taken the role of expert, giving lots of technical advice without necessarily spending much time analysing the problem with the individual? Or have you spent most of the time in a counselling-type conversation, asking open-ended questions and helping the individual to draw their own conclusions? Again, you only need to record a few conversations to begin to develop your own personal plan for improvement.

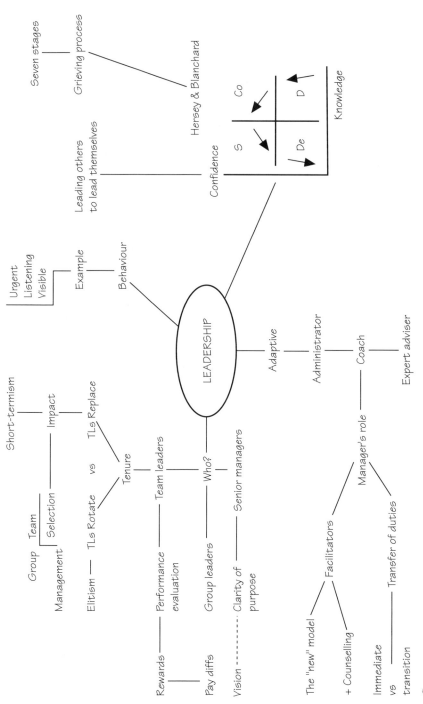

Summary Mindmap 7: Leadership

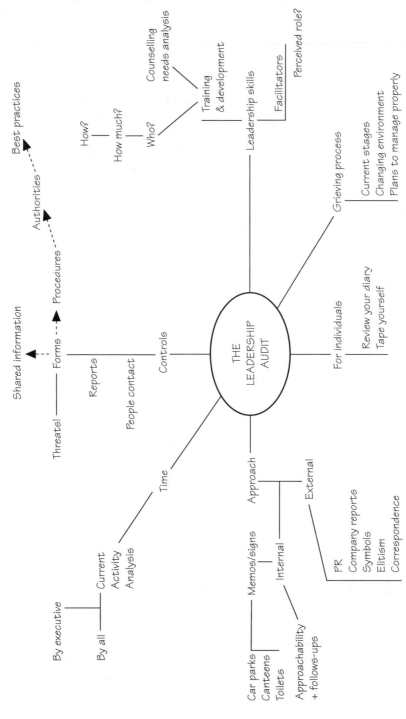

Leadership Audit Mindmap

8 ADMINISTRATION

For many organisations, the administrative systems were introduced years ago and slowly evolved over time. If you walk into most businesses you will find that the administrative systems that are being used are extremely traditional. Many of them were implemented in an almost textbook fashion. This is not entirely unexpected. As the administration systems are most often closely related to legislative requirements, there tend to be more perceived controls over the way in which they should be implemented. Quite how this perception arises is a study in its own right, but it is remarkable the number of times that you will come across a most peculiar arrangement in an organisation and, when challenged, you will be told: 'It's got to be done that way, it's the law!'.

THE IMPORTANCE OF SYSTEMS

If the organisation is to be responsive to its customers' needs it must have effective administrative systems. This is especially the case if you consider that the role of an administrative system is to remove the need for a human to control and monitor. Properly designed systems should ensure that where a problem is encountered it becomes immediately visible, and there should be little need for someone to check and re-check. This is the fundamental assumption which underlies quality management systems and was certainly intended when BS5750 (subsequently ISO9000) was developed.

Sadly, for many organisations, quality systems have become another layer of bureaucracy and the old, inefficient systems which they were intended to replace have been allowed to continue – often in parallel. There is no reason for this and any organisation which finds itself in this position should do all it can to rid itself of the unnecessary burden.

The administrative systems of most companies reflect the core set of perceived operations for the particular function concerned. In the most obvious case, the accounting practices will have been developed as a direct reflection of double-entry book-keeping systems. Although reports such as cash flow, profit and loss and so on, may have been tweaked over the years, their fundamental basis has not changed. Banks, venture capitalists and administrative receivers often report that organisations in difficulty have not got there because of bad systems but usually because systems have only been partially developed and implemented. There is a widespread perception that there is only one way to do certain things.

In a similar vein, many organisations have elaborate personnel procedures. On the face these appear to be rigorous, well thought out and well intentioned. In practice, an extraordinary number of organisations have systems in personnel which have been developed from simple textbooks. These are often developed by someone with very few qualifications in the field and almost certainly little awareness of the developments that have been taking place in personnel over recent years. This is hardly surprising. Organisations with less than two hundred employees are only likely to employ a part-time personnel officer. Equally often the personnel function is filled by someone who has had no formal training. To be fair, many of the developments which have occurred have been driven by much larger organisations.

In many ways the legislators are at fault here. There can be little purpose in developing administrative systems which apply to perhaps a thousand companies, namely the larger ones, when the bulk of the gross national product is in organisations with less than two hundred people. An excellent example of this in the UK is the VAT system. Far easier to operate for larger organisations, most smaller businesses end up employing an outside agency to help them complete their VAT figures – tremendous work for accountants, which could have been avoided had the system been designed in a more sensible manner in the first place.

In our experience, which is not as jaded as may appear from the previous few paragraphs, most organisations embarking on a change process need to thoroughly review their existing administrative systems and purge themselves of this kind of inflexible dogma. Where administrative systems have changed rapidly in recent years this is usually due to a parallel change in the technology with which they are performed.

Any administrative system in an organisation needs to be developed to support the corporate strategies. They should run in parallel and not across one another. An obvious example of this would be that if we were introducing self-managing work teams, our internal accounting practice should not call for a senior manager to 'sign off' expenditure of a certain level. Even today we come across organisations which have been moving down a quality improvement process for many years only to discover that even quite senior managers have negligible signing authority.

The stupidity of signing authorities is clear whenever you talk to the staff in the purchasing function (who are usually fine masters at jumping the system). For example, we know of one very well-established petro-chemical company where the signing authority for an individual manager is £500. During the oil crisis, when the barrel prices plummeted, an embargo was placed on all expenditure of a capital nature while expense items were allowed to continue. Unfortunately, this time coincided with the boom in personal computers (PCs) but the purchasing department helped the managers get round this problem by declaring that PCs were expense items. Nevertheless, at the time most PCs cost more than £500 but again the purchasing department had a simple solution. If you ordered the keyboard separately, and then the system unit separately, and then the monitor separately, and then the cables separately, and finally the software separately, each item came to less than £500 and so you could quite easily buy a complete system without infringing any of the rules!

SYSTEMS TO PARALLEL STRATEGY

So, how do we develop administrative systems that are in parallel to our organisation strategy? Fairly obviously we have to have the strategy in the first place, and we will assume that the guiding light behind this is that the organisation wants to be more responsive to its customers. A useful model to help redesign administrative systems stems from the days of JIT (Just In Time). JIT was one of the few manufacturing strategies which was implemented in a slow, steady, progressive fashion. The analogy which was often used was of sailing a small boat across a pool where there were rocks hidden below the surface. The pool represented inventory in the organisation and the rocks were problems. The model was simple, as you drained water from the pool the rocks came closer and closer to the surface, and therefore closer to the bottom of the boat. In other words, as you reduced the levels of inventory in the organisation, so you exposed more problems.

One approach for resolving administration systems problems is to progressively implement other changes and then, where an administrative problem appears, tackle it. For some organisations this can seem rather like the blind leading the blind, and instead we need some guiding principles to redesign systems from the top down. The purpose of the administrative system in the new organisation is to provide confidence. Confidence, for those who use it, that their processes are working effectively and satisfying their customers. The only way in which this can be achieved is through measurement. Unfortunately, measurement is a word which turns more people off than it inspires. We do not mean that the Purchasing, Personnel or the Maintenance Departments should start using the types of chart and forms that you will see around the production line. Of course, these days many measurements can be analysed and interpreted by computer, but, nevertheless, measurement is a vital part of this 'confidence system'.

We were recently asked to visit an organisation to talk to them about improvement possibilities. They were pretty confident that most of their organisation worked very efficiently. The first question that we asked was what their turnover was and the second one was how many employees they had. Unfortunately, the General Manager in charge did not know the answers and had to send for someone to get them for him. It seems that turnover is a very difficult figure to come up with when you are in an organisation of which you form only a small part. The nearest approximation that he could come to was the size of his annual budget. Even then he did not have the total figure, despite the fact that when we asked him what his principal role was in the organisation he'd said that it was to 'manage the resources in (his) department'.

We asked the purchasing people for performance figures concerning their suppliers, they had none. Simply no records were kept of the time between placing an order and receiving the goods. In the accounts department the situation was slightly better. Although we had been told that turnover was a difficult issue to measure, the accounts people clearly were invoicing external customers. When we asked how many days overdue some of these customers were, we were shown a very straightforward print-out from their accounts system showing age of debtors. The picture was probably no worse nor better than any other organisation, but if they had spent the last three years on a continuous improvement process we asked how they had measured their improvements. It seems nobody had told them that there might be a purpose in reducing the number of aged debtors!

Nowadays, when so many administrative systems are based on computers it seems remarkable that the people who are developing these systems do not build in quality detection processes. An industrial accident recently highlighted just this problem. Despite the fact that an organisation had a highly sophisticated personnel records facility, this did not have an option for flagging impending deadlines. As a result one of the first-aiders attending an incident was found to have an expired first aid certificate. As he said: 'The company sent me on the course, so I expected the company to tell me when I had to do another one'. This should be the sort of problem that computers and administrative systems take care of.

Whatever measurements we use, they should be directly related to our strategy; they should allow us to control pro-actively; they should monitor our performance in certain goals; and those goals should have a relevance to the outputs from our businesses. All large organisations that have gone down the route of improving responsiveness report that they have had to simplify their administrative systems. It is only small companies, that have grown rapidly and not necessarily evolved such systems, who may need to add more.

THE CHANGING ORGANISATIONAL STRUCTURE

The responsive organisation inevitably changes its organisational structure. This has consequences both internally and externally. Most organisations that have taken this approach have adopted larger numbers of partnership agreements. Through these, they have sub-contracted activities which previously they would have undertaken themselves, or entered into a longer-term relationship with companies which would have perhaps been in a competitive tendering situation.

The benefits that accrue from a partnership sourcing arrangement are enormous and are often derived from reduced effort and improved communication. Consider a practical example which, for continuous painting jobs, must come pretty close to the apocryphal maintenance of the Forth Road Bridge, namely the oil rigs. Rather than paint their own rigs, most oil exploration companies that own them sub-contract the activity. Painting a rig involves two main steps; the first one is erecting a scaffold to provide access and the second one is painting using the scaffold. For at least two decades the rig owners have sub-contracted both steps separately. This has involved twice the number of negotiations and often twice the number of visits to assess and make an estimate. Once the contacts are awarded, it involves twice the number of liaison meetings and with two teams of operators on the rigs at the same time, there have been double the transportation costs, not only for the workforce themselves but in particular for their supervisors and managers. Recognising the burden that this administration was creating, oil rig owners decided to sub-contract to an individual company that could offer both services. They put out their invitations to tender specifying a preference for a supplier that could provide both services. Because this was a new practice and had not been carried out in previous years no individual company could reasonably respond. The key players in the market, though, had different strategies to try to overcome this problem. A small group of them took to lobbying the oil companies, pointing out that by taking on such a broad mix of skills they were diluting the quality of the work that they would receive. In other words saying: 'We want to maintain the *status quo*'. Another group of companies tried to swell their own numbers and deliver both services. In one case, a scaffolding company tried to buy-in painters and then offer the single service themselves and in the other case a painting company tried to buy-in scaffolding contractors. But both disciplines are quite different. The training, qualifications, supervision and so on are all very different. In taking this route both companies were committing themselves to a lengthy learning curve.

Only two organisations had been progressively following a change of culture towards Total Quality. Quite frequently they found themselves being offered a sub-contract by the main rig owners because of this culture change. They often found themselves on the same rigs working alongside one another. Their solution was different. Rather than proposing a venture in which a gang of scaffolders arrived, did their work with their own managers and supervisors, then left and were replaced by painters (albeit wearing the same hat), this organisation decided to create mixed teams. Small gangs were pulled together with a supervisor from one or other of the two companies. As they had both been working towards a similar culture the styles and management which were used in both organisations were highly participative and moving towards that of the self-directed work team. It was easy for individuals from one company to respond to the working practices of the other. As a result not only was their operation more efficient, a saving which they were able to pass on to the rig owners, but the collaboration also bought new skills for the individuals in the gangs. This approach became self-reinforcing as, at the next round of tenders, no one could compete on price, skill or for the motivation of the workforce. With each round of tenders so the gang members become more skilled and are able to offer more services such as cleaning, simple electrical work, plumbing work and so on.

Partnerships of this kind are by no means restricted to the manufacturing or construction environment and, although partnership sourcing is in its infancy, there are a growing number of cases emerging around the world. It is important, though, to recognise that partnership sourcing is a result of common cultures and has little or nothing to do with the legal agreements between the two organisations.

As we have said before, as the self-managing teams become progressively more effective and more highly skilled they can become a single business unit in their own right. In just the same way as a business may begin to expand its range of services and look for new niches to operate in, so can these teams. Not only can a team move from one project to another, but individuals within it can also move. The restrictions of a hierarchy and the replacement of the pressure on an individual to try to climb that hierarchy means that people are constantly looking for more exciting opportunities.

Of course the key to success is for the same organisation to offer that variety of opportunities. Growing numbers of these companies are recognising that this process requires a sophisticated approach to monitoring the movement and growth of individuals – a new form of administrative system.

Such systems have not existed before and so need to be developed from scratch. In no instance have we heard one of these organisation complain about the apparent up-front cost. This is usually because they are well down the route of changing culture already and are seeing the benefits of this highly mobile and flexible workforce.

In Case Study 12 (page 201) we look at Xerox and the way in which they have adapted to become more responsive to this growing demand for excitement and innovation on the part of their employees. Apple, as another example, have re-organised their business to focus much more closely on individuals. They are in the process of developing a computer network system called 'Spider' which can be used to provide a manager with instant information about the availability and skills of an employee and where-abouts they are located in the corporation. Becton Dickinson are a firm of high-tech medical equipment manufacturers based in New Jersey. Their CEO is Raymond Gilmartin. He has recognised that in his organisation the structure no longer reflects tasks or products, but instead represents the people within it. Back in 1987 Becton Dickinson were finding themselves under increasing competition despite a period of intensive, fast growth and high revenues of around two billion dollars. The company produces extremely sophisticated diagnostic systems such as blood analysers. This is an area which is constantly looking for new innovations, and in which the technology has dramatically improved in recent years. Although the organi-sation still maintains departments concerned with traditional functions such as marketing, sales and manufacturing, it encourages its people to form teams across these barriers to innovate and go about business in different ways. They are encouraged to challenge existing practices. As Gilmartin puts it, he wants people to say: 'This is the right thing to do around here' and not 'You are going to do it because I am the boss'. In 1990 while they were developing a new analyser system called the Bactec 860 the team leader pulled together a project team of engineers, marketeers, manufacturers and suppliers. The results were impressive, with the Bactec 860 reaching mar-kets some 25 per cent faster than had previously been achieved.

Nevertheless, Gilmartin was unhappy with the level of improvement. He instituted a review of the practices and the way in which the team had operated. Very quickly they found that there had been conflict between Marketing and Engineering: Marketing were seeking additional functionality and Engineering were trying to restrict the product because they were concerned about extensive design times and costly development. Because the team leader was reporting to the head of the Engineering function he did not have sufficient positional power to resolve the conflict. As a result Gilmartin revised the process by which these teams were working. Removing layers of management above the team leader meant that any leader had access to a divisional head, giving them sufficient authority to settle disputes between smaller functions. This in turn resulted in a new change in operating style for the organisation.

Although it is still in the early days, Becton Dickinson are now trying out what they call 'lateral promotions'. By this system, each year roughly 20 per cent of the management team rotate jobs, so a financial person may move into a marketing role or a manufacturing person may move into a financial job and so on. Although the people are given a raise and a change of title in exactly the same way as they would with a normal promotion, at the same time they were being relieved of the number of individuals who would report to them. Another difference, though, is that to get onto this route of higher and accelerated growth within the organisation, you have to have performed well in one of the original teams. This of course calls for a monitoring system of some sort, but again one based on the people rather than on their functions.

Clearly, this is an emerging organisation structure for which firm principles are unlikely to stand. Different companies will have different solutions. The more high-tech the organisation the more high-tech the solutions are likely to be, or if not a high-tech solution, then the more structured it is likely to be. At Cyprus Systems, for example, which employs 1,500 people in an almost structure-free organisation, each individual maintains a list of ten to fifteen goals which they have developed in association with their peers. The goals are deliberately short-term and in a traditional organisation could possibly be confused with a daily to-do list. The process of updating the list takes each employee only a matter of minutes and by maintaining them on a computer network it is possible for the CEO, T.J. Rodgers, to review the goals of every employee in the organisation in the course of only a few hours.

While our organisation has become more flexible, more responsive and the people within it have become more motivated and are developing faster personally, we need to maintain control. We do this by setting a long-term vision, by changing our skills as managers and leaders from the traditional controller-cop model to one in which we allow people to take more control of their lives, and we assume a role of developer. This transition is not easy and inevitably leads to some kind of conflict for the group of individuals who find themselves closest to the middle of the organisation. As Gilmartin at Becton Dickinson discovered, as the teams began to take off and assumed greater levels of responsibility and authority so the middle managers found themselves under increasing pressure. This was compounded by the senior management team who introduced a re-structure into the organisation. The impact was that the middle layers found themselves overloaded with responsibility. They were working long hours simply to keep up with the paperwork that had been used previously as a control measure.

The Vice-President of the organisation, Jim Wessel, summed up the situation neatly: 'We had to get over the mind set that said "I am not in control, so it must be out of control". It took us as much as a year to appreciate what was happening but, eventually and with a degree of support, the managers began to appreciate that they had to delegate responsibility, not just activities'. Similar experiences are reported from all sorts of organisations which have embarked on this process. Not only is there a mind set to overcome but it is also important in this sort of organisation to accept that when a mistake occurs the key is to find a solution that will prevent it happening again, and not to embark on blame and finger pointing.

Case Study 12

Xerox

So much has been written about the development and turn-around of Xerox in recent years. The organisation is a classic case study in its own right of the change process from start to finish.

When they launched the Xerox 194, plain paper copier in 1959, Xerox created a whole new industry. For nearly two decades this underwent very high growth and led to a dramatic internal complacency. The only threat that was perceived at the time was towards the low end of the market and the organisation felt that it could afford to ignore this competition.

It was only in the late 1970s that the trigger to change came from an internal study which revealed that the selling price of Japanese copiers was in fact the same as the manufacturing price of the Xerox machines. As Paul Allaire, then President, commented: 'That woke us up in a hurry. We realised that . . . we had to challenge everything we had done in the past'. In 1981 they launched their 'Leadership Through Quality' programme. In practice, this was little different from any other organisation's quality improvement process. It began with awareness raising and led subsequently to team-based improvement activities. By 1987, 70,000 employees had been sent on awareness-raising courses. In that six-year period, a number of creditable results had been achieved. By 1987 manufacturing costs had been reduced by 20 per cent. The time for new products to reach markets had been reduced by 60 per cent. Billing errors had been reduced from 8.3 per cent to 3.5 per cent and the revenue per employee had been raised by 20 per cent.

Again, in common with most quality improvement programmes, Xerox cascaded its own process to its suppliers. In 1988 they were out-sourcing roughly $2 billion worth of business. Between 1981 and 1987, they reduced their supplier base from 5,000 to 300. In the same period of time, they moved from supplying roughly 30 per cent of out-sourced components direct – raising that to 95 per cent supplied direct. Similarly, of goods received – 92 per cent were defect-free in 1981, a figure that they had raised to 99.997 per cent by 1988. As David Kearns, Chairman and Chief Executive at that time, explained: 'Our goal was to make this group model suppliers – an extension of Xerox'.

In a manner similar to that adopted by Motorola, Xerox introduced a Team Excellence Award designed to stimulate employees to work in groups to solve problems. The Award includes a formal recognition and reward process and to date nearly 75 per cent of employees are involved in the activities. A typical example were the 'Fly-by-Nights'. This group studied the sending of small packages by overnight courier. A problem of poor customer satisfaction had been identified, showing that around 20 per cent of deliveries reached their destination before 9.00 am. As a result of this team's activities, the delivery rate is now 82 per cent and rising. But in addition to the improved customer satisfaction, the group identified a number of cost savings which could be introduced with relatively little effort. In some cases, through simple switches of policy, in other cases by simple education activities to inform individuals of the cost implications of certain decisions, and finally by the investment in new technology. As a result quantified costs have been reduced by nearly $1.9 million. As we have said, the results achieved by Xerox and the way in which they introduced their Change Process is laudable. As a result, in 1989 they were awarded the Baldrige Award.

As we have also pointed out several times in this book, it would be easy for an organisation to achieve such an accolade and to then rest on its laurels! In 1990, Paul Allaire was appointed Chief Executive. As he has said: 'For a variety of cultural reasons, we are never going to out-discipline our major competitors – the Japanese – on quality. The reality is that we will, at best, maintain parity. Quality improvement will not be enough to create a sustainable, competitive advantage'.

Allaire recognised the dramatic improvements that were being achieved in other organisations as they developed the self-managing work-team concept. Allaire is clearly a visionary thinker and does not embark on initiatives without understanding them from first principles. It did not take long for him to recognise the importance of the team concept. As he has subsequently explained:'It assumes that a diverse group of people can do a better job in today's world of constant change than any set of formal procedures administered by remote, centralised management'.

In Xerox the self-managing team concept has been termed 'Productive Work Communities'. These are natural work-groups, organised around natural units of work. They are concerned with the whole work process, have complete responsibility, manage themselves, are responsible for learning new and different skills, and for establishing an organisation with minimal boundaries. Above all else, Allaire is trying to create a culture of enterprise.

No organisation, however, can rely on an anarchic situation. It is important to realise that Xerox has addressed this. To establish a shared vision among all its employees, the organisation has turned to a Japanese technique which has not been widely applied. Known as 'Hoshin Kanri', it is perhaps better recognised in the western world as 'Policy Deployment'. Initially developed in the Rank Xerox, the European subsidiary, Policy Deployment begins with the top management team. Working together they develop specific targets linked to a 3–5 year plan for almost all functional areas. These plans and targets are simply documented in a book available to all Xerox's employees. Translated into a variety of languages, in the UK it is known as the 'Blue Book', while in Germany it is the 'Kursbuch'.

Each year, when the book is produced with its revised targets and projections, a series of annual kick-off meetings are held exposing each employee to the shared vision, and allowing them to develop in a workshop format their own plans to meet the corporate goals. It is in this way that Xerox is able to maintain its leadership while at the same time delegating tremendous levels of responsibility to the majority of its employees.

Case Study 13

The New England

Any Financial Services organisation depends upon two key aspects of its operation for it to be successful. The first of these is its distribution system and the second is its administrative systems. The New England organisation has been operating for more than 150 years. It deals in two specific areas of the Financial Services sector, namely Mutual Funds and Insurance.

Throughout that period of time, by independent assessment, its 'funds' and 'insurance' policies have offered a very high performance. For many years, it has placed a great deal of emphasis on the retention of its agents, who form the main element for the distribution of its policies and funds. The retention rate of New England agents is roughly twice the industry average and reflects the investment that the organisation makes and the very different way in which they are managed. Although the organisation is based in Boston, it services customers throughout North America and further afield.

Soon after it was founded, it recognised the importance of responding quickly and efficiently to local demands. As a result, the organisation developed a structure which was in the form of a loose matrix. In this way local experts, even in complex issues such as disability income, serviced the needs of their local customers. Although an individual agent may not have expertise in a particular area, he could draw rapidly on local sources of guidance without having to refer significant issues to senior management at head office. This approach has had not only a very positive effect on the retention of agents, but is also highly customer-centred – especially when coupled with a fast and efficient delivery system for completed policies. The organisation has not only had a high retention rate for its agents, but has also always measured its success in terms of the growth rate of renewal premiums for policies.

In the late 1980s and early 1990s, the New England launched a quality improvement process, known internally as 'Continuous Improvement Methodology' (CIM). As James Mederios, Vice-President for Quality Commitment, described at the time: 'The CIM focuses on the customer and the process by which products and services are delivered. The goal is continuous measurement and process improvement'. CIM launched a number of initiatives and, as a result, a large number of task forces comprising between three and five individuals were established to fundamentally review the way in which the organisation carried out various aspects of its quality process. For example, one task force examined client communications. For most financial services organisations, client communications involve four elements: information about new products, routine information, reports about an existing policy, and statutory notices (such as tax and state laws). Given the history of investment in its agents, the natural route for delivering this information within the New England was either direct or through its sales people. In the past, most client communications had been driven by the sales force. This was potentially patchy.

This time, the team tackled the problem of communication from the customers' expectations. A thorough survey of customer opinions about the communication that they received from the New England led to the identification of a number of key criteria or critical success factors from the customers' perspective. Typical of the sort of information that they gleaned was that most customers felt a need to feel in control of the communication that they received. The task force set about modifying existing practices and progressively measured its improvement in hard financial terms with the growth of renewals of annual and monthly policies according to different communication strategies.

The organisation was broadly satisfied with progress and was justifiably proud of the achievements which had been made by the task forces. However, in the period between 1990 and 1991, the senior management team under the direction of Robert Shafto, the Chief Executive, set about intensifying their search for a clear vision for the organisation. By this time the Baldrige Award had become established as the USA's national quality award and already a small number of select organisations, having won, were promoting the importance of the Award. Shafto and his senior management team visited all of these organisations. As a result of their de-briefing process after each visit, they began to formulate a view that the critical element to the success of their organisation, regardless of how it was measured, was the strength of its workforce. They made it clear at the time that they did not necessarily intend applying for the Award. Instead they were interested in an improvement for the sake of the customers. This effectively removed the competitive element that would have been introduced when they began to develop their own targets for measured improvements based on the Award criteria.

Between 1990 and 1991, they embarked on the first of their audits. Having recognised the importance of their workforce, the first audit to be carried out was one of employee attitudes and views. The methodology that was adopted by the Audit team was to carry out a series of focus-group activities, coupled with a company questionnaire. Two primary areas for improvement were identified by the employees through the team. The first of these was for increasing involvement in decision-making processes within the organisation and for a greater share of information. The second was for the specific development of problem-solving skills for most of the organisation's employees. Among the other recommendations made by the team, was the need to improve the recognition of ideas and suggestions made by employees which would help the organisation.

As a direct result of the audit, a number of initiatives were set up. The first – and possibly the most visible – was that Shafto himself met, in an open forum, with every employee in the organisation. In this way it was possible for him to discuss developments as he saw them in the financial services sector, in their organisation and among the customers that they served.

Another initiative was the introduction of problem-solving skills training for every employee. This has taken the form of a week-long intensive course in the systematic solution of problems. They have also launched a monthly internal communications newsletter targeted around the quality improvement process. They have replaced the previous recognition programme and introduced an alternative which focuses much more clearly on the results of improvement activities. They have also developed a formal suggestion scheme known as 'Ideas for Quality'. With the employees clearly motivated to improve and being equipped with the relevant skills, it was vital for the organisation to demonstrate that it was prepared to make significant changes if they were necessary. Thus in 1992, again under the direction of Robert Shafto, the organisation set about performing a process analysis of its entire operation. Being conducted in a formal way, more than 70 employees have been trained as Process Analysis Consultants. They are currently working through eight key processes with the various sub-branches that each of these stimulates. For each independent process, an owner is identified who works with the Process Consultant and a team of 'Experts' – in other words the people who are responsible for carrying out the task on a day-to-day basis. In this way, the organisation is committed to revamping its internal bureaucracy and reorganising itself through workflow processes.

Case Study 14

Technology for a Structureless Workplace

As we have seen in chapter 4 and elsewhere in this book, organisations have progressively replaced the methods of control that they have used in previous years with alternatives. At its simplest level, this transition began by attempting to implement controls on people and processes. The controls were initially retrospective and then progressively moved up the production process in an attempt to prevent waste.

In the 1970s and 1980s, there was a boom in 'systems' – that is paper-based approaches to implement control by ensuring that people operated in a straightforward and well-defined manner. The technology of these approaches has developed over the years and, with the initial inspection-based controls, we began to see the development of online, highly elaborate, statistical process control systems. On the paper-based front, our systems became sufficiently sophisticated that they would satisfy the criteria for BS5750. In a few organisations, the technology was further developed and the Quality Systems paperwork was transferred to a computer-based application.

As they have begun to recognise that the secret of responding to our customers' requirements revolves around empowering our employees, organisations have tried to achieve control by developing their technology. Whereas in the earlier systems, the technology was intended to supplement the control (in other words to provide a mechanism by which mistakes could be trapped), the new technology which we are seeing emerging to satisfy the needs of work-groups aims to provide a tool for those work-groups rather than acting as a control over them. In short, the systems, and now the technological systems, are being used to provide structure in an otherwise structureless environment. The problems of such an environment can broadly be divided into two types. The first is the difficulty of 'routing', that is transferring messages from one person to another or from one work-group to another. The second issue concerns coordination, that is how do we ensure that groups can gain access to shared information and in turn use that information for more effective decision-making. The decision-making process is further disrupted by the fact that many of these work-groups do not routinely meet together. And so a solution has to be provided to allow these organisations to benefit from group-process, even though the individuals may be widely distributed.

Work-flow technology, as it is now described, is the software and hardware solution to this growing form of application. The role of work-flow technology is to allow us to facilitate and manage business processes in a networked computing environment. Whereas before, the business processes required human involvement to ensure that they were adequately managed, work-flow technology frees those humans to allow them to become involved in more innovative and constructive use of their time. Applications of this new work-flow technology include: tracking sales orders; managing product design; research and development processes and coordinating improvement activities. The work-groups themselves use these systems to enhance collaboration, to improve group productivity, and above all else to shorten business cycles. Unlike their predecessors, which would have attempted to automate parts of a system, work-flow technology is concerned with bridging barriers, and with crossing between departments and boundaries to ensure that the full process is being actively managed.

Work-flow applications usually require four forms of software. The Work-flow Server which forms the heart of the system, allows us to manage, track and report business processes. The Work-flow Server is used to monitor progress and status of processes and to provide us with analysis and reports on the processes and their performance statistics. Based around this Work-flow Server are Communication Tools which allow us to transfer information from one place to another, between individuals or between groups, and between departments and processes or machines. In one sense, these Communication Tools are electronic-mail applications for both people and machines. The second group of tools operate on this Work-flow Server and the Analytical Tools; they are the Reporting Systems. These allow us to generate graphical reports and statistical data about production or service-delivery processes.

Finally, we need a set of tools to enable us to build and implement work-flow applications based around the Server, and these are called 'Development Tools'. At first sight, you could be forgiven for thinking that the new concept of work-flow technology is simply a re-packaging of existing applications by smart marketing people in IT businesses! In practice, we are re-thinking the entire concept around which existing computer systems and applications have been developed. By crossing boundaries, and by reconsidering the work-flow process from initial order to delivery and invoicing, we are able to create tremendous benefits and no longer force our people to conform to an artificial system.

Among the pioneers in this technology is a technical partnership formed by Lotus Development. Lotus were formed in 1982 and one of their best selling products, Lotus 123, now has an established user-base of over 20 million people. Lotus 123 is one example of a decision-making tool which has become well-established in industry. As the basis for decision-making in the work-flow technology environment, Lotus 123 is a natural choice. Ironically, it was other Lotus products which led them into this market. As Cliff Conneighton, Director of Marketing for Lotus Communications Products Group explains: 'Many of our customers are implementing work-flow applications, with the current versions of Notes and CC:mail, and re-engineering the way they do business'. The technology partnership that they have entered into builds on the strengths of their own products and those of two other organisations. Action Technologies Incorporated was founded in 1983, a year after Lotus. They have become internationally recognised for their work-flow management systems; a suite of software components that allow applications to be run across work-flow processes. It is their technology that provides the Server at the heart of such systems. The third member of the partnership is Quality Decision Management. Although Lotus 123 provides a tool that will provide probably 95 per cent of user requirements for decision-making and reporting, Quality Decision Management have a suite of products that allow widely distributed individuals using a computer network to carry out group-process activities, such as brain storming, conferencing, and opinion gathering.

Working together, the three partners promise to deliver exciting new products that will allow work-flow applications to be developed by small groups of individuals within many organisations. It is hardly surprising that Lotus and its partners should wish to move into this marketplace. Not only do they have an established product range that complements it, but they are also aware that an independent survey conducted by International Data Corporation showed the work-flow technology market to be likely to be worth $2.5 billion by 1996!

THE ADMINISTRATION AUDIT

The Administration Audit team will probably begin by reviewing the activities of the customer audit. Most of the issues with which the customer team are concerned externally are equally relevant internally.

It is important for the administration team not to trivialise their role. Of all the audit's roles, this is probably the most significant and is likely to lead to the most dramatic change. The focus of the administration team is one of reduction. They have to reduce waste and at the same time reduce lead times. Their concern is with making sure that the organisation operates in the most efficient manner, and that it does so whenever it is called upon.

Unlike other Audit teams, the administration one will probably last longer and will need to involve far more people at various stages in its activities as, without the results of each step, it would be difficult to plan the next one.

1. Housekeeping

Despite the popular image of the absent-minded professor living in a world of clutter, most of us cannot work effectively in this way. Not only do our minds find it difficult to handle so many items at any one time, they can also create considerable levels of physical stress. From the customers perspective, this can also mean that errors occur. In an office where chaos abounds, papers go missing and sadly so too do customers. Housekeeping is everyone's responsibility. The rules are very simple. There should be a place for everything and everything should be in its place.

It is the role of the Administration Audit team to institute a programme of improving awareness and progressively reducing the amount of 'flapsy-hapsy' as it has been so graphically described by the Scandinavian Service School. The team will need to identify the right means of raising awareness; to plan a programme of briefings or talks probably accompanied with posters and newsletters. Photographs of the companies against which you are bench-marking can often provide a useful trigger for this change as, of course, can site visits. One of the simplest tricks to use is to visit most departments with a Polaroid camera and take a few snap shots of what they look like – with the cooperation of the inhabitants. But don't let people turn it into a joke. The picture should be an accurate record. Too many silly examples with deliberately shuffled papers, loose wires and open filing cabinets will just undermine the process.

Many people who work in a fairly tidy environment will tend to think that this activity is trivial. Sadly, it isn't, and the effort that can be required to get people to tidy their own space can be very great.

Marcus Sieff, of Marks and Spencer, recognised the vital role of the top person in this process. Not only did he purge his own office to set an example but he had delivered to each branch of their operation (throughout the UK) a large industrial skip. He then paid for his staff to come to work on a Sunday and everyone was given the same instruction: 'Take each piece of paper that you would normally use and ask yourself whether you know how it is used and who receives it? If you do not know the answer to either of these questions throw the paper and all of the duplicates into the skip. If you do know who owns the paper then pick up the telephone and call them. Ask if they know what it is used for and where it is sent. Again, if the answer is "no" then put it, and all of the copies into the skip'. This must have been an incredibly bold step and most of the staff, though finding it hilarious, will have been worried about the level of chaos that would have ensued the following day. In practice there was none and the organisation operated far more effectively.

Some industries almost pride themselves on their levels of poor house-keeping, though in most cases this is an old attitude which is being worn down through more aggressive, quality-focused competition.

2. Quality improvement

With a clearer environment and more visible work, most organisations report that their quality improvement activities undertake a step change. Often, while they were still coping with poor levels of housekeeping, they were able to introduce measurements and controls. Now they are able to make the real change to a prevention culture. When something has not gone right it becomes very visible. The key is for time to be created for the individuals in each department, or each area, or each team, to resolve problems. In the much maligned Japanese manufacturing environment, this is one of the key roles of Team Briefing; namely, communicating a solution to problems across the organisation rapidly.

SGB, the international scaffolding company, as part of its ongoing total quality process, recognised that improvements which were being identified in one depot often took several months to percolate through the organisation to other depots. With the introduction of the team briefing process they were able to make sure that such improvements could be communicated within a matter of days.

Quality improvement is never a rapid process. It is the role, though, of the Administration Audit team to assess the progress that has been made so far, to stimulate renewed activity, and to achieve the shift in culture. Again, the way in which they tackle this will vary from organisation to organisation and depend upon the activities which have gone before. Most Administration Audit teams begin with a carefully designed attitude survey. Unlike their cruder counterparts which may have been carried out in the past, this survey is concerned with helping individuals to become aware of the much greater scope for improvement that exists in most organisations.

3. Sales rate centring

As the culture moves to one of flexible teams so the demands for individual resources in different areas will be seen to vary. The Administration Audit team will be responsible for looking at this under-employment.

Unlike traditional work-study methods, they will not go round with a stop-watch, but it will be their job to encourage the people in particular areas to do so. Where activities consist of a series of discrete steps, for each one the volume of resource which is necessary needs to be assessed. The driving force for this should be the sales rate. If we are to respond to our customers then every activity has to be capable of taking place at the same pace as sales are occurring. If we start with a team of five people, each performing slightly different activities, all of which form a whole process, usually there will be one person whose activity takes slightly longer to perform. In traditional organisations it will have been this person's activity that determines the pace at which the organisation can produce. The goal is to shift resources so that other individuals can help out and so reduce the actual time it takes to produce to the level at which sales are occurring. This has the effect of increasing some of the work load for people who would have otherwise been under-utilised while relieving the individual who is forming the bottleneck. If shifting resources does not achieve the desired result then it is likely that there is a bottleneck created by the equipment.

One role of the Audit team is to flag these bottlenecks. Either the process will need redesigning or new investment will have to be made for those particular areas. If neither can be done, then the team structure needs to be changed so that the individuals who would otherwise be under employed are used in a larger team for other activities.

4. Redesigning the process

Again the role of the team is as much to raise the awareness and transfer skills as it is to do the work itself. The object of this phase is to make processes faster and more flexible, while giving feedback. Where possible we should make them 'hands-free' by automating the drudgery and routine, and make them 'floor-free' by reducing the amount of space that they take to achieve the same output.

An excellent starting point in this process is to develop a map of the activities that are involved in each process. This can be done directly or by transferring the items on a flow chart to a physical map of the site or the office area. Enormous benefits can be achieved almost overnight using this process. One factory, occupying a site of nearly four acres, reduced the amount of space it needed by 50 per cent. As the site was split by a major trunk road they were able to sell off the land on one side of the road, retaining only one part of the site. Not only did they improve the speed of the process and its flexibility but they also netted a huge capital investment. Frequently, when you look at a factory or a warehouse, you will find people whose job is mainly just to shift goods from one location to the next. Almost always where there are transit operations of this kind there will be two stores; one at each end of the movement. There is rarely a need for this. Usually one would be better and would also minimise the damage to the product while it is being moved.

If you think that this is just a problem for organisations who deal in fork-lift trucks, think twice. One German sales company sent its secretaries on a quality awareness course. Over lunch two of the secretaries drew a map of their office area and showed the flow of headed stationery through the organisation. Working as accurately as they could using knives as rulers they showed the path of paper in their offices. Entering through a rear entrance, headed stationery was received from a commercial printer in palettes of twenty boxes, each consisting of a number of reams of paper. The boxes were split down and stored in the 'goods inward' area. When the staff in any part of the office required more stationery they would call this area and a ream would be sent up. It would be placed in a stationery cupboard and small wadges would be taken and put into the input tray of their laser printers. As each letter was printed the secretary would get up from their desk, go to the printer, collect the sheet of paper, bring it back to their desk, place it with its envelope, together with the other two or three letters which were intended for signature by the manager who had prepared them. Throughout the day the secretaries would take small numbers of these sheets in their folders to their managers' offices. As the managers were frequently out of the building, it had been decided some time before to accommodate all the secretaries on one floor under the supervision of an Office Manager. Consequently, each time some letters had to be delivered for signature the secretaries would take them up one floor of the building to their individual manager's office. They would then return.

The two individuals carrying out this exercise estimated that most secretaries made four trips in the course of a day, though some of their colleagues felt that this was an underestimate. As the managers were often on the telephone there could be considerable delays while the secretary waited for the paper to be signed. Returning downstairs to their desks they would fold the letters, place them in their envelopes and put them into an out-tray. Throughout the day, wandering around the building, was the 'mail-boy'. He collected the envelopes, took them downstairs to the mail-room where they were franked and then taken outside to a nearby postbox. Again the two of them marked this mail-boy's route around the office with the number of times that they knew he visited each person. They also knew how many letters were written each day from the consumption of headed stationery. It took only a few minutes to estimate the amount of distance and time which was being wasted by people travelling around the offices from one place to the next.

Despite the fact that their office was quite small with only a matter of forty or fifty people in it, the excess effort amounted to nearly four or five man-years each year! Although the process of redesigning the offices

TRADITIONAL PUSH SYSTEM

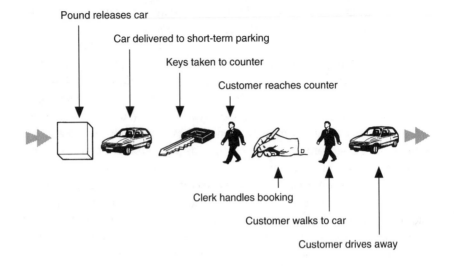

ALTERNATIVE PULL SYSTEM

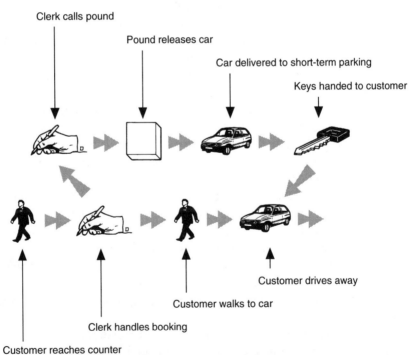

Figure 8.1   Examples of push and pull systems in operation

obviously took considerably longer to achieve, these simple calculations provided the basis for some well thought-out improvement actions.

5. Pull processing

Now is the time for the audit team to begin the process of developing alternative administrative systems. The object of each stage in this process is simple. Whereas in most organisations people continue working at their particular job, almost regardless of what is going on around them, in the responsive organisation we work on the basis of not doing anything unless there is a demand for it. Thus the administrative systems need to trigger activities. The most effective way of achieving this is by not having 'reservoirs' between different stages in the process. In a manufacturing environment the reservoirs would be called 'Work In Progress'. How this works in a service organisation is often harder to perceive. In Figure 8.1 we illustrate a simplified version of a pull system in operation in a car-hire station.

6. Partnership sourcing

With the organisation's in-house processes working effectively, now is the time for the Audit team to review the supplier base. This is not an excuse for a witch-hunt of bad suppliers. With a clear picture of the process on which they are working, the team should be looking for opportunities to involve suppliers more substantially. Prime targets obviously would be suppliers who service several stages within a particular production process, or who provide a number of services as part of your own service delivery. The Audit team needs to assess the culture of these organisations. To what extent have the improvements, at the supplier's premises, mirrored those that have been taking place within their own organisation?

The Audit team will be looking for examples of services that are currently being carried out by people in-house and which could perhaps be more professionally delivered by outsiders. Although this may sound like an out-sourcing process, in fact it is not. What we are concerned with doing is identifying opportunities for people with greater skills to join our own teams. With time it is likely that their skills will transfer to our own team members and it may no longer be necessary to involve outsiders at all. This transfer should be two-way and the team grows as its success stimulates further work.

Entering into partnerships of this kind usually calls for changes to some of the interfaces. The most obvious examples are the buying process and the delivery process. Firstly, as we are now 'buying' a supplier and not a product, many of the technical specifications which we might have previously issued are no longer required. 'Goods inwards' inspection can usually be dispensed with, as we are adopting the standards and inspections carried out by the supplier prior to delivery. The delivery process itself may change. In some cases, suppliers are given space on our own site, minimising the transfer times and transport costs. This allows them to integrate more fully into our processing systems. Alternatively, the Audit team may recommend improved communications between the two organisations, possibly through direct computer lines and/or shared access to computer systems.

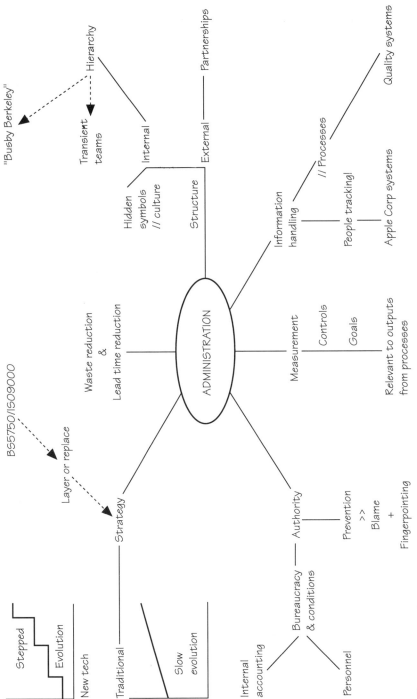

Summary Mindmap 8: Administration

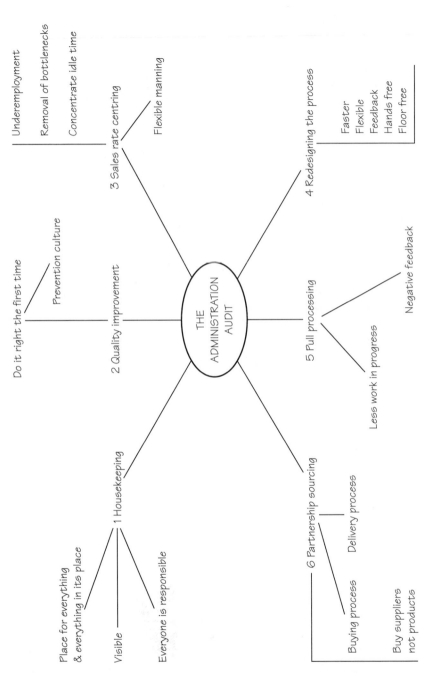

Administration Audit Mindmap

9 CONCLUSION

We explained at the outset that this was a book with four parallel themes. It may be that your organisation has yet to appreciate, or at least openly discuss, the extent of the changes that will face it in the next decade or so. If that is the case, you would be far from unique, as for most organisations, survival in the short term is far more urgent than long-term strategic planning. It is our experience that by following the internal auditing approach, you can provide the trigger for change in your own organisation by highlighting the practical changes that need to take place, rather than focusing on generalisations that may mean vastly different things to different people in the organisation.

You may, on the other hand, be an organisation that has already recognised the need to change, may have taken some steps to do so, but perhaps feel that there is a lack of credible alternatives to the traditional approaches to management. As we have explained, for many years it has been expected that there was an enduring model of management which required little or no adjustment. As you will have seen, for many organisations this is no longer acceptable. To be flexible to your customer's requirements, the organisation itself must be fluid. At the present time, the structure which appears to reflect this most accurately is that of self-managing teams. These groups of highly skilled and developing individuals are able to respond more effectively and more efficiently than any cumbersome traditional bureaucracy-based organisation. They not only make good business sense, they are also highly motivating for the individuals involved. It is important to recognise though, that they are not another steady state, but that instead, they, and you, will be constantly on the look-out for opportunities to reshape them.

By its nature, this book has focused on some consistent and important topics to ensure flexibility of response in the modern organisation. Any one of them – and certainly all of them together – represents a significant change to the organisations that most of us know. We have therefore examined the reactions that you can expect from your colleagues, from parts of the organisation and indeed, from the organisation as a whole. Having reviewed this and tested it out, we expect you to find that it's consistent with your own experiences. You will then be in a position to apply your own resources to managing that change process. We have highlighted the key steps that are involved in most organisations and we shall review these to highlight the opportunities for your organisation to evolve more effectively.

The fourth theme that we explained ran throughout the book was that of implementing self-managing work teams. While you may use internal auditing to provide the trigger for change, you may also use it as one of the stages in the development of self-managing work teams. As we explained, in most organisations, they have evolved from management-led cross-functional groups through a re-definition of the word 'functional' and the adoption of team working as the natural approach for problem-solving and day-to-day management. In the traditional organisation that has done little to reshape its functions and persisted with the approach of management control, these teams were known as 'quality circles'. In the new, fast, responsive organisation, they are self-managing work teams. The material provided in the form of the five audits described in this book is an excellent starting ground to sow the seeds for the implementation of self-managing work teams – provided that the objectives of re-designing functions, reshaping the organisation and relieving management of its control responsibilities go hand-in-hand with the audits.

THE INFRA-STRUCTURE OF THE NEW ORGANISATION

We have looked at five aspects of the infra-structure of a business throughout the course of this book and our fundamental assumption is that giving good customer service leads to the long-term success of the business. Service has long been the forte of a small business which relies more on the skills of its employees than on capital value. That we are entering the era of the small business is an indication that firstly standards will continue to rise for service, and secondly that this strategy will need to be constantly re-visited in an ever increasing spiral to provide more flexibility in our products and service. Through automation almost anybody can make a service faster and more responsive, but to achieve real flexibility, we need a constant source of new ideas. Unfortunately for many organisations, the very systems that have enabled them to control their business and grow in the previous generation now impede innovation, either indirectly through bureaucratic control or overtly through a failure to recognise the inter-personal constraints on the expression of new ideas. The recognition that the way in which we treat our employees is critical to the success of the business is hardly new, and yet remarkably few organisations have systematically attempted to review their entire organisation and make the changes that are necessary truly to empower their employees. There are many reasons why this should happen, and the audits are intended to flush them out if they are operating in your business.

Fundamental to all of these is a need for a change in the attitudes and behaviour of all managers. Even today, most managers will describe their responsibility in terms of control – responsibility for controlling budgets, controlling profits, controlling output, controlling quality, and so on. Relatively few couch their role in terms of development, especially of people. We suspect that we are still mentally many years away from the routine delivery of people-development skills training for new managers. With the perspective that managers are responsible for control comes the need for paper-based or computer-based systems enabling them to influence wider groups of people or corporate-wide systems. Time after time, it is these administrative processes that most managers will report as the main encumbrance in their present jobs. Thus the Administration Audit is intended to review and revitalise the company's systems.

Few organisations will embark on all five audits simultaneously. It is not exceptional, though, for an organisation to begin with one and then follow it with a couple more. The audit is, in this case, fulfilling different roles. The first demonstrates the approach and delivers satisfactory results. It's often on the basis of the success of this first approach that subsequent audits begin to provide the trigger for change in organisations. As senior managers and directors see the messages from the first repeat under different guises, confronted repeatedly with the same messages, it is difficult to deny their importance. Equally though, it is vital to recognise that the audits are only one stage in a change process.

WHERE DO WE GO FROM HERE?

If it hasn't already done so, frequently after the self-assessment stage, the senior management team will adopt the title of 'Steering Group' when describing their role in connection with the change process. This is especially likely if the audit team or teams have identified a need to change the structure of the senior management team. By adopting the steering group title, the senior managers are able to co-opt or change the structure of their group without fully buying into a new structure for full management decision-making. This interim position will normally persist for about twelve months, during which time the first full cycle of the change process should occur.

1. Cascading aims

With a clearer picture of the tangible changes which are necessary to begin the transition to self-managing teams, the senior managers will begin the communication process with the rest of the organisation. This may have already begun with simple communication and the goals and aims, possibly the vision, of the new organisation. If it has done so, it will need to be followed up very quickly with a simple statement of the clear changes that the senior management team envisage. If there has been a significant delay between the statement of vision and the first changes to be introduced by self-assessment teams, then it's often necessary to restate the vision.

2. Developing skills

In the first wave of the culture change process, many organisations attempt to merge the cascading of aims with the initial development of process awareness or analytical skills among managers and employees. If this is the case, they should not be too ambitious about the outcomes of the skills development step. On the other hand, if the vision has already been clearly communicated and senior managers are now disseminating the results of the self-assessment teams, considerable emphasis can be placed on the development of skills.

It's vital to separate in the senior managers' minds the idea of training and development. Training is something that can be provided on a two-to-five-day course, but skills development is a much longer process. Certainly, changing the habits of a lifetime for a controller/'cop' style of manager is a process that can take years in its own right, and is very unlikely to happen over the course of a few days.

Now is the time to plan systematically the training and development of managers at all levels in the organisation. If the culture of the organisation equates development with training, then a large budget can be expected to be incurred, because most of the activities will be off-site and involve extensive periods of training courses. On the other hand, if the culture is one of development, then much of this budget will be swallowed as the effort will be focused on on-the-job activities. Either way, the people responsible for managing the change process – whether it is the senior management team, the steering group or an individual who has been given a role such as a Total Quality Director – need to think carefully and plan how this development process will be measured and monitored.

3. Supporting teams

As the new skills are developed, so members of the organisation will be constantly seeking opportunities to establish teams. The transition can be a controlled one, from the cross-functional, multi-disciplinary teams which form an audit for self-assessment, to the self-managing teams. Alternatively, it may need to be staggered and specific activities introduced to encourage cross-functional teams, then functional teams, teams driven by managers to teams that spontaneously suggest ideas for investigation. Again, the management of this activity is important.

Often, simple logistic problems can block the transition. After all, there's no point telling a group of people that they can get together and work as a team if they wish to, if you don't then provide them with the basic facilities that they need, such as a room, desks, chairs, flip-chart, paper, and so on. On one occasion, though, we do know of a group who got together in a member's home, because the company didn't provide the relevant facilities!

It's also important at this stage for the people managing this process of change to be aware of the difficulties that some managers may have when teams of employees, who previously reported in to them, assemble as a group. If they have done so without involving the manager, it can create considerable fear, especially among more traditional managers. For this reason, part of the process has to involve an avenue of support for managers in department that are changing. This was one of the roles of British Telecom's Department of Management Counselling.

4. Counselling members

At the senior management level, the provision of counselling is often a difficult issue to appreciate, especially in organisations that are particularly technical or structured in the work that they do. It is here that the role of a process skills consultant is essential, and even if the organisation eschews the idea of using consultants for the majority of its culture change process, it will almost certainly need to do so either overtly or covertly for the senior management team. We often find that in organisations more than one counsellor is working at this level. Ironically for many, it is far easier to spend large sums of money supporting many man-years of consultancy at lower levels than it is to bring in a process skills consultant for the senior management team for only a few hours, despite the fact that the results of the latter will be far greater.

Failing to provide counselling support for the middle managers in the organisation verges on negligence and is a certain way to make sure that change will not happen. This is the real role of a facilitator. Eventually, as the change process goes through several iterations, the facilitator's approach will have been adopted as a role model for the rest of the management team, and the counselling responsibilities will have been adopted by the managers as part of their duty for the development of others.

5. Ongoing review

We've stressed the fact that in successfully changing organisations the clarity of vision coupled with critical success factors provides the basis for an ongoing review, carried out by a senior management team, usually called the steering group. Some organisations try to define where they will have reached by a given time. Unfortunately, this rarely works as it assumes that the senior managers have a clear understanding of the nature of the changes that will be taking place in their organisation. In practice this rarely happens. A more effective approach to the ongoing review can often be to assess satisfaction with the current state of progress – whether people are happy with the pace and with the nature of the changes that they witness going on around them. This usually leads to a more fruitful discussion.

6. Targeted marketing

Throughout this process, it is important that the management team constantly re-market the concepts, the implementation, and the result of the change process, to the people in the organisation in an appropriate manner. It is important, too, not to forget the outside world as often, internal marketing can be coupled very effectively with external marketing.

Recent examples of this problem in practice have been highlighted by police forces throughout the UK. Many have adopted a new style of organisation, resembling the embryonic stages of self-managing teams. Known by some as 'geographic policing' this approach places far greater responsibility and authority at local levels, typically in the care of an inspector with a number of sergeants and constables. Ultimately the reason for the change process is to improve satisfaction levels on the part of the public with the nature and style of policing that is being provided in the local community. For the change process to be successful in an organisation that has been steeped in a culture very different from that of the geographic policing model, it is important for the officers to receive feedback that the public are satisfied with the changes that are taking place. Sadly however, budgets for external marketing of the police forces' activities are out of their hands as they rest with the local county council.

It's only when the importance of this aspect to pull through the change process is appreciated that adequate investment can be made, and although the Chief Constables and their staff try to make do with the limited resources that they have available to them, a well-designed campaign is essential for the success of the culture change.

IMPLICATIONS

The implementation of self-managing teams has impacts on the organisation. We've highlighted some of these through this book, but there are many others – not only affecting the organisation, but also society around it. We shall look briefly at some of these.

1. The sales process

By its nature, the Sales Department is very often widely distributed geographically. It's often expected that sales representatives will work alone, with limited contact with the parent company. In the mid-1980s, many 'Rah-Rah' events were organised as a motivator for these distributed workers. In the 1980s as many organisations moved towards the total quality culture; the sales force was often the last group to be addressed. This sometimes led to elitism and a perception that the sales team were beyond 'TQ'. For the organisation implementing self-managing teams, an important aspect to address is how employees from the factory or production area will become involved in the sales process, as it is only by this means that they can begin to understand the problems of the use of their products in the customers' business.

2. Partnerships

Just as self-managing teams are a natural extension of the TQ process for most organisations internally, so partnerships sourcing is the extension externally. We have looked elsewhere in the book at the importance of partnership sourcing, but the implications of it need to be thoroughly understood and appreciated both at senior management level and in the areas of purchasing as it can radically affect the way in which the firm does business.

For example, IBM at its Havant location in the UK recently entered into a contract with a returns re-engineering company. Where components manufactured abroad are imported and incorporated into IBM's products, small quantities, especially of moving parts, can become liable to wear and damage. If these fail during warranty, the organisation will replace or repair them. The cost, however, of returning them to the original manufacturer is prohibitive and so IBM agrees with the manufacturer in its supply contracts that it can sub-contract the repair to local providers.

One such organisation, which was established as a reliable sub-contractor found itself under increasing pressure to deliver to the tight schedules required by IBM. Among the constraints acting on it were the lack of physical space in its existing plant, the need to invest in more sophisticated and expensive capital equipment, and the desire to reduce the time taken to transport defective components to the company and back. IBM's Purchasing Department introduced into the equation of the negotiation process the provision of spare plant space and loans to purchase capital equipment from IBM's far greater resources. This partnership has tied the two companies far tighter together, ensured the success of a small business during a major recession, and avoided the need to involve third-party financing. This is just one example of the countless types of partnership arrangements that can be introduced by organisations as they extend their culture change process to their suppliers.

3. Education

One of the hardest aspects for many managers to appreciate is that as self-managing teams become established in the organisation, so the individuals in them begin to clamour for greater and greater involvement in the development of the business and its products. Inevitably this means that individuals who have previously received no formal skills training in technical aspects of the business find themselves in need of this knowledge if they are to continue to develop the self-managing team. The organisations that have been most successful find that the traditional route to providing training and development is no longer capable of supporting their demands.

Let's be clear about the level at which this educational requirement is taking place. Obviously, organisations that employ large numbers of less skilled workers, find that the need for education includes basic skills, such as reading, writing and arithmetic. Many American organisations have been pioneers in the adult literacy movement, recognising its critical importance for the empowerment of individuals. However, as automation takes place, many employees who previously could have relied on basic skills require significant technical knowledge. One example of this is Johnsonville Sausage where employees attend graduate level courses in microbiology, electronic engineering, design and advanced manufacturing technology.

All organisations report that investment at this level is amply rewarded. One that we're aware of has audited this using independent auditors. Motorola found that for every dollar spent on the education of its employees, $33 were returned. As more and more organisations begin to implement self-managing teams we see a shift from the idea of individuals being seconded to a university or offered day-release, to a university attending the company with large numbers of employees receiving similar training at the same time. This has serious implications for the management of higher education. Already we see partnership programmes developing in the UK, particularly with the newer universities (formerly polytechnics), and there are moves afoot to introduce franchising of courses so that a university course can be provided locally at a plant and accredited in the normal way. There are instances in the USA of universities that are 'campus-free', where all the education is provided away from site.

4. Responsibility

Many traditional management practices revolve around assigning formal responsibility for a particular activity to an individual. A good example of this, ironically, is that of Quality Management Systems, where BS5750 (ISO9000) expects an organisation to appoint an individual who is ultimately responsible for quality. Other instances include accounting practices where the Companies Act places responsibility on individuals, and legal practices where the Company Secretary, for example, has formal responsibilities. The institutions setting these requirements need to be aware of the fact that in a short time it will be difficult to identify an individual who has this unique responsibility.

We have seen some changes of this emerging, particularly with the recent Companies Act in the UK, where the responsibilities for direction of the business were shared among the directors, and a broader category of shadow director was also identified. In this case, the purpose of the legislation was negative rather than positive in that it was trying to identify individuals who could be held accountable should things go wrong. This is an interesting example of external controls being applied on organisations. In the case of international standards, the continuing practice of identifying responsible individuals is alarming as the concept of team working has become well established in many organisations. That this should be the case in BS5750 is understandable given its heritage. Hopefully however, the new generation of standards, and ideally the next re-write of 5750, will encompass changes that no longer place individual responsibilities.

5. Organised labour and representation

Throughout the last two decades the 'power' of the unions has been eroded. Much of this has been deliberately introduced from within by unions seeing their responsibilities shifting from their original protective responsibility to one that involves greater development and decision-making. In many cases this has been forced by external changes including legislative controls which have been introduced by successive governments. We know of no union that does not endorse the concept of self-managing teams, but it is particularly important for organisations to understand the impact that their introduction will have on traditional practices that have involved union negotiation and representation.

We are not talking about an employer-led shift to single-union or no-union status. We recognise, too, that the unions have many vital roles to perform, although lots of these have not been exercised because of more pressing requirements. There is no reason why unions cannot become more heavily involved in the provision of social facilities. Another development is the independent management of the formal education process by union representatives, supported throughout by the organisation's resources.

The steering group needs to consider very carefully how it will respond and reorganise salary negotiations, and other benefit packages, and how it will involve the union representatives in the self-managing team implementation. Certainly most senior management teams decide to co-opt a representative of the employees on their steering group, though this may not necessarily be a member of the union.

6. National government

There are two aspects worth highlighting here. First, the problems of introducing self-managing teams in government bodies. Many government organisations operate under different rules from those that are effective in a commercial environment and the decisions that can, perhaps, be delegated to empowered employees in a commercial world may not be feasible within the government at the present time.

For instance, in a factory, a team of employees may decide to make a significant capital investment and the organisation may have given them spending authorities of many thousands of pounds. They will research their investment. They will make their decisions on normal accounting grounds and will go ahead and purchase. In a police force, most purchasing decisions have to be made by a Chief Constable. In many forces, even senior officers with many hundreds of men reporting in to them, have little or no budget and are therefore not in a position to delegate authority for spending to lower levels in the organisation. Another example is the Department of Health and Security benefits offices where, at the present time, benefits are allocated according to very strict rules and there can be little empowerment of employees to make changes to these rules. In the future, we can expect to see small teams of employees in individual benefit offices making decisions about the allocation of funds to claimants. Obviously this calls for step changes in thinking – not only on a local management level, but nationally at government level too.

The second aspect of national government involvement in self-managing teams is their responsibility to promote them. In the UK the highly successful Quality Initiative has done much to encourage organisations to take a far greater interest in developing and promoting themselves on the basis of good quality. As the benefits of self-managing teams become evident, it is to be hoped that national government will continue to support this natural extension of the TQ process. As organisations take more and more responsibility for provision of educational resources, for example, will the government reimburse them for their efforts? Or provide long-term and short-term tax advantages? There is a great deal that the government can do to stimulate a transition of this kind and in the next five years we can expect to see major developments in this area.

7. International teams

Just as we have highlighted for the sales force, where many individuals are likely to be working independently, so in organisations that have a high international focus, liaison is often between individuals in different countries. We have highlighted earlier in the book the importance of cross-functional communications and the developing breed of software solutions to enable this. The tremendous power of electronic-mail to provide rapid communication across time zones and its proliferation in international businesses is one instance of this occurring. We offer no solutions at this stage, but it is important for steering groups to consider the impact of the introduction of self-managing teams in international environments. The technology is slowly emerging to allow us to manage this, with video conferencing and on-desk video telephones becoming cheap and easily available. It is not inconceivable that in the near future, small teams of employees will be operating alone and yet as a team, holding team meetings by video telephone. No doubt somebody, somewhere, will be reading this and saying 'But we already do it!'.

INDEX

Further titles of interest

FINANCIAL TIMES

PITMAN PUBLISHING

ISBN	TITLE	AUTHOR
0 273 60561 5	Achieving Successful Product Change	Innes
0 273 03970 9	Advertising on Trial	Ring
0 273 60232 2	Analysing Your Competitor's Financial Strengths	Howell
0 273 60466 X	Be Your Own Management Consultant	Pinder
0 273 60168 7	Benchmarking for Competitive Advantage	Bendell
0 273 60529 1	Business Forecasting using Financial Models	Hogg
0 273 60456 2	Business Re-engineering in Financial Services	Drew
0 273 60069 9	Company Penalties	Howarth
0 273 60558 5	Complete Quality Manual	McGoldrick
0 273 03859 1	Control Your Overheads	Booth
0 273 60022 2	Creating Product Value	De Meyer
0 273 60300 0	Creating World Class Suppliers	Hines
0 273 60383 3	Delayering Organisations	Keuning
0 273 60171 7	Does Your Company Need Multimedia?	Chatterton
0 273 60003 6	Financial Engineering	Galitz
0 273 60065 6	Financial Management for Service Companies	Ward
0 273 60205 5	Financial Times Guide to Using the Financial Pages	Vaitilingam
0 273 60006 0	Financial Times on Management	Lorenz
0 273 03955 5	Green Business Opportunities	Koechlin
0 273 60385 X	Implementing the Learning Organisation	Thurbin
0 273 03848 6	Implementing Total Quality Management	Munro-Faure
0 273 60025 7	Innovative Management	Phillips
0 273 60327 2	Investor's Guide to Emerging Markets	Mobius
0 273 60622 0	Investor's Guide to Measuring Share Performance	Macfie
0 273 60528 3	Investor's Guide to Selecting Shares that Perform	Koch
0 273 60704 9	Investor's Guide to Traded Options	Ford
0 273 03751 X	Investor's Guide to Warrants	McHattie
0 273 03957 1	Key Management Ratios	Walsh
0 273 60384 1	Key Management Tools	Lambert
0 273 60259 4	Making Change Happen	Wilson
0 273 60424 4	Making Re-engineering Happen	Obeng
0 273 60533 X	Managing Talent	Sadler
0 273 60153 9	Perfectly Legal Competitor Intelligence	Bernhardt
0 273 60167 9	Profit from Strategic Marketing	Wolfe
0 273 60170 9	Proposals, Pitches and Beauty Parades	de Forte
0 273 60616 6	Quality Tool Kit	Mirams
0 273 60336 1	Realising Investment Value	Bygrave
0 273 60713 8	Rethinking the Company	Clarke
0 273 60328 0	Spider Principle	Linton
0 273 03873 7	Strategic Customer Alliances	Burnett
0 273 03949 0	Strategy Quest	Hill
0 273 60624 7	Top Intrapreneurs	Lombriser
0 273 03447 2	Total Customer Satisfaction	Horovitz
0 273 60201 2	Wake Up and Shake Up Your Company	Koch
0 273 60387 6	What Do High Performance Managers Really Do?	Hodgson

For further details or a full list of titles contact:

The Professional Marketing Department, Pitman Publishing, 128 Long Acre, London WC2E 9AN, UK

Tel +44 (0)71 379 7383 or fax +44 (0)71 240 5771